"A masterpiece of research and narrative."   —*Yale Alumni Magazine*

"A wonderful book . . . *Fatherland* achieves a catharsis of its own."
—*The Economist*

"The admired *New Yorker* writer has turned his reportorial skills on his own family [in this] powerful new memoir."
—NPR, *Weekend Edition with Scott Simon*

"[A] powerful investigation of morality . . . a vivid portrait of [Bilger's] grandfather and his times [and] a fascinating, deeply researched work of Holocaust-era history . . . a moving, humane biography."
—*Kirkus Reviews* (starred review)

"A fascinating excavation of the twisted veins of good and evil in one man's soul."   —*Publishers Weekly* (starred review)

"Exceptionally well-written and compulsively readable."
—*BookPage* (starred review)

"In this gripping, beautifully written memoir . . . the history is frank and insightful . . . the storytelling evocative and richly detailed."   —*Booklist*

"A deeply personal family portrait and an insightful and fascinating war-time history."   —BookBrowse

"Anyone struggling to write their own problematic family histories could learn a lot from the ingenious narrative fashioned by Bilger."
—*The Anchorage Daily News*

"A fascinating read, beautifully told."
—ROBERT PHILPOT, *The Times of Israel*

"Engrossing . . . The fascinating journey Bilger takes his readers on is part family story, part detective mystery. . . . [An] emotionally candid book, expressed with reflective clarity."   —*The Times* (London)

"An intimate, searching examination of guilt, complicity and moral complexity."
—*The Sydney Morning Herald*

"Burkhard Bilger has long been one of our great storytellers: an acute observer, an intrepid reporter, and a writer of unmatched grace. *Fatherland* is that rare book—a finely etched memoir with the powerful sweep of history."
—DAVID GRANN, author of *Killers of the Flower Moon*

"A profoundly haunting work of historical investigation, a reporter's dogged inquiry into the tangled history of his Nazi grandfather . . . *Fatherland* is an unflinching, gorgeously written, and deeply moving exploration of morality, family, and war."
—PATRICK RADDEN KEEFE, author of *Empire of Pain*

"*Fatherland* is the book we need right now. Gripping, gorgeously written, and deeply humane, it's both a moving personal history and a formidable piece of detective work."
—ATUL GAWANDE, author of *Being Mortal*

"What a remarkable book, full of insight and unfailingly honest. I was caught up in the author's search from the first page. An extraordinary accomplishment."
—TONY PHELAN, creator and producer of *Grey's Anatomy* and *A Small Light*

"*Fatherland* is an unforgettable book: a family saga set on a global stage. I could not put it down."
—REZA ASLAN, author of *Zealot* and *An American Martyr in Persia*

"A penetrating account of one Nazi official and his family that takes us to the very heart of what it is to be human when trapped in the labyrinth and horror of war."
—JULIA BOYD, author of *A Village in the Third Reich*

"*Fatherland* is a masterful and riveting weave of the personal and the monumental, of ordinary Germans' struggles with questions of identity, responsibility, and sheer survival in a world gone mad."
—JOEL F. HARRINGTON, Centennial Professor of History at Vanderbilt University and author of *The Faithful Executioner*

BY BURKHARD BILGER

Fatherland

Noodling for Flatheads

fatherland

A MEMOIR OF WAR, CONSCIENCE,
AND FAMILY SECRETS

BURKHARD BILGER

RANDOM HOUSE

NEW YORK

Library of Congress Cataloging-in-Publication Data
Names: Bilger, Burkhard, author.
Title: Fatherland: a memoir of war, conscience, and family secrets / Burkhard Bilger.
Description: First edition. | New York: Random House, [2023] |
Includes bibliographical references.
Identifiers: LCCN 2022035829 (print) | LCCN 2022035830 (ebook) |
ISBN 9780804173308 (trade paperback) | ISBN 9780385353991 (ebook)
Subjects: LCSH: Gönner, Karl, 1899–1979. | Ex-Nazis—Germany—Biography. |
Teachers—Germany—Biography. | World War, 1939–1945—France—Bartenheim. |
France—History—German occupation, 1940–1945. | Bilger, Burkhard—Family.
Classification: LCC D802.A45 .B55 2023 (print) | LCC D802.A45 (ebook) |
DDC 940.53370944393 [B]—dc23/eng/20220803
LC record available at https://lccn.loc.gov/2022035829
LC ebook record available at https://lccn.loc.gov/2022035830

Printed in the United States of America on acid-free paper

randomhousebooks.com

9 8 7 6 5 4 3 2 1

Book design by Jo Anne Metsch

For my mother

CONTENTS

AUTHOR'S NOTE

This is a work of narrative nonfiction, part history and part storytelling. The scenes I describe are based largely on primary sources and first-person accounts, drawn from interviews and archival work in Germany and France. The translations from French and German are mostly my own. Where I've had to navigate between contradictory accounts, I've tried to make that clear in the text. Where details are scarce, I've used contemporary sources to fill them out. In some cases, I've relied on people's memories alone, as imperfect as they are indelible.

Like many men of his generation, my grandfather wasn't much for self-expression. He left behind no soul-searching diary or final testament, no war stories buffed and polished like lucky stones in his pocket. He wanted to forget, not remember. Yet he left traces of his passage everywhere: in memories, anecdotes, and letters from prison, in court records, school reports, and police interrogations. This book is one path through those sources: my mother stumbling behind her father, he behind his, and I behind them all. I've tried my best to go where they lead.

Fatherland

1

SUSPECT

THE MAN IN THE INTERROGATION ROOM HAD ALL THE MARKS of a dangerous fanatic: stiff spine and bony shoulders, lips pinched into a pleat. He wore brass spectacles with round, tortoiseshell rims and his head was shaved along the back and sides, leaving a shock of brown hair to flop around on top, like a toupee. When he posed for his mug shot, his expression was strangely unbalanced. The left eye had a flat, unwavering focus, edged with fear or grief. The right eye was glazed and lifeless.

The French inspector, Otto Baumgartner, paced in front of him reading from a typewritten sheet. "In October of 1940, you moved to Alsace and set yourself the task of converting the inhabitants of Bartenheim to National Socialism," he began. "You established yourself as *Ortsgruppenleiter* in order to become the town's absolute master. . . . You brought to your duties a zeal and a tyrannical fervor without equal. In the entire district of Mulhouse, you were the most feared and infamous of leaders!"

Baumgartner paused after each charge to let the prisoner respond, while another inspector transcribed the exchange. It had been nearly a year since the German surrender, and these men had heard their share of pleas and denunciations. The countryside seethed with military courts and citizens' militias, lynch mobs and makeshift tribunals. For four years, the Nazi occupation had divided France ever more bitterly against itself, turning neighbor against neighbor and Christian against Jew. Now the days of reckoning had come. More than nine thousand people would be executed as war criminals and collaborators over the next five years, in addition to those denounced and beaten; the women shorn and shaved and paraded through towns for sleeping with German soldiers. *L'épuration sauvage,* the French called it: the savage purification.

The facts in this case were not in question. They came from a seemingly unimpeachable source: Captain Louis Obrecht, an adjunct controller in the French military government and president of the local Purification Commission. Obrecht was a veteran of the French army and a former prisoner of war. When German forces invaded Alsace in 1940, Obrecht was the school principal in the village of Bartenheim, where the prisoner later became *Ortsgruppenleiter,* or the town's Nazi Party chief. For four years, Obrecht insisted, the prisoner had been the terror of Bartenheim. "But it was above all in the last year of his reign that he became menacing and dangerous."

Obrecht went on to accuse the man of crimes ranging from sabotage to using French children as spies. But the investigators zeroed in on a single incident: the murder of a local farmer named Georges Baumann. On the morning of Wednesday, October 4, 1944, a German military police chief named Anton Acker ordered Baumann to report for a work detail, building wooden pallets for the German army. Baumann refused. The war had turned against Germany by then and the Allies were on their way. He had no intention of working for "those German swine," he said. When Acker tried to arrest him, a scuffle ensued, and Baumann and his family disarmed the officer.

Their victory was short-lived. Within the hour, Acker returned with five other policemen. Baumann was arrested, as were his wife and daughter later that day, while his son fled into the fields. The three prisoners were taken to a police station, where they were detained and beaten. By that evening, Baumann lay half dead. "I found him on the floor of the station, unconscious, his hair, cheeks, and forehead covered in blood," a local doctor later told investigators. "His scalp was split open, without a doubt from blows of a rifle butt, and he also had a bullet wound in his pelvis, with tears in his intestines and probably an artery as well." Baumann died in the hospital that night. By then, bruises from the bludgeoning had begun to appear all over his body.

The death of Georges Baumann could be traced back to one man, Obrecht believed. It was set in motion by a direct order from the prisoner in the interrogation room. "For four years, he made thousands of innocent people suffer," Obrecht said, and the inspectors had no reason to doubt him. The war had been over for nearly a year and fresh horrors were still being unearthed in mass graves and killing fields and concentration camps across Europe. There was more than enough guilt to go around.

Yet the inspectors had also heard rumors of a different sort. There was talk that this gaunt, bespectacled bureaucrat—this "perfect Nazi," as some people described him—was the opposite of what Obrecht claimed. That far from terrorizing two villages, he had shielded them from the worst Nazi excesses during the occupation.

That without him many more might have died. It was an unlikely story. But in those days of furious judgment, justice could be hard to tell from self-justification, and purity was often code for revenge.

The inspectors would look into the matter. In the meantime, the case would be remanded to the military court in Mulhouse, and the prisoner—my grandfather, Karl Gönner, forty-seven years old and a father of four, one of them my mother—would be sent to solitary confinement in Strasbourg. To await judgment in the Citadel, the seventeenth-century fortress along the River Ill, where the worst German war criminals in Alsace were kept.

2

SUBJECT

FAMILY HISTORY IS A HAZARDOUS THING, FOOTPATHS THROUGH a darkening wood. It's a shout in the night and a dash through dim trees, in thin slippers and an old flannel robe, with only a flashlight beam to guide you. You get short of breath and circle back, change your mind and stop in your tracks. Was that a cough behind you, a muffled sob? There's something moving back there—a hunched figure heaving into shadow—but you can't bring yourself to follow. And when you go back in the morning and peer at the trampled ground, the trail is lost in a confusion of prints, most of them your own.

I'm an American, born in Oklahoma, taught to be unafraid of history—to believe that God is on my side, or at least willing to forgive my lapses. But I also have German blood, so I know that forgiveness doesn't always come easily. Every country has its dark past, my mother always told me, its historical rap sheet. Scratch today's gentle Danes and you'll find Viking longships still coursing through their veins. The Swiss were Europe's deadliest mercenaries long before they were counting deposit slips. And those jolly Dutchmen, faces flushed over tankards of ale in their portraits, probably owed their fortunes to shiploads of slaves. Each of us carries the seeds of murder and mercy within us, my mother said. What takes root depends as much on circumstance as character.

There was more than a little defensiveness to all this. My mother was born in 1935, in the foothills of the Black Forest in southwestern Germany. She was too young to serve in the Third Reich or even to join Hitler's League of German Girls—though she used to pine for their smart white blouses and black neckerchiefs. Too old to not witness and register the horror of war. If she believed that any country, any people, could turn criminal under the right conditions, it was because she was a careful student of history. But it was also because she saw it happen all around her as a girl. If her own neighbors, her own father, could become Nazis, couldn't anyone?

.   .   .

The question never really came up when I was a boy. Like most Germans her age, my mother rarely talked about the war—or she talked about it as she might tell a sinister fairy tale: in rough, woodcut images, black and white gouged with red. Of a narrow escape from a witch's lair or a huntsman who had come to fetch her heart. After she and my father moved to the United States in 1962, they seemed to relegate those memories to a high shelf, spined in leather with dark Gothic script. In full view yet out of reach.

The country they had left behind was a sullen, dispirited place, shoulders hunched as if against the next blow. The railroads had been rebuilt, the rubble cleared—more than seventeen billion cubic feet in all. But the people still seemed shell-shocked, half asleep. What had been a place of fearsome modernity—Autobahn, Volkswagen, V-2, Wehrmacht—felt like the old country again. More than half its young men lay dead on the battlefield, and the cities had been bombed back to a previous century. In the Catholic villages to the south, the streets smelled of coal smoke and sour milk.

My parents were luckier than most. My mother was an elementary-school teacher like both her parents. Not long after she and my father married, in 1958, she was offered a job in the village of Inzlingen, not far from her hometown of Weil am Rhein. Tucked into a cul-de-sac along the Swiss border, flanked by neutral territory on three sides, Inzlingen had survived the war as if protected by a force field. Its moat-ringed *Wasserschloss* was left untouched. When air-raid sirens would go off at night, people on both sides of the border would douse their lights and pull down black shades. By the time the British bombers arrived, there was no telling where the border lay, so they flew on to safer targets. Even so, more than a decade after the war, the buzz of an airplane could still set my mother's heart hammering.

Her posting came with a two-bedroom flat in the attic of the schoolhouse—a rare luxury in those days. Other young couples had to live with their parents or share quarters with refugees. They came from East Prussia, Silesia, eastern Pomerania and other former German territories, from areas like the Sudetenland that had been annexed by the Nazis, and from Hungary, Romania, Yugoslavia, and other countries that simply didn't want Germans around anymore. More than thirteen million ethnic Germans were expelled and resettled throughout the West. The refugees and their hosts spoke different dialects, ate different food, and prayed differently to their God. Yet suddenly they were sharing the same stove, bathroom, and couch. In a village like Inzlingen, even newcomers from a neighboring valley could take years to fit in. And beneath it all, like a dark current winding under the floorboards, lay the knowledge—repressed, denied, or suddenly, cripplingly accepted—that they had brought it all upon themselves.

They had seen the photographs from the death camps at Buchenwald and Bergen-Belsen. They had heard the stories of forced abortions and human experimentation. They knew that they had allowed this horror among them—had invited it into their homes, then watched and followed as it moved from house to house, denouncing this neighbor and arresting that one, herding mother and child into the same doomed cattle cars. Yet they tried to thrust those thoughts from their minds. "We in Germany must find a way, together, to set our spirits to rights," the philosopher Karl Jaspers told his students in Heidelberg in 1946, in a lecture later published in his book *Die Schuldfrage* (The Question of Guilt). This was a task not just for the mind but for the heart, Jaspers believed, but he feared that Germans were too beaten down to undertake it. "We don't want to hear about guilt or the past. We're not affected by world history. We just want to stop suffering, to escape this misery, to live but not to think."

The habits of war were hard to unlearn. The guarded speech and mutual suspicion, the fear, bone-deep, that a handful of ration stamps and a hundred grams of beef tallow might be all that kept your family alive for another week. In the small stores where my mother went shopping every afternoon, food was still weighed and parceled from behind a counter, one meal at a time; meat cut from a carcass at the butcher's discretion. My mother would note each expenditure in the tobacco-colored *Haushaltsbuch* that she used to keep her budget: *Eier:* 1 pfennig, *Speck und Leberwurst:* 2.90 mark, *Brötchen:* 50 pfennig. It was a life measured out in milligrams.

·   ·   ·

I would often try to picture it, from whatever carpeted, air-conditioned room where we were talking. It seemed so much more than a generation away: the attic apartment with no bathtub or hot running water, the bedrooms without heat through the long German winter. My mother got up at 5:30 in the morning and tiptoed down to the basement in the dark, to keep from waking my older brother in his crib. She filled a large black kettle with water and set it boiling, feeding the fire with egg-shaped lumps of coal known as *Schwarze Eier,* then dumped in a load of diapers. When they were scrubbed clean and hung to dry, she went back upstairs to feed my brother, handed him off to the young war widow who took care of him during the day, and headed downstairs to teach her class—fifty first-grade boys, a few of whom always seemed to be waiting in line to have their loose teeth pulled. On Saturdays, she boiled some extra water for the family bath.

You wouldn't have thought, to look at her, that she was so strong. Raised on rations of pork fat and potatoes, skim milk and cheese, she had grown up small and watchful, with a pale, moon-shaped face. Her eyes were so weak that she wore bottle-thick glasses; her skin was nearly translucent in places. Her hands were warm, the veins so close to the surface they could make bread dough rise while she was still kneading it. When she was a girl, the other kids in her village used to say that her bright-red hair was the mark of a witch. But she was more like some shy household spirit, fierce only when backed into a corner. She had learned early on when to defend herself and when to hide.

She and my father had come up through school together, in the same graduating class of twenty-eight. Both were excellent students—top of their *Oberschule* in an era when only a handful earned a full high-school diploma. But though she was the valedictorian of their class, he was the one who went on to university. Had the world been opened wide to her, she would have liked to study law. The drive toward justice was deeper in her than anything else—even, at times, a kind of rigidity. But her parents couldn't afford the tuition. She had seen the young women in town who had paid their own way through

college: shabby and careworn, too overworked to find a husband, too
poor to buy a decent pair of shoes. She'd had enough of that sort of
existence.

And so, while my father earned his PhD in physics in Switzerland, she pulled her first-graders' teeth and had three children in
three years. My brother, Martin, came first, in 1959, then my sisters
Eva and Monika. At night, when my father returned home on the
train from Basel, a bottle of milk or a tin of coffee under his overcoat, his mind was still spinning from the lab. He would pace the
kitchen as she cooked, waving his arms and talking about signals and
noise, Gaussian beams, gravitational waves. She listened quietly at
the stove, turning occasionally to ask a question or point out some
seam of illogic, sending my father into another gale of analysis and
hand waving. Her knowledge of physics was mostly intuitive, color-
coded by their nightly conversations. But he was happy for her
prompting, and she was hungry for any talk at all.

It was a gift, this life. She knew that better than anyone. After the
howling sirens and concussing shells, even boiling diapers could seem
a blessing. But a darkness still clung to things. In my parents' wedding pictures, taken in an apple orchard in my mother's town, she
holds close to my father's side. He looks like a young Kafka, with his
big ears and smoldering, deep-set eyes, and stares at the camera as if
he doesn't quite trust it. Her hair is tousled by the wind, her eyes lit
with faint surprise, as if she had only just grasped her good luck. But
her dress is black velvet, his suit almost funereal. There's a sense of
the past floating quietly in the wings, still too close for comfort.

It had been two years since her mother died of ovarian cancer
and eleven since her father had returned from France. She knew that
he had been imprisoned there for more than two years, first in
prisoner-of-war camps in eastern France after his arrest in Alsace,
then in solitary confinement in Strasbourg, after he was arrested
again under suspicion of war crimes. She remembered him putting

on his uniform when she was a girl—the brown one with the eagle on the cap and black swastika on the sleeve. But she had never asked him what he did during the war. And that question, unasked when he was in the room next door, began to be answered only years later, when she and my father had crossed the ocean and seemed to have left their history far behind.

·   ·   ·

They meant to stay for only a year or two. A postdoc in the United States had become something of a rite of passage for the physicists in my father's lab—a brief adventure before life got down to business. One evening when my parents still lived in Germany, they were walking to the village dump, pulling a cart full of their old belongings behind them, when my father stopped and pointed at the sky. What was that light shining there? It was too bright for a star, too slow for an airplane; it drifted along the horizon like a will-o'-the-wisp. "I think it's a Russian satellite," he said.

The Soviets had sent Sputnik and two successors into orbit in the past few years, propelling America into space behind them. American rocketry had long been a German affair. Wernher von Braun and his staff, inventors of the V-2, had surrendered to the Allies in 1945 and carried on their missile research in American labs. Now von Braun was director of NASA's Marshall Space Flight Center and German physicists seemed to be in demand in every engineering department and federal lab. The map of the continent lay unfolded before them; the only question was where to go.

My father had grown up in the era of Einstein and Heisenberg, Bohr, Dirac, and Bethe, all of whom had crossed the Atlantic like von Braun. Though he wasn't really of their generation, his work partook of their glamour in my eyes. He told stories about them the way other fathers told stories about Mickey Mantle or Johnny

Unitas—wily, impudent geniuses who had outfoxed the rules of physics. Relativity and quantum theory, in his telling, were like Willie Mays's over-the-shoulder catch in the '54 World Series. "Ah!" he would say, jabbing a forefinger in the air and widening his eyes. "But then Bohr, *der Saukeip*, that crazy bastard, proved all those *Dreckskerle* wrong!"

The stories that most drew him to America, though, were of a different kind. Growing up, he was obsessed with the Old West and the cowboy novels of the German writer Karl May. Cribbed from James Fenimore Cooper or invented from whole cloth—on his only trip to America, May never went farther west than Niagara Falls— the books sent generations of German boys galloping across the dusty plains in their minds. My father dreamed of being Old Shatterhand, the German frontiersman who was the hero of May's most famous novels, even more than he did of being Einstein or Bohr. Like Old Shatterhand, my father was happiest when thrown back on his wits, improvising from available materials. He was less a theoretician than an engineer, less an engineer than an experimentalist— a tinkerer, a tamperer, a builder of ring lasers and other oddball devices. He would have been good with a buck knife and a bag of black powder. And so, as strange as it later seemed to us—as wrongheaded from a career standpoint—when given the choice of working anywhere in America, he chose Oklahoma State University. It was in the heart of what Karl May knew as Indian Territory.

My mother just hoped that they could find a place to live. If housing was as scarce in the United States as it was in Germany, they might have to turn around and fly back home. A backyard, a bathtub with hot running water, a grocery store nearby: Her dreams were of a practical sort. In Germany, there always seemed to be only one right way to do things—cross a street, wear a hat, raise a child—and if you dared to do otherwise, someone was sure to let you know. The windows glimmered with inquisitive eyes. She needed an escape as much as an adventure.

On the night of their transatlantic flight, my parents were waiting with their children for a connection at Idlewild Airport in New York, when a lady with purple hair sat down across from them. My mother gave her a sideways glance—*Mensch!* Are people really so strange here?—but she was soon distracted by my brother and sisters. They were sprawled on the bench beside her, wrung out from the long propeller flight over: Martin was now three; Eva, two; and Monika, less than a year old. (My younger sister, Andrea, and I were born later, in the United States.) Their fussing and whining had built to a squall when my mother looked up to find the lady with purple hair standing in front of her. She had walked over to a nearby vending machine—itself a wonder—and had brought back a handful of candy bars. My mother and the three children stared up at her. They weren't sure what to make of this bizarre stranger bearing treats. Then the kids grabbed the candies, tore off the wrappers, and ate them contentedly all in a row. It was November 22, 1962: Thanksgiving Day.

.   .   .

Only seventeen years had passed since the war ended. Seventeen years since American soldiers liberated the prisoners in Dachau and Buchenwald, and witnessed the atrocities in Ohrdruf, Gunskirchen, and Mauthausen. Nearly half a million Americans had died in the war, and some fifteen million veterans came back to tell of it. But they had also seen the ragged streams of refugees, the cities leveled and families broken and children starving by the roadside. They had shared rations and cigarettes with the survivors, danced the Lindy Hop with German girls, and sometimes brought them home. They knew the doubleness of war firsthand—how innocence and guilt are so often intertwined.

My parents' names were almost comically German: Hans and Edeltraut Bilger. Their accents were a dead giveaway. Yet they found Americans unaccountably welcoming. The war rarely came up. When it did, people could tell that my parents were still children at the time, so the conversation turned to a great-grandfather from Schleswig-Holstein, a niece who had studied in Heidelberg. It was a kind of miracle.

By the time I was born, a year and a half later, my parents had settled in the United States for good. Oklahoma State was a land-grant school focused on the practical trades—agriculture, economics, engineering, and football, not always in that order. It was located in Stillwater, a town of twenty-five thousand, half of them students. The roads turned to red clay well shy of city limits, and the university's main drag ran for all of four blocks—mostly pool halls and cowboy bars, serving watered-down, 3.2 percent beer. The town was too small for a McDonald's or a Burger Chef, much less a Chinese restaurant. It was just what my parents wanted.

In the faded Kodachromes of those years, the bricks in our ranch house are still raw from the baking, the backyard fenceless and treeless, its Bermuda grass burned yellow by wind and sun. Sitting on their shadeless patio, surrounded by kids in cowboy suits and summer dresses, my parents have the clear smiles and unburdened eyes of people cut loose from history—blown across the continent like prairie schooners. As far from what they had known as they could get.

They weren't, really. Oklahoma had its own version of the history they had left behind. The Nuremberg Race Laws were based on Jim Crow codes passed in the United States after the Civil War and still widely enforced when my parents arrived. Oklahoma was the first state to segregate phone booths. Forty years earlier, white rioters in Tulsa had burned down more than twelve hundred Black-owned houses and killed as many as three hundred Black residents. Inter-marriage was still illegal between Blacks and those of other races, and the Black citizens of Stillwater were effectively consigned to the flood-prone bungalows southeast of downtown. (When my friend Doug Mitchell and his family moved into a house a few blocks from mine—his parents were the first Black homeowners in the area—the neighbors sent them hate mail.) Crystal Plunge, the only pool in town when I was a boy, was sold after the Civil Rights Act was passed. The owners, it was said, were afraid that they would be forced to let nonwhites into the water.

We hardly noticed. When I think back on the Oklahoma of my childhood, my memories are full of blind spots. I never thought to ask why all my neighbors were white—the one exception was a col-league of my father's who was from India—when my classes usually had Black students in them. I learned about the Trail of Tears in school: the sixteen thousand Cherokee who were forced to take it to Oklahoma from the Southeast, and the four thousand who died along the way. But the lesson ended when they arrived at their reser-vation. We never heard that some tribes lost most of their new land to forced allotment. Or that the Osage were the wealthiest people in the world, after oil was found on their reservation, but were system-atically murdered or defrauded by oil speculators, bankers, lawmen, and prosecutors. Our teachers stuck to what they called the "Five Civilized Tribes"—the Cherokee, Choctaw, Creek, Seminole, and Chickasaw—as if the others hadn't quite made the grade.

We lived in the odd intersection between the America of my par-ents' imagining and the Germany of their memories. Something in them couldn't leave the past behind. They stayed in the United States on green cards, spoke German with us at home—an obscure south-western dialect called Alemannisch—and socialized mostly with other Germans. (My mother's best friend was a hairdresser; my fa-ther's best friend was her husband, a retired boxer and assembly-line foreman.) When I was in elementary school and again in junior high, my father took long sabbaticals in Germany and France and enrolled us in public schools, as if for the long haul. We always came back to Oklahoma, but my parents kept their German citizenship just in case.

Our house in Stillwater felt like a world unto itself: a tiny, land-locked principality with its own laws and invisible borders. A prairie Liechtenstein. We drove the same roads as other people and some-times spoke the same language, but only for diplomatic purposes. On weekday mornings before school, I used to watch the guitar pickers and bluegrass fiddlers on the local cable station. I had no idea what they were yodeling on about, but I had a nagging sense that the real world lay with them and not us—along the county roads east of town, in rodeo arenas and country dance halls, cockfighting pits and gas stations reborn as Pentecostal churches.

Still, we stuck to our customs. On my first day of elementary school, my mother sent me to class in lederhosen. That tradition thankfully didn't hold, but most others did. We ate *Bratkartoffeln* and *Gurkensalat*, played skat and listened to German pop hits by Alexan-dra and Hildegard Knef. On Christmas Eve, my father and I would chop down a cedar tree in a nearby cow pasture. We would prop it up in the living room, parched and hunchbacked from the rainless fall, and festoon it with candles as German tradition required. The branches would be tinder-dry, the needles raining onto the carpet. But we would set the candles blazing anyway—the family crouched in ready position around the room, in case the tree went up like a torch.

I was the closest thing in the family to an assimilated American, though you wouldn't have guessed it from my Wagnerian name: Burkhard means Powerful Fortress. My brother's and sisters' names were of the more neutral, postwar type, with their plain-sawn Scan-dinavian sounds: Martin, Eva, Monika, Andrea. No Trautwig or Ermintrude, Dagobert or Baldemar. No Edeltraut, Gernot, Sigmar, or Winfried, as my mother and her brothers were called. There was too much myth and history, tribe and bloodline bound up in those names. Too many Aryan identity cards.

.   .   .

I was twenty-eight years old when my mother first told me that her father had been imprisoned as a war criminal. I would give almost anything now to talk to my German relatives who were alive then, and hear their version of the story. My mother's oldest brother, Gernot, had a mordant wit and might have talked about his father with all the bitter devotion of an eldest son. And Sigmar, her middle brother, was closest to his father after the war. But though my grandfather's story only grew richer and stranger over the years—"like ripples from a stone," my mother said—I kept my distance from it. Germany was too close to home.

Like my parents, I had spent my twenties trying to get as far from what I'd known as possible: I came east for college then worked as a writer and editor, covering stories in Africa, South America, Southeast Asia, and Eastern Europe. But I never wrote about Germany or my family history. Collective memory isn't much good at forgiveness. The further events recede from view, the more we flatten and simplify them in our minds, till history is just a series of cautionary tales: crime and punishment, heroes and villains. Someone else's bad behavior. I had always been touched by the goodwill that Americans showed my parents when they first arrived. But I knew that the war had never really left people's minds. If anything, their feelings about it had hardened. I could hear it in their voices when I mentioned my background. How old are your parents? they would ask, then count back silently to 1939.

I knew better than to talk too much about my heritage. Some

forty million Americans claim some German ancestry, according to the 2020 census—nearly twice as many as have English roots, and more than any other ethnic group in the country. Yet culturally, German Americans have long gone underground. More than once, I have had friends or students confess that it took them a while to completely trust me, given my background. There is something inherently different about Germans, they had been taught growing up. Something enduringly suspect.

The summer after I graduated from college, I helped lead a group of high-school students on a six-week tour of France. About a month into the trip, one of my favorite kids in the group—a sharp, spunky fifteen-year-old with a huge head of curly auburn hair—came up to me after dinner. "I've decided that you're all right," she announced, with a defiant grin. She wasn't sure at first, she added. She had grown up on Manhattan's Upper East Side, in a conservative Jewish community. She had been taught all her life to be wary of Germans, she said. But she'd been watching me closely these past few weeks, and she had decided that she would make an exception.

I laughed, a little startled. I appreciated the vote of confidence but bristled a bit at the assumption that I needed it. Still, I could see why she had had her doubts about me. The horrors of Auschwitz and terrors of *Kristallnacht* had never been far from her classroom and television set. My people were the murderous thugs of *Sophie's Choice* and Anne Frank's diary, the officious buffoons of *Hogan's Heroes* and *Stalag 17*. They were warlike, humorless, chillingly methodical. They were not to be trusted. "The notion that ordinary Danes or Italians would have acted as the ordinary Germans did strains credulity beyond the breaking point," the historian Daniel Goldhagen wrote in his bestselling book *Hitler's Willing Executioners*. "The Germans were not ordinary men."

Goldhagen's book was written in 1996, when Germany was once again a subject of anxious hand-wringing. The fall of the Berlin

Wall had given rise to a unified country alarmingly reminiscent of its former self: educated, efficient, economically dominant. What would keep it from falling back on its old authoritarian habits? Not much had changed since Hitler's days, a group of historians convened by Margaret Thatcher had declared in 1990. The German character was still an amalgam, "in alphabetical order," of "angst, aggressiveness, assertiveness, bullying, egotism, inferiority complex, and sentimentality." Or so Thatcher's private secretary, Baron Powell of Bayswater, declared in a private memorandum afterward. For good measure, he added a "capacity for excess" and a "tendency to overestimate their own strengths and capabilities."

Even later, after the new Germany had proved to be the most reluctant of superpowers, its decisions were seen in this same orange-alert light. When the Germans refused to forgive the Greek government's crippling debts, or temporarily closed its borders to Syrian refugees, or Volkswagen was caught cheating on car emissions, these weren't just heartless decisions. They were windows into the country's soul. "Germany is never quite what it seems," the columnist Roger Cohen warned in *The New York Times* in 2015. "There is a strain between its order and its urges. Formality may mask frenzy. When things go wrong, they tend to go wrong in a big way."

To be German, it seemed, was always to be one part Nazi. In my case, that part was my grandfather.

·   ·   ·

Had you asked me as a boy what I thought of him, I would have told you that he made me a little nervous. When my family visited Germany, I always felt more comfortable around my father's father— a red-faced, barrel-chested railroad man who was always telling funny stories and pressing sour candies into my hand. My mother's father was a sterner sort. Tall and gaunt, with a shock of peppery gray hair, he had a glass eye that would swivel unnervingly out of line as he spoke. He would ask me questions in a grave, deliberate voice, like an astronaut meeting a Martian, and sometimes give me a piece of beeswax with honey to chew—strange, like him, with its chambered secrets, its amber depths, but also sweet. I remember watching him tend to the hives behind his house, never flinching as the bees swarmed over his neck and arms.

The older I grew, the more my mother's stories about him changed. At first, she described him through her eyes as a child—as a good man caught in barbarous times. He had served in two world wars, she told us, first as a foot soldier, then as a political functionary, and nearly lost his life both times. Then, when I was a teenager, my mother went back to school to study history. Her doctoral work was on the Vichy regime and the German occupation of France in the Second World War. And though she rarely mentioned her father's role in the war, I began to see him through her scholar's eyes. Why did he join the Nazi Party in 1933? What was he thinking two years later, when Hitler introduced the Nuremberg Race Laws, depriving Jews of citizenship? Why was he imprisoned in Strasbourg after the war? My mother never said, though we talked about her research all the time, and the omission seemed telling. In our loud, gleefully argumentative family, she had always been the voice of reason, of scrupulous fair-mindedness. It must have been a torment to her, trying to square what she learned about the war with her memories of her father. How could he have been both the man she loved and the monster history suggested?

She was his favorite child, my German relatives said. They had heard my uncles grouse about it for years. There was an intensity to my mother's relationship with him—a cautious tenderness, as if they knew each other's weaknesses too well—that he didn't have with anyone else. If my uncles brought out the disciplinarian in him, my mother disarmed him. Perhaps she reminded him of his first wife, who had died young. There was a melancholy in both women, an abiding sense of pity, that tempered the fierce principles beneath. Or maybe he saw some of his own bleak idealism in his daughter—his stubborn belief in the world's perfectibility and even deeper sense of how he had failed it. "Life can't be cheated," he wrote after Sigmar, his middle son, started his first job in 1957, "and every little error comes back to take its revenge."

There were no little errors in wartime Germany. The choices you made put you on one side of history or the other. Yet the more I learned about my grandfather, the harder he was to categorize. His life seemed to sprawl beyond the bare facts of his biography, twisting and bending and doubling back like an oak root beneath a sidewalk. I found myself thinking about him more and more as I got older. At first, this was just idle speculation: He was a story to tell, a riddle to solve, a piece of dark family gossip. Then I began to feel myself bound up in his twists and turns. I got married, had three children, and began to get a visceral sense of how the past lives on inside us. How some of my own character had taken root in my kids, and how much of my parents was lodged in me.

Did my grandfather's past still have a claim on us? I hoped not. At best, I thought, he was a passive accomplice to one of history's most criminal regimes; at worst an eager participant. But no one seemed to know for certain. My mother and her brothers were getting older, their recollections weakening. More than that, they belonged to a generation that was taught never to ask questions about the war. The answers would only be dismal or self-incriminating—or worse, self-justifying. Even my mother, with her historian's mind and intense affinity for her father, never dared to ask him about Alsace.

Was it even possible to uncover a story like his anymore? What was left of Germany's countless *Kleinbürger*—the ordinary citizens who witnessed the war but did their best to bury its memory? Not much, it seemed. Then, one July afternoon seventeen years ago, my mother received a package of letters from one of my aunts. They were postmarked Bartenheim, the village in Alsace where my grandfather was stationed during the war, and they turned his story inside out once again.

It was that package, and an old memory of my mother's about an encounter she'd once had in Bartenheim, that finally drew me back to Germany.

3

FATHER

THE VILLAGE OF BARTENHEIM LIES IN THE LOWLANDS OF southern Alsace, in the unquiet heart of Western Europe. From the belfry of the Catholic church, you can see the spires and smokestacks of Basel to the south, the textile mills of Mulhouse to the north, and the hills of the Black Forest to the east, shouldering above the horizon. *Le pays des trois frontières,* the locals call it. The land of three borders: France, Germany, and Switzerland all within a ten-mile radius. To one side of the village, the Rhine flows north through some of the best farmland in Europe, its fields incandescent with sunflower and rapeseed. To the other side, clay-tiled villages cluster in the foothills of the Vosges, each with a steeple lifted above it like a mother goose watching over her goslings. It's a place of such self-satisfied prosperity, such unruffled repose, that it's hard to imagine it knowing anything but peace. Yet everything here is haunted by the ghost of its former self.

Every Sunday afternoon during the war, my grandfather Karl rode his bicycle to Bartenheim from Germany, to stay in a boarding-house during the week. His path took him over the bridge at Weil am Rhein, where my mother and the rest of his family lived, past small plots of asparagus and tobacco, down *allées* of white-barked syca-mores, and around country graveyards patrolled by swaying cy-presses. From Germany to what had been France and was now Germany again. The landscape looked like it hadn't changed in a thousand years, yet everything in it bore the mark of its divided soul—checkpoints and armed guards, repainted street signs and hushed voices in roadside cafés. Even the castles that clung to the high ridges carried double-barreled names, like children of twice-married parents: Haut-Königsburg, Saint-Ulrich, Château Flecken-stein.

Bartenheim lay squarely on the Maginot Line, on the contested border between Europe's bitterest enemies. After the First World War, the French built fortresses and bunkers up and down the Rhine to repel German attacks, just as the Germans had once built bul-warks against the French. To no avail, as it turned out. Alsace was too lovely and too valuable—too deeply embedded in each country's self-image—to be left alone for long.

On the night of June 14, 1940, German forces crept into position along a forested stretch of the Rhine, some forty miles north of Bartenheim. As a thick fog and then rain drifted over the river the next morning, they bombarded the French bunkers on the opposite shore with heavy artillery, reducing them to rubble within minutes. Then a fleet of motorized assault boats set off under cover of smoke and howitzer fire, crossing the river with regiments of infantry and combat engineers. The invaders soon overwhelmed the French de-fense. Within days, they had built pontoon bridges across the water and broken the enemy line. Within a week, they were marching through Alsace unopposed, singing songs as they went.

Karl followed soon thereafter: He was stationed in Bartenheim from 1940 to 1944. He was forty-one years old when he first came, married with four children, and had been a schoolteacher for eighteen years. He was too old to be on the front lines but not to serve the Reich. Alsace was now part of Germany again, after two decades as part of France, and Karl had been ordered to help reeducate its children. Schools were the vanguard of the *Kulturkampf*—the place where young Alsatians could be cultivated from seed to sprout, like new plants in a nursery. It was Karl's job to turn Bartenheim's beret-wearing French children into sturdy, hardworking Germans—to convince them that the disaster of war was a kind of salvation.

The question was whether he believed so himself. On those Sunday evenings when he wheeled into town, the villagers remember, his uniform was always crisply starched, his boots polished to a gloss. But what was in his heart?

.   .   .

It was that thought, or some half-formed version of it, that brought my mother back to Bartenheim forty years ago. She had been there only once before, in 1943, when she was eight years old. But she had never returned. Then, in the spring of 1983, my father was invited to give a talk on white noise at a physics conference in southern France. Afterward, he and my mother and my sister Andrea were driving across Alsace, on their way to Germany to see relatives, when my mother suddenly sat up straight in her seat. "Could you take the next exit?" she asked. She had seen a name flash by on the highway, like a jump cut in an old film, grainy and overexposed: Bartenheim.

Why hadn't she come before? When I asked her that question once, her reply was a little testy. "Oh, it was just so far away," she said. "It would have been too expensive to bring the whole family from Oklahoma. Five children!" But we had spent years in Europe when my father was on sabbatical, I said. On Saturday mornings when we were living in France, my mother would herd us into our yellow Volkswagen bus and drag us to anything of historical interest within a hundred miles. To ruined abbeys and Roman aqueducts, Cathar fortresses and Romani sanctifications in the Camargue. To Carcassonne and Béziers and the papal palace in Avignon. On holidays, we would take red-eye drives to Lake Constance or the Black Forest to see relatives, while the Bee Gees and Rod McKuen sang their lamentations from the cassette player on the back seat. *Adieu, Emile, it's hard to die / When all the birds are singing in the sky.* Alsace would have been an easy side trip, yet she could never bring herself to go.

When my parents drove into Bartenheim that day, my father stayed in the driver's seat, his yarn cap pulled over his ears. How long was this going to take? They had been on the road all day and were less than an hour from my uncle's house. "Just wait in the car," my mother said. She knew he would be happier there, doing equations in his head with my sister in the back seat to keep him company. And she needed some time alone.

The village was just as she remembered it, yet nothing was the same. The long, winding main street was lined by workaday shops and a village green with budding tulip trees. The houses mixed German propriety and French deshabille, their walls newly plastered here and crumbling picturesquely there. Her father's schoolhouse, which doubled as the town hall, still stood at the center of town, fronting the square. It was the grandest building in Bartenheim, its Gothic windows trimmed in pink sandstone from the Vosges, its stair-step gable like an Alsatian girl with bows in her hair. A school bell hung from the top, and when she stepped inside, the dark, paneled halls still smelled of stove oil and eraser dust, mucilage and pencil shavings. But the children had long since moved to another building.

My mother walked past the reception desk and out to the courtyard, where the students used to play at recess. She thought about
the last time she was here, in 1943, and how ashamed she had felt.
Her father had brought her over from Germany for a day and told
her to sit in with his third-grade class. He was hoping, perhaps, to
impress his students with her sharp mind and rigorous German
schooling. She had always been his most studious child—the one
who took to her education with the same high seriousness he had,
the same zeal. But when the moment came in math class, and he
asked her to calculate a sum, she failed him. Rather than spring up
smartly and recite the answer, she could only give him a blank,
round-eyed stare.

Sitting on the back steps of the old schoolhouse, four decades
later, she remembered the disappointed twist in his mouth that day,
the dry way that he told her to take her seat, then moved on to another student, who answered the question correctly and without
hesitation. There's nothing more for me here, she thought. Her father had died four years earlier, in a nursing home in Germany. Were
he alive, she might have asked him about that day, and the four years
he had spent in Bartenheim during the war. But it was too late for
that now: This old place was just filled with bad memories.

She was heading back to the car when something caught her eye.
Across the courtyard, on the sidewalk behind the back gate, an old
man was walking by. He was pulling a toy wagon behind him with
two small boys inside it, most likely his grandsons. He looked about
as old as her father would have been if he were still alive.

My mother stood still for a moment, hesitating. Then she hurried
across the courtyard. "It was as if my father had given me a shove,"
she told me later. "He said, 'Go look at the school. Go look at the
courtyard. Okay, now you have to say something.'" By the time she
reached the old man, she was too flustered to introduce herself. She
just bid him good day and came to the point, speaking French at first,

then German when she heard the man's accent. Her father, Karl Gönner, had lived here during the war, she said. He was principal of this school during the German occupation. "Do you happen to re-member him?" The old man, whose name was Georges Tschill, just stared at her. "*Ha jo!*" he said, finally. "*Ich ha doch si Lebe grettet!*" Well, of course! I saved his life, didn't I?

.   .   .

Georges Tschill was French; Karl was German. The war had made them enemies, but they could just as easily have been countrymen. They lived fewer than twenty miles apart and shared the same tradi-tions and Catholic faith. Their ancestors had settled the same pine forests and river valleys, and had passed kindred dialects down to them. Tschill's Alsatian had a rich, rustic sound. It was very old Ger-man but laced with French borrowings, like a potato soup swirled with crème fraîche—"*Vielmols Merci.*" "*Répétez noch a mol.*" Karl's Ale-mannisch was softer and more musical, with the singsong cadences of the Black Forest. But the two men would have understood each other perfectly. They just happened to live on opposite sides of the river.

The Rhine was less than half a mile wide at that point, yet people had fought over it for two thousand years. Blame it on Caesar. When he marched his four legions into eastern Gaul in 58 B.C., it had no single national identity or established border. The pagan tribes who inhabited it—the Sequani, the Treveri, the Leuci, the Suebi—were more Celtic in their language and culture in some cases; more Ger-manic in others. But the difference wasn't always clear. People on both sides of the river hunted and farmed, forged iron and bronze, revered nature, and were said to perform human sacrifices. The Celts, according to Caesar, believed in the transmigration of souls, and their property may have changed hands as often. If the river froze one winter and some warriors stormed across it, it wasn't long before someone chased them back.

The Romans put an end to all that. To govern effectively, they needed their colonies well defined, their borders clearly drawn. Rather than try to parse the differences between a dozen Celtic and Germanic tribes, Caesar tossed them all into a few clearly labeled sacks. "The whole of Gaul is divided into three parts," he declared in *The Gallic Wars*, his summary of his campaigns there between 58 and 50 B.C. "These all differ from one another in language, custom, and law. The Gauls are divided from the Aquitains by the river Garonne, and from the Belgians by the Marne and the Seine. . . . They are closest to the Germans across the Rhine, with whom they are always at war."

Germanis, qui trans Rhenum incolunt: the Germans across the Rhine. With that one passing phrase, Caesar drew an indelible line in the river bottom and seeded a durable set of stereotypes. The Gauls were "tall of body with rippling muscles," the Greek historian Diodorus Siculus later wrote. They had white skin and blond hair, which they bleached in lime water. The Germans were thickset and coarse, according to Tacitus, with "fierce blue eyes, red hair, and huge frames, fit only for sudden exertion." The Gauls were a little soft but susceptible to civilization. The Germans were hotheads, fearsome in battle. Best to keep them on the far side of the river.

Caesar invented Germany, some historians say. Yet even the Romans changed their minds about where its borders lay: Caesar drew the line at the Rhine, but later maps lumped both sides of the river into *Germania Superior*. The Rhine was easier to cross and less culturally isolating than the Vosges Mountains to the west and the Jura to the south. And even if Gaul did end at the Rhine, as Caesar claimed, and most Gauls stemmed from Celtic rather than Germanic stock, the Celts themselves had come from across the Rhine hundreds of years earlier. Their ancestral homeland lay in what is now Austria and southeastern Germany.

Where, then, did Germany end and France begin?

The names didn't help. The Franks conquered Gaul in the fifth century, and Charlemagne was crowned emperor of Francia in 786. But the Franks were a Germanic tribe, and Charlemagne seems to have spoken an archaic form of High German. (The Germans call him Karl der Grosse and claim him as their own.) When Charlemagne's empire was divided up by three of his grandsons, the western third became the basis for modern France and the eastern third for modern Germany. But it was the middle kingdom that was the most coveted. It ran from what is now the Netherlands to Italy and included Rome and Aachen, the seats of the Pope and the Holy Roman Emperor. France and Germany had distinct languages and natural borders: the Alps, the Pyrenees, the Atlantic, the Baltic. But the middle kingdom was a random patchwork of territories and tongues, and Alsace was at the center. It wasn't long before its neighbors were playing tug-of-war over it.

And so it went: French and German, Frank and Goth, Gaul and Alemann—all flip sides of the same coin. Yet nothing mattered more than which side you were on. Alsace became the great fault line of Western Europe: a strip of land only thirty miles wide that changed nationalities six times in twelve centuries. The Germans annexed it in 870, ceded it to Louis XIV in 1648, then took it back in 1871, after the Franco-Prussian War. The French reclaimed it in 1918, lost it to the Germans in 1940, and got it back on November 23, 1944, when Allied troops marched into Strasbourg.

· · ·

My mother knew most of that history on the morning she met Georges Tschill. In her quiet way, she had been circling Alsace and her father's past for years. As soon as her youngest child went to first grade, she went back to school to study history. She started out slowly, taking a couple of courses at a community college. Then in the summer of 1978, she brought a rumpled copy of her *Abitur* diploma—the German baccalaureate—and teaching certificate to the admissions office at Oklahoma State University. They had no idea what to make of the documents, but they had a vague respect for German schooling. So they shrugged and enrolled her as a master's candidate.

She was in her forties then, twenty years older than most of the students in her program. She had a house and five children to manage along with the classes she was taking or teaching as a graduate assistant. Although her English was fluent and precise, it couldn't match her eloquence in German, so the writing came hard. It was a constant tussle with words, with never quite saying what she hoped to say, always feeling like she was running behind, letting her children down, missing the last years of their youth. "I don't like to think back on that time," she once told me. *"Es war a bizli von a Alptraum."* A bit of a nightmare. But then something more than ambition was driving her.

I was fourteen when she went back to school full-time and mainly recall the steep drop-off in dinner quality. My mother had always been a wonderful cook, trained in a Swiss culinary school in Basel before she married. But her *Spätzli* and *Kohlrouladen* soon gave way to Pillsbury Bake-Off recipes, then to frazzled calls from her cubicle in the history department. Could I put the pork roast in the oven? She hung a chart of rotating chores for us on the refrigerator and abandoned our bedrooms to teenage entropy, but she was still up past midnight most weekdays, leafing through French documents or folding laundry as we slept.

Literature had been her first love—her valedictorian address was on Hermann Hesse's long, cerebral novel *The Glass Bead Game*. But now she focused on history and the two World Wars. She began by stalking their periphery, like an arson investigator picking through charred beams and broken glass. Rather than write about the fighting in Europe, she studied its effect on emigrants like her, five thousand miles away. Her master's thesis looked at German American communities in Oklahoma during the First World War. When the war began, she found, the state had seven German-language weeklies. By 1920, only two were left. Anti-German sentiment ran so hot that Oklahoma banned the use of German in public. Some towns changed their names—Kiel to Loyal, Bismark to Wright. In others, schoolchildren held German book burnings, and German sympathizers were beaten, lashed, hanged, or tarred and feathered.

By the end of the Great War, the new country had lost its luster for the émigrés. "There was no way back to the secluded and isolated German communities of prewar times," my mother wrote. When I read that passage, I caught my breath at the buried longing in it: She was so clearly talking about herself and her own family, too. "The new generation spoke English at school, on the playground and often even at home," she went on. "They grew up as Americans, fully assimilated. While their parents still carried with them a little piece of Europe with which they never would or could part, their emigration from the homeland had become final and irrevocable in the children."

·   ·   ·

Patriotism was her true subject. Patriotism and prejudice and the ways the two can amplify and distort each other. When the United States went to war against Germany in 1917, she wrote, the problem wasn't one of conflicting loyalties but of conflicting loves. Whichever side the emigrants chose, they were betraying themselves. The people of Bartenheim would face a similar decision twenty-five years later. To be true to your country was the one inviolate rule of war. But what if that country had already changed hands twice in your lifetime? Or, like my mother's father, you took orders from an ever more criminal regime? What did disloyalty mean then?

My mother wasn't ready to answer those questions, much less write about her father. But step-by-step her research was drawing her closer, tightening the circle of police tape. I have her doctoral dissertation in front of me as I write, bound in black buckram, its edges gone sepia with age. Reading it now, I can see her wrestling with her family's legacy on every page. But her dissertation isn't about her father. It's about a man who must have reminded her of him, however uneasily: Henri Philippe Pétain, chief of state of the Vichy regime during the Second World War. Like Karl, Pétain was Catholic, the son of a farmer, and a veteran of the First World War. He was an idealist who insisted on the rule of law, an elitist who championed the working class. He was willing to die for his convictions, no matter how wrongheaded they were.

My mother looked at Pétain through the reporting of American war correspondents, and her writing has some of the same blunt urgency. She was too skeptical of her own English to be seduced by jargon, too late to academia to worry about impressing colleagues. She needed to pin down her own unsettled mind. I was a freshman in college by then and still remember her voice over the phone—the weary, conflicted sound of it. At one point, I went door-to-door in my dormitory to scrounge donations for a (pretty skimpy) care package to send her. She needed one more than I did.

As the French commander in chief in the First World War, Pétain had rallied his forces to victory in 1918. Yet the same qualities that made him a hero in that war proved his undoing in the next. On June 17, 1940, three days after Hitler's armies took Paris, Pétain asked the French people to lay down their arms: "It is with a heavy heart that I tell you today that we must cease hostilities," he declared, in a national radio address. Churchill wanted the French army to retreat to Brittany, fight a guerrilla war, or make a stand in Paris. Charles de Gaulle, the leader of the Free French Forces, wanted the government to rule from exile in North Africa. But to Pétain, those options were unthinkable. To flee was dishonorable; to keep fighting was madness. France would be reduced to ruins. Worse, the French people might be won over by Nazi ideology. It had taken just a few years for the Germans to come under its spell, and for the Russians to be swept up by communism. The only defense, Pétain believed, was to revive and unify French culture. To reaffirm its Christian and patriotic values—by force if necessary. Otherwise, France could "lose her soul."

On June 22, 1940, France signed an armistice with Germany. It divided France into two zones: The north and west would be occupied by Hitler's armies; the south would be governed by the puppet Vichy regime. Within a month, the French parliament had disbanded and granted Pétain absolute power to lead the new government. His regime went on to impose strict censorship and create a paramilitary force, known as the *Milice*, to hunt down those who resisted. It barred the children of immigrants from civil service jobs and Jews from working on newspapers, in schools, or in high government positions. Then it went further, confiscating Jewish property and arresting its owners. By war's end, the Vichy regime had helped deport more than seventy-five thousand Jews to death camps in Poland. Fewer than three thousand returned. If Pétain began by trying to save his country's soul, my mother concluded, he ended up trying to "beat the Fascists at their own game."

Before the armistice, *Time* magazine described Pétain as the "shining symbol of French courage and resistance." Five years later, on August 15, 1945, he was court-martialed and condemned to death as a traitor. He had hoped that the armistice would lead to a peace treaty. But the Nazis just tightened their grip on France. In Alsace, which was annexed outright, the occupation had a strange double edge. The Germans took prisoners, seized food and lodging, and drafted young Alsatian men into the army. Yet they framed it as a homecoming. The French had deported two thousand Alsatians to Germany after the First World War and forced the rest to carry identity cards based on degrees of French ancestry. Now the Nazis brutally reversed course. French families were deported and Germans brought in. The rest of the population was once again issued identity cards, this time to prove their German ancestry. Those who resisted were sent to the reeducation camp at Schirmeck, an hour and a half north of Bartenheim, or to nearby Natzweiler-Struthof, the only death camp in France.

•   •   •

All of this must have weighed on my mother's mind that morning in Bartenheim. She had finished the first draft of her dissertation just a few weeks earlier. In her years of research, she had never dared to ask about her father's role in the war. Hadn't I avoided it, too? Perhaps it was because we both knew part of the answer already: Karl wasn't in France just to teach schoolchildren. He was also Bartenheim's Nazi Party chief.

That was what she and Georges Tschill talked about that day behind the schoolhouse. Tschill's grandsons were squirming in the wagon behind him, and my father was waiting impatiently in the car, drumming his hands on the steering wheel. But my mother wasn't thinking about them. She was imagining the scene in that same village during the war. When French troops reclaimed Bartenheim in November of 1944, Tschill told her, her father was among the leaders who were rounded up and tied to a tree to await execution. This was Karl's true moment of judgment—long before the lawyers and interrogators and war crimes tribunals could weigh in—and Tschill was in charge. He was the leader of the local Resistance in those days, he said. When it came time to decide who should live and who should die, the choice fell to him.

4

ANCESTOR

HIDDEN INSIDE KARL'S UNIFORM, TUCKED FLAT AGAINST HIS chest as he awaited a verdict of life or death, was a small book with blue-gray binding. A single word was stamped on the cover in gold Gothic print: *Ahnenpaß*. Below it, a coat of arms bore a sword, a spade, and the open-handed Nazi salute. As a civil servant and party member, Karl had to have Aryan blood and an "ancestry passport" like this one to prove it. The pages were filled with his strong, clear script, in royal-blue ink from a fountain pen. He must have spent countless evenings and weekends working on it, digging through church records, village archives, and his relatives' spotty memories, filling page after page with births, deaths, baptisms, and marriages. It was a step-by-step account of how this man came to be bound to that tree.

"Anton Gönner," the first entry read. A master tailor born on

January 15, 1741, Anton was my great-great-great-great grandfather. He was married at thirty-one to Ursula Hall, twenty-six, in the Catholic church in the village of Ippingen, on the eastern edge of the Black Forest. The Gönners never wandered far from their roots. The generations that followed were all born and baptized within twenty miles of that same church. They were farmers, glassblowers, day laborers, or simply "burghers," as Karl noted in his book: citizens. But they were of unimpeachably German stock. On the last page of entries, my mother's name appeared, the third of his four children: Edeltraut Luise Gönner, born June 14, 1935. "*Dein Blut, dein höchstes Gut!*" the facing page declared. "Your Blood, your highest Good!"

Genealogy was more than just a duty under Hitler. It was a national obsession—a kind of religion. By 1937, the historian Eric Ehrenreich notes in his book *The Nazi Ancestral Proof,* the Reich Genealogical Authority was sifting through more than a million identity cards. By 1939, it had nearly a hundred and fifty employees. Kinship offices were created, document agencies established, bookstores filled with blank *Ahnenpäße* and manuals on how to complete them. At first, only Nazi Party members and their spouses, and members of organizations affiliated with the party, had to provide proof of ancestry. (Nazi leaders had to trace their families back to 1800, some members of the SS to 1750.) Then soldiers, students, civil servants, lawyers, doctors, dentists, and others were added to the list. By 1945, Germany had more than two thousand race-based laws and ordinances, and nearly every citizen had some form of ancestral proof. At one point, the state-run publisher Westfalia warned the government that its supply of genealogy books was almost gone. The printers were running out of paper.

Often, a birth certificate and a sworn statement were all the documents that authorities needed. But on occasion—if someone claimed that the Jewish father who raised them wasn't their birth father, for instance—a heredity exam had to be administered. First a blood test (often inconclusive) to see if they were born out of wedlock. Then a study of their fingerprints, facial features, eye color, skull shape, skin color, and sometimes mental attributes. Once the data had been gathered and analyzed, the candidates were slotted into precise (though largely fictional) racial categories: Aryan, Jew, Alien, and *Mischling* or Mixed-Race. Hitler's Nuremberg Laws left no room for ambiguity. Anyone with three or four Jewish grandparents was barred from citizenship, civil service, and sexual relations with "true" Germans. "The blood that bore us is no indifferent matter," one of the epigraphs in the *Ahnenpaß* insisted (it was written by the German poet Isolde Kurz, who wrote the eulogy for Hitler's fiftieth birthday). "Our forebears move quietly beside us through life and, unknown to us, color all that we do."

Like so much of my grandfather's story, his ancestry passport induces a double vision. It's both a simple family history and a symbol of collective madness, a product of coercion and complicity. Its pages reduce history to a straight line: Anton begat Johann begat Martin begat Thomas begat Karl. They presume that DNA is destiny and genealogy is a road map to the future as well as the past. But the Nazis soon found otherwise. Carrying the *Ahnenpaß* may have offered safe passage in Germany, but doing so could get you killed in France, after it was liberated. The fact that Karl still had it with him when French troops reclaimed Alsace—that he was in Bartenheim when he could have stayed safely at home across the Rhine—was an act of both pride and conscience, obedience and suicidal atonement.

This is who I am, it said. Or who I used to be, before the war remade me.

·   ·   ·

One July morning in 2014, I took a walk up an old logging road in the Black Forest, to the village of Herzogenweiler, where my grandfather was born. I had moved to Germany that summer with my wife, Jennifer, and my youngest daughter, Evangeline, retracing my parents' path to America half a century earlier. Evangeline would be in the eighth grade that fall, at a bilingual school in Berlin. My two older children, Hans and Ruby, were in college and would join us later that year. They had heard me speak Alemannisch with my parents and siblings all their lives, and Hans had taken a year of German in school. But none of them spoke the language fluently or had spent any time in Germany. It was nearly as foreign to them as America once was to my parents.

I thought of the family history Karl had traced so assiduously in his *Ahnenpaß:* five generations of farmers and laborers circling these same woods. That heritage seemed to end with us. My sisters had re-created a version of it in the United States: They had all moved within twenty minutes of one another in Madison, Wisconsin, along with my parents. My sisters spoke Alemannisch with their children, but I lived in Brooklyn, far from family, and my dialect seemed too rusty and secondhand to pass along. I had tried teaching it to Hans when he was a toddler, but I had only a few hours a day with him after work, and I couldn't bear the baffled look on his face. Moving to Germany was a way to both wrestle with my heritage and reclaim it. I was there to gather stories about my grandfather, but also, I hoped, to show my children something of the country I had known as a boy—a place as darkly romantic, in its way, as the American West was to my father.

When I first came to the Black Forest at the age of five, it felt immeasurably older than the surrounding country. It had a brooding, secretive air, like a sleeping castle covered with thorns. In high summer, the trees had a hand-painted look, at once enchanting and faintly menacing, and the air was scented with elderflower and wild rose. When you stepped off the path and into the woods, the moss was so thick underfoot that it bounced beneath your feet, and you felt like little Hansel or Rose Red striding gallantly into the gloom. Even at midday, the branches turned the sun to twilight.

Herzogenweiler lay an hour up the hill, at close to three thousand feet. I passed an old forester's hut like a hobbit's home, its windows fringed with moss, and a deer stand perched above the slope like a child's treehouse. Then the path leveled off and emerged into a moon-shaped clearing, hemmed in on three sides by dark ranks of pines. When I came there as a boy, the village had the rough, homely look of a farming community. The air was edged with coal soot and wood ash, the houses crowned by haylofts spilling their stuffing onto the street. Inside my great-aunt's house, at the heavy oak table in the kitchen, you could smell haunches of double-smoked *Speck* hanging from rafters in the attic, and feel the heat from the huge ceramic *Kachelofen* in the corner. It was a place that bore the scars of its history as well as its comforts.

That sense of the past alive in the present was getting harder to find in Germany. Before coming south that summer, we had rented an apartment in Berlin, on an elegant old street off Savignyplatz in Charlottenburg, where parts of *Cabaret* were filmed. It had been twenty-five years since the Wall fell and Berlin was newly seamless. The death strip where defectors were once shot on sight was now green with parks, the city's history not so much forgotten as put under glass. The Brandenburg Gate was washed clean, its bomb-pocked parade grounds replaced by shiny new government buildings. "Transparency" was the watchword that the tour guides all used, in their impeccable, lightly accented English. In place of fascist colonnades, the new buildings had walls of clear glass. Standing under the dome of the Reichstag, you could peer straight down into the chambers of Parliament. Germany, once the scourge of the Soviet Union and Western Europe, was now a crucial bridge between them. Angela Merkel, fluent in both Russian and English, was said to be the sole Western leader that Vladimir Putin could abide.

Yet if Germany's borders were unified, its spirit was still divided. It wasn't just that the East was poorer and older than the West—millions of young workers having fled west across the border after it opened—or that it had higher unemployment and less immigration. It was that the two halves of the country had a different relationship to the past. East Germans, as members of the Soviet bloc, had been taught to believe that they shared little blame for the Nazi era. Never mind that people in eastern Germany cast more votes for the Nazis than for any other party in 1933. Their descendants saw themselves as spiritual heirs to the Berlin communists of the twenties and thirties: the heroic resistance.

Reminders of the past lay in wait around every corner in Berlin, like a schoolmaster with a switch: memorials, bunkers, and fragments of the Wall, Stasi prisons and the former headquarters of the SS, rebuilt as an exhibit called "The Topography of Terror." Yet the city felt oddly at ease with its tortured history. Even the Russians, long gone and little mourned, had been allowed to leave their monuments behind: a forty-foot soldier crushing a swastika underfoot; rows of white sarcophagi carved with gilded quotes from Josef Stalin. Inside the Reichstag, the walls were scrawled with Cyrillic graffiti, carefully translated for visitors: "Death to Germans."

In the West, the opposite was true. The past seemed to weigh on everything, yet reminders of it were hard to find. This was partly a function of prosperity—West Germans could afford to rebuild more thoroughly than East Germans—and partly of deliberate erasure. In Berlin, the sidewalks glimmered with small bronze plaques, embedded in the cobbles. Known as *Stolpersteine*, or stumble stones, they each bore the name of a German Jew who had once lived at that address, usually followed by his or her deportation date and manner of death. In Munich, the city council wouldn't allow the stumble stones. They were an eyesore, some Bavarians said, an affront to the very people they were meant to honor. "People murdered in the Holocaust deserve better than a plaque in the dust," Charlotte Knobloch, a former president of the Central Council of Jews in Germany, declared in 2015. In Villingen-Schwenningen, the nearest city to Herzogenweiler, the district council twice rejected the plaques.

The farther south we went, the more the past seemed to disappear. Beyond Stuttgart, in the green foothills of Baden-Württemberg, the villages had a toylike perfection: roads freshly paved, gardens neat as needlework. Even the forests looked carefully groomed. The makeover was so complete, the surgery so free of scars, that it could be a little unsettling. "It's like a giant miniature golf course," my son Hans said. But its benefits were hard to deny. Germans worked less and lived longer than Americans. They had less poverty and a third less violent crime. They had a balanced budget, at least four weeks of vacation, and twelve to fourteen months of maternity or paternity leave. A few months after we arrived, a poll of more than twenty thousand people in twenty countries voted Germany the world's most admired nation—if still far from the most beloved. As Britain's *Daily Telegraph* put it: "The world voted and the best country is . . . Germany?"

Herzogenweiler hadn't escaped the change. In the years since I first visited, the village had become a prosperous bedroom community, far removed from the clanking rhythms of farm life. Its haylofts were mostly gone, its farmhouses rebuilt or updated, their rubble walls replastered and whitewashed. The village had celebrated its eight hundredth birthday in 2008, but you never would have known it. The buildings were as stubbornly uniform as most modern homes in Germany: tile roofs, stucco walls, dark wooden window frames. One style fits all. The problem of housing had been solved, apparently, as had the problem of governance (centrist), transportation (Mercedes), and salad (the dreaded "mixed plate"). There was an admirable logic to all this—German houses were built as stoutly as bomb shelters—but also a nagging sense of diminishment. The downside of erasing history is that you lose what's beautiful as well as what's hard to bear.

·   ·   ·

My mother spent almost every childhood summer in Herzogenweiler. It was her family's second home, where their oldest friends and most trusted relatives lived. It was where they fled in wartime and spent their holidays in times of peace. The Black Forest seemed to contain all that Karl admired most about his country: its deep history and natural beauty, poetry and rough-hewn practicality. Yet it was also where his faith in German society was first shaken, and where the seeds of his politics were planted.

Every year, as soon as school was over, Karl would pack up the family and make the two-hour drive north from Weil am Rhein. My mother's memories of those summers seem to belong to another age. Heading out to the fields before dawn with her brothers, scythes balanced on their shoulders. Gathering currants in the woods in July, blackberries in August, then cranberries and plums in the late summer heat. They would wheel home on their bikes as the sun set, baskets brimming, then separate the fruit from its prickly leaves around the fire at night. When they came back to visit in October, the potatoes were in the cellar and the granaries full. Then the air grew crisp and smoky, and it was butchering time. I've never seen my mother's eyes glow as they did when she talked about making fresh blood sausage. By late February, the villagers were in the fields again, gathering stones churned up by frost heaves, clearing the ground for the next crop of hay as the seasons spun round again.

It was an entrancing cycle for a city girl—the earth's rhythms made manifest—but a relentless one for the villagers. Their only break was on Sundays, when the women would take turns going to church and making soup for dinner, then spend two hours in the afternoon visiting. My mother was a fair-weather guest by comparison—a bird that flew off as soon as the berries were gone. One day in the fall, she was walking across a field with her aunt Elise, gleaning the last of the hard red Russian wheat, when she made the mistake of telling Elise about her dreams. She wanted to be a historian one day, she said, to travel the world and excavate the pyramids in Egypt, and . . . her aunt cut her short. Elise had always had a clenched, *verwurzelt* quality—like a hard root wrapped around a stone—and she had no patience for such talk. "You'd do better to explore your stocking drawer," she told her, then bent back to her task.

Mit dir rede ich nimi, my mother remembers thinking. That's the last thing I'll tell you. Still, Elise was an exception. Most of my mother's relatives in the Black Forest had a surprising delicacy about them, their tact of a piece with their toughness. They would never say they loved you, but might murmur that you had such fine, soft hair. They were *stille Menschen*, she said, but they went deep. "They don't say a lot, but tears come easily. You don't have to talk when you're crying." There was dapper Otto Hug, whose family had owned the village inn for three centuries, and my mother's cousin Manfred, who used to play his harmonica in the potato fields as they dug. His hair was so black that soccer players from other villages mistook him for a visiting Italian. And there was Hedwig, her cousin Gerhard's aunt, whose room my mother shared during the war. They would lie awake at night, when the work was finally done, and talk about *Tod und Teufel*— the devil knows what—and the books they had read. How would it be to wander on the open plains like Karl May's Winnetou? Or to live for art and pure experience like Hesse's Goldmund?

My mother would follow her daydreams across the ocean, but the others never left the Black Forest. When I drove there with my family that summer, Otto Hug still had a house in the village, though the family inn had been sold to an innkeeper from a neighboring town. Manfred lived in an apartment nearby. He was a confirmed bachelor, his long silver hair swept back, his eyes a little wild. And I spent a few memorable afternoons with Hedwig, now eighty-eight, the last of the eight children in her family who was still alive. Her eyes were cloudy and her hearing poor, her circulation sputtery and her gait unsteady. She hated wearing hearing aids or using a walker—"that little wagon," she called it. But she seemed to remember everything.

Hedwig liked to receive me in her sitting room, with cut flowers from her garden on the table and glasses of apple juice from her own trees. She was always dressed for company, her snowy hair neatly combed, her round face crinkled with smile lines as she told stories in a faint, papery voice, like a breeze through dry leaves. She talked about the endless work of the farm: bringing in harvests after midnight and plowing fields in her bare feet—the horse stepped on her toes so often, she said, that one of them was still wider than the others. Then she talked about the dark secrets of the war. Her uncle Franz-Josef was a driver for Field Marshal Paulus at Stalingrad, she said, and came back soul-sick at what German troops had done. But his brother Oskar, who had also fought in Russia, refused to believe him. And then there was the neighbor girl, Amalie, lovely and bright but not always right in her mind. She was sent to an asylum during the war and returned to them two weeks later, ashes in a box.

Hedwig's stories were beautiful and terrible—a century reduced to its rough, bittersweet essence. But to know the history behind them, and how it shaped my grandfather, I had to go somewhere else. I had to see Gerhard Blessing.

·   ·   ·

Gerhard was my grandfather's nephew, his half brother Heinrich's son. He was an eccentric by local standards: bookish but talkative, with a sweet, snaggletoothed smile. He had a long face with sunken, liquid eyes and a hungry gaze, like a stray who couldn't quite trust the bone set before him. In a village full of thick-skinned farmers, he was a wordy, sensitive soul, used to feeling far more than he could say. Yet the villagers always spoke of him with a gruff respect. If anyone knew the history of this place, they said—if anyone could tell me its secrets—it was Gerhard.

When he came to the door that morning, he seemed surprised to see me. I had called ahead to arrange the visit, but perhaps he didn't think I would really come. He gave me a sidelong, searching look, then nodded and shambled down the hall ahead of me. I half expected to find a hermit's cave inside—dim and dusty, with piles of old magazines and coffee-stained newspaper clippings. But the house was sunlit and airy, its white walls trimmed with blond wood in the modern German fashion. Gerhard's wife, Rita, came out briefly to greet me—she had spiky brown hair and a brusque, bemused manner, as if well accustomed to her husband's odd visitors. Then Gerhard and I sat down for tea in the back room, surrounded by his most constant companions: the books of philosophy and military history that lined the walls.

When Gerhard was born, in 1950, Germany was still in its postwar hunger throes. Vegetables were scarce, meat reserved for Sundays, and the lack of vitamin D and other nutrients gave Gerhard a bad case of rickets. He had pigeon toes and a chicken chest and wore boards tucked into his shoes to straighten out his bandy legs. He was ten years old before he could ride a bike. "I always wondered where I came from," he told me. "I was a nervous boy. I had this chaos of feelings. I wasn't good at dealing with stress and I didn't have much willpower. So I had to organize my spirit. I had to understand it, to structure it. And then I started to realize that literature could help me."

He stood up and pulled a slim brown volume from the bookcase beside the couch, then handed it to me. "There are things that I have to undo so that I can find peace within myself," he said. "Things that don't come easily. And for that I need philosophy." The book was *The Question of Guilt* by Karl Jaspers.

· · ·

Gerhard was a '68er, a member of the generation of Germans who came of age amid the political bonfires of 1968. He turned eighteen that year, when close to a hundred thousand protesters marched on Bonn and student rioters filled the streets of Paris, hurling cobblestones and Molotov cocktails. Police brutality and government repression, like foreign wars and a conservative press, were the predictable outgrowths of the West's authoritarian roots, they believed. Germans had been taught to turn their backs on the two World Wars—to forget that their culture was nearly destroyed and get on with rebuilding it. But the signs of their parents' complicity were all around them. The government, military, and universities were still riddled with former fascists. Even the chancellor himself, Kurt Georg Kiesinger, was once a member of the Nazi Party. The old guard had never left, it seemed; they had simply traded in their uniforms.

Gerhard could remember tense meals in his parents' kitchen in those years, grilling his father and Karl about the war. He wanted to hear their stories, now that he was old enough to bear them, but not necessarily to lay blame. "My generation was extremely critical," he told me. "And I completely understood why: That was when those lies were exposed. But I always had the feeling that my experience didn't really match what people were saying. That there were more truths than just the one."

Gerhard knew a family in Herzogenweiler that had lost all three sons to the war in 1942—one in Leningrad, one in Moscow, and one in Germany from diphtheria. The mother was a thickset woman with arms like ax handles, but she grew so weak from grief and illness that she began to tremble uncontrollably. "I couldn't stand there and judge them," Gerhard said. "It wasn't my job to judge. I couldn't know how I would have reacted in their situation. I could only determine what happened, and that was bad enough."

Gerhard's father was mayor of Herzogenweiler in those years, but Gerhard saw my grandfather as the true voice of authority. He called him *Götti*, the local term for godfather, and the two of them would often go walking together in the forest in the evening. Karl would fish a Blue Ribbon cigarette from his pocket—one of his few indulgences—and smoke it as he listened quietly to Gerhard's troubles. "He was *Aufgeschlossen*," Gerhard said—open, unlocked—both the most learned man in the village and the easiest to talk to. When Gerhard, at sixteen, fell for a local girl—a poor but beautiful relation who arrived one summer wearing tight jeans and other city clothes—it was Götti who was brought in to set him straight. Sixteen was no age to be falling in love, Karl said, and not with this girl. When he was a young man, he told Gerhard, he was once tempted by a girl, too, but he managed to fend her off.

Gerhard ignored him, but not without a pang of conscience: "Götti, he knew everything. But he was an idealist, and to be an idealist is to believe in something so strongly that you want it to be perfect. And if you go far enough, it becomes totalitarianism." He paused and glanced up at me. "I've never been to America," he said. "But I've read that you tend to put people on a pedestal or tear them down. They're heroes or traitors. But man is by nature flawed, and he has to live with the fact that he contradicts himself. That's what makes him a man. Otherwise, he would be a cuckoo clock. Götti had terrible things happen in his life, so when we talked about the war, I didn't want to accuse him. I just wanted to know what happened. What did he do?"

.　　.　　.

The question went deeper than guilt or innocence. "*Etwas ist nur wahr wenn das Gegenteil auch wahr ist,*" Gerhard said, paraphrasing the poet Friedrich Hölderlin: Something is true only if the opposite is also true. To understand what happened in Alsace or the Black Forest during the war, you had to understand the history behind those events. Yet Herzogenweiler seemed adrift in time, unmoored by the epochal events that had blown through it. "No one knew anything about the past," Gerhard said.

He went on to earn his *Abitur* diploma and study education in Freiburg—where Karl Jaspers had studied law—then speech pathology in Reutlingen. Yet he always came back to Herzogenweiler. "I wanted to know where I was from," he said. "And I began to realize that there was such drama in this little village, both high and low, and I was part of it."

Gerhard thought he would start by looking in the village archives. There was just one problem: They no longer existed. All but a few of the village records had been lost in 1945, when they were burned by locals desperate to erase their Nazi past. The archives in the neighboring city of Villingen had survived the war, but their contents were mostly bureaucratic: ration cards, enlistment forms, lists of the dead and wounded. The real stories lay in people's memories. The question was how to access them. About the distant past, Gerhard's neighbors seemed to know very little—a few family stories and funny anecdotes, hard to tell from apocrypha. About the recent past some preferred not to talk at all.

Herzogenweiler was a small village, and Gerhard had known most people in it since childhood. Still, it took him twenty years to get their stories. He plumbed people's memories over *Kaffee und Kuchen*. He bought rounds of Fürstenberg at the village tavern and sifted through crates of old papers in attics and basements. He organized a working group of local history buffs and met with them every week to share findings. It was a never-ending process, he told me on that first visit. If you wanted to understand the Nazi years, you had to understand the crushing poverty in the village after the First World War. To understand the war, you had to understand Prussian authoritarianism and the bitter persistence of the German feudal system in the Black Forest. Gerhard cast his eyes around at the roomful of books. The longer you followed the story, he said, the further back it led, like a ball of twine unwinding in a labyrinth.

5

SON

TO A BOY LIKE KARL, BORN IN 1899, THE VILLAGE MUST have seemed a haunted place. Year by year the population fell, till fewer than a hundred people were left in 1910. Herzogenweiler was becoming a ghost town. Compared to gas-lit, factory-filled cities like Stuttgart and Saarbrücken, these Black Forest villages had hardly changed since the Brothers Grimm wrote about them a century earlier. Those tales were like yesterday's gossip. The same ragged cow pastures lined the dirt roads. The same peasants scythed the fields. The villagers still couldn't buy their own land, hunt for their own larder, or kill the wild boars that marauded through their crops. The boars, like everything else, belonged to the Fürst of Fürstenberg.

In the rare moments that Karl had to himself, when he wasn't pulling weeds or peeling potatoes or any of a dozen other chores, he would wander the fields around Herzogenweiler, finding traces of the life that used to be: cracked vases and crystal schnapps decanters, ruby red and cornflower blue; fire bricks, bottle molds, crucibles, and flow pieces, still smudged with cinders from the furnace. The village was founded by six glassblowers in 1721, when the area was still primeval forest. To the east, the land fell away toward the Brigach Valley and the ancient town of Donaueschingen, then rose again to the pale peaks of the Swabian Alps. To the west, vast forests of oak, fir, spruce, and pine stretched to the horizon, dotted with beech, chestnut, hazelnut, and deer elder. That was why the glassblowers came. They needed wood to fire their kilns, and this forest seemed to have an endless supply.

Herzogenweiler meant "Duke's hamlet"—as if the new settlers needed reminding. The Fürst of Fürstenberg, who owned it, was now a prince of the Holy Roman Empire. (His descendants still live in Donaueschingen, in a palace of the Belle Époque with a fountain said to be the source of the Danube. "They're stone rich," my mother once told me. "They fly to Switzerland in the morning just for coffee and rolls.") The Fürst owned not only the glassblowers' land but their houses and any surplus of their labor. He charged a tax for every hog butchered and field fenced in, every marriage performed and child baptized. It was all there in the lease. The glassmakers had to swear an oath of fealty to the Fürst and agree to send their children to Sunday school. If a man died, his family owed the Fürst their best cow; if a woman died, her best dress.

This suited the settlers fine at first: There was profit enough for everyone. The *Waldglas* of Herzogenweiler—a pale forest green, etched, fluted, or hand-painted with woodland scenes—wasn't as prized as Bohemian glass, but it sold well in Swabia, Switzerland, and France. The same trade routes, later adopted by local clockmakers, would stretch as far as Genoa and Tunis, bringing back silks, saffron, and Persian ouds, frankincense and Egyptian canaries. By the nineteenth century, the village had become a fashionable way station for aristocrats on holiday. They rode up by carriage with their stiff-backed retinue, the men in knee-high boots and red hunting jackets, the women in silks and brocaded satins from Paris. They took rooms in the village inn, *Zum Hirschen*—named for the twenty-point buck whose head was mounted inside—and hired a guide for what to him were a month's wages. They shot deer, wolf, and wild boar, and rose before dawn to creep up on wood grouse, asleep in their roosts deep in the woods.

In their heyday, the glassworks had ten kilns running all day and much of the night. The radiant heat was so intense that the glassblowers strapped wooden boards to their thighs to keep them from blistering. To live next to the factory was like having a lit bomb beside you, with a fuse of uncertain length. Everything in the village was flammable: the buildings, haylofts, workers' clothes and hair. To contain the fires, the glassworks were built in a clearing, with houses gathered in a horseshoe around them—close enough for a frantic dash with slopping buckets; far enough to stay clear of sparks.

By 1871, when Karl's mother was born, the Black Forest had been thinned to a gray second growth. For every goblet the factory produced, it consumed a whole tree. In a year, it burned as much as 150,000 cubic feet of wood. As the forests fell, the workers switched from hardwood to soft to keep the furnaces fed. They rafted in trees from neighboring regions and carted them up with teams of oxen. They planted fir, then even faster-growing spruce, and still the wood ran out. Mired in debt, some of the workers joined a tax strike from 1838 to 1843, and the failed German Revolution five years later. Once the Prussian army had restored order, the Fürstenbergs increased the rebels' tenancy fees and allowed another glassworks to open in a neighboring village. Soon, rail lines were snaking deep into the forest, carrying factory-made glass from the Rhineland, sold at a fraction of the cost. The glassmakers of Herzogenweiler, squeezed from all sides, shuttered their business in 1880.

It was a social catastrophe—just one in a ruinous cascade that would sweep through Germany for the next half century. "For more than a hundred and fifty years, the people of this small village had basked in the ever-dimming light of the factory," Gerhard would later write, "only to stand, in the end, in the dark."

.   .   .

When Karl was five years old, in 1904, a team of inspectors came to his village from the state agricultural office in Villingen. They were appalled at what they found. The living conditions were medieval, the people as impoverished as serfs. They should be allowed to own their own land, they reported, but the Fürstenbergs waved them off. These peasants weren't capable of paying property tax. Best that they remain in the family's care.

Jobs were scarce and most often went to men from Pfaffenweiler and other neighboring villages, who were willing to work for less. In the depths of winter, when the *Speck* was long gone and even the bitter black turnips were running low in the larder, some children would eat the plaster from their walls, just to fill their bellies. "When you live like a slave, it's not just that you're hungry," Gerhard told me. "It hurts your soul. People are always against one another, and things happen that poison the atmosphere. They can't do anything about it. They're prisoners of their situation."

Karl lived with his mother, stepfather, and three siblings. He couldn't remember his real father, who had died when Karl was just a year and a half old. The villagers didn't like to talk about him. They were a taciturn bunch on the sunniest days, but when the name Thomas Gönner came up, they turned mute as oysters. He came from the village of Ippingen, on the next hilltop over. When he first met Karl's mother, Luise Mahler, he was working at the tavern in Herzogenweiler. He was six years older than Luise and had been married once before, but he had lost his wife and first baby to child-birth. He had neither land nor inheritance.

Luise was as close as the village came to gentry. Her ancestry stretched back to Hans Georg Mahler, one of the glassblowers who founded Herzogenweiler. He and his brother Philipp first negotiated terms with the Fürstenbergs, then built a sawmill along the Wolfbach and opened the tavern that later became *Zum Hirschen*. But the Mahlers, for all their history, were as poor as most. They had little education or hope of advancement, no sense of brighter days ahead. If they stored every seed and worked till their backs gave out, it was just to keep their families alive.

Thomas didn't have the patience for that. Like a lot of men in the village, his hopelessness led him to drink and then to gambling. The glassmakers had made a similar mistake, borrowing money for new kilns and lumber, only to be forced to sell the company when their debt redoubled. But Thomas had nothing to sell. He couldn't afford to lease more land, and his family was expanding by the year. He and Luise's first child, Elise, was born in 1894, then Franz Josef two years later. By the time Karl was born, on January 12, 1899, the land could barely support them. Thomas always seemed to be behind on his rent, one failed crop away from losing his lease. When he did get a windfall—from cutting lumber in the winter or selling the berries that his children gathered in the woods—his first stop was *Zum Hirschen*.

The tavern had become a haven of lost souls. Gone were the days of skittering fiddles and mad country dances, with the local gentry cavorting among the glassblowers. The aristocrats had long since left the premises, more at ease in their own drawing rooms. On dark nights when their work was done, weary cowherds and sharp-eyed laborers now filled the tables, hunched over their ale playing skat, trading bitter gossip as they hid their hands.

The night before Karl's father died was no different than most.

He just reached a snapping point. The more he drank, the wilder his wagers grew, until he had tossed in all the money he had and some that he didn't. There must have come a point, late in the night, when the numbers no longer appeared real: His debt was so deep, his luck so abysmal, that it all seemed a twisted farce. How else to explain the disaster he had made of his life? There was nothing for it but to make one last, desperate bet. If he lost the next hand, he declared, he would give the winner all that he had left: his house and garden.

A moment later they were gone.

Early the next morning, Luise took her children to Sunday mass in Pfaffenweiler. When they came back to the house at noon, they found Thomas curled up on the living-room floor. An empty bottle of disinfectant lay on the ground beside him, the bitter scent and smear of it still on his lips. Karl was just a baby then and Franz Josef was a toddler. But Elise was almost six and could tell that something was terribly wrong. She climbed onto her father's chest and hit his shoulders again and again with her fists. *"Papa wach auf, Ich hab' Hunger!"* Papa, wake up, I'm hungry! Later, when the men from the tavern heard what had happened, they were confounded. The last bet of the night was just a joke, they claimed. They never would have taken a man's house and garden.

.   .   .

Luise and her daughter would carry the sight inside them for the rest of their lives. Elise never married, though she had offers. She stayed home to take care of her mother, went to church every morning in Pfaffenweiler—an hour's walk to the east—and sometimes lapsed into the dark, bitten-off moods that my mother learned to avoid. (Elise was the one who told her to mind her stocking drawer instead of dreaming of Egypt.) Luise remarried and had two more sons,

Heinrich and Xaver. She was a sturdy, commonsensical soul in most
ways. She was a midwife, so she took care of all but the most grievous
injuries in the village—the closest doctor was in Villingen, two hours
away on foot. Like Thomas, many of the men in Herzogenweiler cut
lumber for added wages, and mishaps were common: falling timbers,
piercing splinters, blades that skipped off bark and bit into ankles and
thighs. Luise got used to sending bodies large and small to the graveyard in the meadow below the village, only to meet them again later
in town. She would see their shades sitting by the side of the road
when she walked to her garden in the morning, or waiting by the
crossroads at dusk, a look of mournful reproof in their eyes. Whether
the sight alarmed or consoled her, I can't say. But I like to imagine
that she took the visitations in stride: old friends and neighbors stopping by to pick up the conversation where they'd left off.

Something about Herzogenweiler had always instilled a sense of
the supernatural in people. Maybe it was its solitary setting, high on
a windblown plateau, or the dark woods that encircled it. But the village was unusually devout even for southern Germany. A century
later, a priest from Freiburg, making the rounds of the Black Forest
for a religious survey, would find that belief still burned hottest
among the villagers here. Theirs was a pre-Reformation sort of
Catholicism—a murky brew of folklore, superstition, and pitiless religion. Even the boldest farmers sometimes hurried home from the
fields before nightfall, lest a dire spirit overtake them, and the devil
was more than an idle threat. He was the dark stranger who might
come knocking at your door some stormy night; the man with the
hooded eyes at the end of the bar, lazily flipping a coin in the air.

Before Luise was born, there was talk that a man named Aloïs
Sigwart practiced witchcraft in the village. His spells were mostly of
a harmless, mundane sort, people said. If a farmer lost his hayfork,
Sigwart might murmur a few words over a candle that night. The

next morning, there the hayfork would be, leaning against the barn door. But Sigwart's end came badly, with howls of such agony that the villagers were certain that his soul was damned—torn from his chest by the devil and cast down. When he was buried, only the priest and his acolyte accompanied the body to the graveyard.

.   .   .

Karl grew up surrounded by these uneasy spirits. The house where he was born had once been Sigwart's. After the man's death, the family discovered a hidden *Rumpelkammer* upstairs, like a secret study. A small writing table and chair stood inside, cloaked in dust, along with an old chest full of decaying leather volumes. Among them were *The Sixth and Seventh Books of Moses*—notorious heretical texts compiled by the German occultist Johann Scheible in 1849. They claimed to contain the spells by which Moses had defeated Pharaoh's magician-priests in Egypt, turning his staff into a snake and parting the waters of the Red Sea. The books so frightened Luise that she picked them up with a pair of tongs, dropped them into a sack, and brought them to the village priest to burn.

Karl was a pious boy even by village standards, preoccupied by sin and the devil's snares. Late one afternoon, when he was nine years old, his mother sent him to the graveyard to leave some flowers in the chapel. Karl raced there and back as fast as he could— a twenty-minute trip, though it felt much longer—desperate to get home before sunset, only to realize that the chapel key was still in his pocket. His mother had told him to leave it on the altar for the priest to find. When his stepfather heard what had happened, he erupted. He was a decent man at heart—a small, quiet figure, as my mother later remembered him, hunched by the fire playing cards with his grandchildren. But fatigue and stress could make him cruel, and his youngest stepson often got the brunt of it. He ordered Karl to return the key in the dark.

The boy knew that the dead were always with him. His mother's visions had made that clear. She could see them slouching beside him at the breakfast table or hovering at his bedside as he fell asleep. Some were old friends; others were kept at bay only by his family's prayers. To walk among them on a starless night was almost more than he could bear, my mother told me.

The graveyard was enclosed on four sides by stone walls. Veiled statues stood along its inner perimeter, gazing out at him as he stumbled among the tombs. Some were carved with Gothic script; others bore the mark of a mystical chalice, symbol of the glassblowers buried there. Karl could feel their spirits gathering around him as he groped his way in the dark—he could almost feel their breath on his neck. When he reached the chapel, its altar lit by a single candle, he flung the key down and fled home through the gate.

God's grace was said to be the only protection against such spirits, but the village church was a dour, disgruntled place, steeped in thwarted hopes and declining fortunes. It had neither organ nor tabernacle, reliable heat nor decent lighting (the village only began to be electrified in 1917). There was just a wheezing harmonium and two bells that called the village to service. The vicar came only once a week, complaining of the "Siberian cold" when a sled came to fetch him from Pfaffenweiler. His successor didn't even get that. He had to make his way to the plateau on foot—an hour and a quarter's trudge through snow and scouring wind—only to gaze out on the threadbare congregation as the sweat froze on his skin. "I have a duty to promote religious life," he wrote. "But what can and should I do when the chapel is so far away that so few people come? There aren't even enough for a noontime service on Sunday."

Karl was one of the stalwarts. The swell of hoarse voices around him on a Sunday morning, singing hymns and intoning psalms, was one of the few things that could loft his mind clear of its foreboding. *Beim frühen Morgenlicht, erwacht mein Herz und spricht.* When morning gilds the skies, my heart awakening cries. Music would always be both a refuge and a release for him—a taproot to the eternal—and the church suited him despite its discomforts. Its discipline and doctrinal rigor, its self-denying spirit, matched his own meager circumstances. It gave them purpose.

For a boy of Karl's means, the priesthood was one of the few paths to an education, and he came to it naturally. Even as an old man, long since strayed from his faith, he had an ecclesiastical air about him, with his probing eye and measured speech, his way of framing the world in parables and maxims. By age ten, he was studying with the village priest; at fifteen he was at a boarding school for future seminarians. Then war intervened. In the summer of 1917, Karl received a letter from the German military command. He was to report immediately to the army base in Radolfzell, forty miles to the southeast—part of a last great surge of German forces that would punch through Allied defenses before the Americans came.

He was eighteen years old and certain, for all his faith, that the letter was a death sentence.

6

SOLDIER

THEY WERE CAMPED OUTSIDE THE VILLAGE OF MOREUIL ON
the Western Front: the Third Company of the First Battalion of the
114th Infantry Regiment of the 199th Division of the Third Army
of the German Empire—one small cog in a great, clanging war machine of more than eleven million men. Their company counted a
scant two hundred soldiers, mostly from southwestern Germany like
Karl. They had been trained in haste and thrown raw into the field
to revive a sputtering war effort. The Reich was at the threshold of
glorious victory, they were told. *"Es gilt die letzten Schläge, den Sieg zu
vollenden!"* as a poster for German war bonds proclaimed, above an
illustration of a warrior beheading a roaring lion. To seal the victory,
the final blows must fall!

They hardly looked like a conquering army: hollow-eyed and list-less, underfed. At the beginning of the war, a day's field rations had consisted of more than a pound of bread, half a pound or more of meat, three pounds of potatoes and other vegetables, and a few tea-spoons each of coffee or tea, sugar, and salt. Every soldier got two ci-gars and two cigarettes, or an ounce of pipe or chewing tobacco, along with wine, beer, or spirits at the commanding officer's discretion. By 1918, the rations had dwindled to a cup or two of turnip stew.

Still, they seemed to be winning. The last offensive in France, at Chemin des Dames in May, had ended in disaster for the French—a hundred thousand soldiers dead and sixty thousand captured. The British, in their own botched offensive in Flanders, had lost a third of a million men, and their supply lines were beginning to unravel under German submarine attack. And the Russians, weakened by revolution, had surrendered altogether in March, freeing a million German troops to return from the Eastern Front.

It was time for a final hammer strike to end the war. Eleven days before Karl arrived at the front, the Germans had launched the *Kai-serschlacht*. The name meant "emperor's battle," but it had the same root in Old High German as *schlachten:* to slaughter. Backed by fifty of the infantry divisions from Russia, German stormtroopers had torn through the exhausted French and British defenses. In the Somme alone, they had taken forty miles of new land, killing 164,000 Allied soldiers and taking another 90,000 prisoner. The day before Karl arrived in Moreuil, the regiment had launched an attack from the vicinity of Villers-aux-Érables. Scrambling over flatland and hol-low, through the shattered remnants of a French cavalry position and a forest whistling with passing shells, they had seized a strategic over-look from the French. It was Easter Sunday, March 31, 1918.

Moreuil was just seventy miles north of Paris. From Karl's trench, he could see the steeples of Amiens hovering above the horizon to the northwest, shrouded in rain. The kaiser's men had been bombarding the Gallic stronghold for more than three years and never come this close before. But no sooner had they taken the hill than they were under attack themselves, pummeled by enemy fire from ground and sky. The big German guns had fallen silent behind them, destroyed or out of position, and the enemy was out of reach of rifle or machine-gun fire. The sky droned with enemy fighters, far outnumbering the German planes, as the British launched a furious counterattack against the regiment's right flank. Some German soldiers hunkered in foxholes and covered themselves in dirt-smeared tarpaulins for camouflage. By the time Karl reached his company, they were losing radio contact and running low on food and ammunition. April Fool's Day: He had arrived just in time to retreat.

"The ordeals of the previous days had a poor effect on the troops," the survivors of the regiment would later write. "Especially the never-ending rain, which had turned the land to a soupy, yielding mass of earth on which the feet could find no purchase." The storm troops had advanced too quickly for reinforcements to keep up. Trucking supplies across these vast, devastated plains was treacherous under enemy fire, so the division command sent word for the troops to fend for themselves. For meat, they could butcher their fallen horses. Soon the roads and ditches were littered with long white ribs curving beneath the mud, picked clean.

Three days later, unable to gain any ground, the company fell back to Villers-aux-Érables, while others stayed to defend the front lines. They joined up again after a few days, then slogged steadily eastward, across the killing fields of the Somme, past Mézières, Beaumont, and Rosières to Vauvillers, where the supply trucks met them. They marched through Framerville, Rainecourt, and Foucaucourt-en-Santerre, Estrées, Villers, and Éterpigny to the town of Péronne, where they huddled among its charred ruins and slept. Along the way, in the village of Caix, they passed a Gothic church that had been riddled with gunfire. A placard hung below what remained of the steeple: *Elle est détruite par le bombardement anglais*. Destroyed by British bombers.

.   .   .

The recruit Karl Gönner was a hundred and seventy centimeters tall, his military records show. About five foot seven. He had a medium build and boots twenty-eight and a half centimeters long. His chin was "ordinary," his mouth ordinary, his nose . . . ordinary. He had brown hair and no beard, wore wire-rim glasses, and bore a scar on his right thigh. He was unmarried, Catholic, and a high-school graduate. A small cross on the record indicated that his father was dead; his stepfather was identified as a farmer. On June 19, 1917, Karl had reported for duty in Radolfzell, on the shores of Lake Constance, as a *Landsturm* soldier in the German infantry.

The Great War was the most assiduously documented event in the history of the world—at least until the next war. It was the trauma that its survivors couldn't stop reliving. Poems, memoirs, monographs, and novels, songs, symphonies, photographs, and films were left in its wake, along with letters and diaries beyond counting. In 1932, a group of veterans from Karl's regiment published a 656-page memoir of the war, meticulously accounting for all its miseries. They would note not just their daily meals, movements, sleeping quarters, weather conditions, battle tactics, victories, and retreats, but the marching songs they sang and the poems they wrote in the trenches. Some were high-flown and romantic: "At Tahure, death rode / From dawn to dusk / So that heroes averted their eyes / And from the distant vale of home / Pale lips sent greetings once more / With their last, soft breath." Others were touchingly blunt:

I stand at my post all alone
And wonder where my girl is now
And as I think about my girl
I suddenly notice that there is blood on my scalp
From a grenade that pierced the roof
Of the trench where I stand guard
And lodged—Ach! what a poor sod I am!—
Three fragments in the back of my head

And yet, for every would-be Wilfred Owen or Georg Trakl, writing poems at the front, or Henri Gaudier-Brzeska carving a Madonna and child from the butt of a German rifle, a million soldiers died in obscurity, leaving little trace of their experience. My mother knew next to nothing about her father's time as a soldier, aside from the story of how he had lost his eye. Her brothers remembered only that he was wounded in Verdun. The truth, as it turned out, was both less familiar and more dramatic. The battles that Karl fought, I learned, took place well west of Verdun, in the hills and forests of Champagne. They were part of the Meuse-Argonne campaign—the single bloodiest military offensive in American history. American forces alone suffered 120,000 casualties, the French 70,000, and the Germans 126,000. Yet even in the United States, which at least has victory in hindsight, the Meuse-Argonne has been largely forgotten.

"The standard narrative of World War I doesn't mesh with the American idea of what war is supposed to be," the military historian Edward Lengel, who wrote about the Meuse-Argonne in his book *To Conquer Hell*, told me. "We have this idea that war is good guys and bad guys. That it has a clear beginning and a clear ending, and in particular that it's supposed to move—to have dashing, exciting elements to it. But the Meuse-Argonne just seems brutal. This was a vast charnel house of slaughter, and I think most people just don't want to hear about it."

Lengel calls the Meuse-Argonne the most understudied of all major American battles. What little has been written about it is generally wrong: that the French were cowardly and fought without conviction; that the Germans were too sick and spent to offer much resistance; that the Americans were sole authors of the Allied victory. To Karl, it was a disaster of both mind and spirit. Without even a victory to redeem it, the war revealed its true senselessness—and the emptiness of the prayers and promises that had encouraged it. Before he became a soldier, Karl wanted to be a priest; afterward, a schoolteacher.

·   ·   ·

What was left of this one earnest teenager among the eleven million Germans who fought in the war—from Angola to the South Pacific, Malaysia to the coast of Chile? What record of his conflicted soul? When I first came to Berlin to trace Karl's story, I put together a list of military archives in Germany and their holdings. I noted my grandfather's name and hometown, date of birth and death—everything I knew—and sent my emails into the ether like so many messages in bottles.

The biggest hurdle, at first, was linguistic. The dialect I grew up speaking, Allemannisch, was perfect for getting around the Black Forest but useless for official communication. Every call I made or letter I wrote had to be in High German, and often of a specialized sort. English has its share of jargon, but in Germany, where the trades are all licensed and professionalized, every business seems to have its own vocabulary—common enough to Germans but completely foreign to me. Banks have their banking terms (*Einlagensicherungsfonds, Namensschuldverschreibungen*), the rail service its train terms (*Schienenersatverkehr-Haltestelle*), the phone service its phone terms (*Rahmenbedingungen für Festnetzanschlüsse*). Even our handyman liked to stud his explanations with arcane carpentry words, carefully dovetailed together. To get anything out of the archives, I had to learn to talk like an archivist.

I've always loved the sound of spoken German. It's a language of forest and soil, sorrow and exultation, full of wind and weather and earthy rumblings. Its umlauts and throaty consonants are its horns and woodwinds. Still, after six months in Berlin, it began to grate on my ears. Compared to Allemannisch, with its simplified grammar and more coarse-grained vocabulary (the word for potato, for instance, is *Grumbüre*, or "ground pear"), High German seemed in love with its own abstraction. It was all prefixes and suffixes, conjugations and declensions, like English stripped of Anglo-Saxon, with only the Latinate superstructure left standing. It was all "utilize" and no "use." A writer like Rilke could both elevate the language and ground it in particulars. But the High German I heard in stores and offices seemed correct to a fault. Its chief satisfaction seemed to lie in solving its own grammatical puzzles.

Or so I told myself, as I struggled to find the proper wording. Then, late in the winter—on my birthday, as it happened—I got a note from an archivist named Manfred Hennhöfer: "*Sehr geehrter Herr Bilger*," it began, "We have been able to identify the unit in which your grandfather performed his military service in World War I." Hennhöfer was a section manager of the state archive in Karlsruhe. He was also a native of the region, which meant that when we spoke on the phone he could hear the singsong traces of Allemannisch in my High German and tactfully fell into dialect with me. I was back among my people.

Hennhöfer sent scans of three pages of military records from the archive, and I later went to see them in Karlsruhe. The first two included only my grandfather's name, rank (musketeer), and date of discharge (February 15, 1919), along with some brief notes on his health and family history. The third page was the key: a detailed summary of his military service, by date and location. The only catch was that I couldn't read it.

The notes on the page were clearly written, but the clerk had used an outdated Prussian script known as *Sütterlinschrift*. Modeled on old German chancery script, it has an almost whimsical look on the page, full of loop de loops and letters round as smiley faces. But even older Germans find it indecipherable. Some letters resemble their Latin equivalents, others do not. The lowercase *h* looks like an *f*, the *x* like a *y*, the *s* like an *l*. The lowercase *m, n, u,* and *w* all look pretty much the same, aside from the occasional squiggle. Strung out in a row, in a word like *Weltanschauung*, they go by like waves in a pool. You have to count the humps to guess the meaning.

Sütterlin went on to become a subject of furious debate in Germany: a culture war writ small. Commissioned by the Prussian Ministry of Science, Art, and Culture in 1911, it was designed to convey the grandiloquence of Gothic type with a modern, handwritten fluidity. From 1915 to 1940, it was taught in German schools. Then, abruptly, the Nazis banned it. German nationalists had long sworn by Gothic lettering—Bismarck refused to read anything else—but Hitler never much liked it. The style was too backward for a nation destined to rule the world, he declared at the *Reichsparteitag* in 1934. It was "ill-suited to this age of steel and iron, glass and concrete, of womanly beauty and manly strength, of head raised high and intention defiant." The Nazis later claimed that Gothic lettering was a Jewish creation, even as they deemed Jewish publishers insufficiently German to use it. Finally, in 1941, the use of all Gothic fonts and scripts was forbidden in schools and publications. The secret note that first announced the policy to party leaders was printed, ironically, on Gothic letterhead.

The date of the ban turned out to be significant. It meant that my mother, who was born in 1935, was just old enough to be taught Sütterlin in school. "We learned to write that damn script with blood and sweat," she said when I sent her a copy of her father's war records. "Then one day the teacher said, 'From now on we'll write a different way.' And suddenly everything was easier. It may be the only good thing that Hitler ever did."

She and I had become practiced, if somewhat scattershot, collaborators. We talked on the phone almost every day. There was nothing more reassuring to me—no better reminder of the irrepressible pulse of ordinary life—than to find her and my father at their usual posts in the kitchen, drinking coffee and debating the news. My mother would answer the phone and do most of the talking from the kitchen table. My father would sprawl on the couch next to her, yelling jokes and indelicate asides. I knew a good deal of the family history already, but it grew more detailed and convoluted as we spoke—full of odd tangents from my sidewise attempts to unlock my mother's memories. What did your father wear to school when he was a teacher? What was his favorite song to play on the organ? It was part storytelling and part safecracking.

Sütterlin was a confounding example. When I first sent my mother her father's records, she couldn't decipher them. It wasn't that she had forgotten how to read the script; she just couldn't see it. She was eighty years old now and slowly losing her sight. Her right eye was nearly blind; the left one myopic and clouded by glaucoma. She tried blowing up the images on her computer screen, but even at the highest setting the handwriting still registered as a dark smudge, a swirling inkblot. It was only when she took a magnifying glass and held it up to the monitor that the words came into focus.

And then, letter by letter, she traced her father's path through the battlefields of northern France.

·   ·   ·

By late April, the weather had broken and all of Picardy was in bloom. Along the banks of the Somme, the hawthorn and horse chestnut were in flower, the marsh grasses showing their first pale shoots. After weeks of numbing wind and rain, Karl's pack and shoes were dry at last, his body loose and warm beneath his uniform. Yet the clear skies were a mixed blessing: They also increased visibility and robbed the company of its cover. The air was full of reconnaissance planes and enemy fighters, tracking their movements and swooping low to strafe them with machine-gun fire.

This was when his training really began. The days of boredom edged with constant vigilance. The screams of horses struck by mortar fire. The chlorine gas that crept into your trench as you slept, searing your eyes and lungs as you fumbled for your mask, recalling, with surreal precision, the exact wording of the leaflet sent down from central command: "It has been determined that people with very small heads, for whom mask No. 3 is too big, can usually use mask No. 3 with a chinstrap shortened by 2 cm."

One morning in early May, just before daybreak, the company was marching along the Rue de Bray-Corbie, due east of Amiens, when a thunderhead of artillery erupted nearby. They barely had time to grab their rifles before the enemy was rushing in from both sides. Australians, they later heard—elite infantry that had circled half the globe to kill them. The raids seemed to come from a new direction every day, sometimes in such pitch dark that it was hard to tell whom to shoot. Rumors of enemy tanks rippled through the trenches, while bombers blasted the trees to every side. By the third day, everyone's nerves were so frayed that one corporal, patrolling the encampment at dusk, mistook a field kitchen for a row of tanks and shot them up.

The fighting would flare on for two weeks, in thickets and hollows and forest clearings, like coals from a kicked fire, till the company was finally relieved by the 227th Regiment. They took a transport train to Cambrai, thirty miles to the northeast, then marched to Mortagne, twenty-five miles to the north, with the last of their strength. It was a "friendly, clean little town" just south of the Belgian border, the veterans later recalled. It would be their final rest of the war.

·   ·   ·

Nearly five hundred thousand men died in the *Kaiserschlacht*, half of them on the German side, including many of the emperor's best shock troops. The survivors slept and played Doppelkopf and other card games, mended uniforms and cleaned rifles, while new recruits streamed in for training, even greener than Karl had been. The young officers took riding lessons; their superiors met for tactical meetings and organized war games. By late June, when the company was ordered east to the Ardennes and the battlefields of Champagne, the war had come to seem a strange sort of fiction. In Charleville, the men attended a parade before the crown prince, followed by an awarding of medals and demonstrations of the latest flamethrowers and engines of war.

Karl didn't make the trip. Like hundreds of thousands of other German soldiers, he was too sick to fight. The day before his regiment left, he was sent to a military hospital near the Belgian border, in Saint-Amand-les-Eaux. Built by the French for wealthy and high-ranking officers, the hospital was on the site of a seventh-century monastery. The ancient wood that once surrounded it had been largely razed by the Germans for war construction. Its sulfur springs were said to work wonders on sprains, contusions, gout, rheumatism, pleurisy, ulcerations, gunshot wounds, and diseases of the skin and bone. But Karl was neither hobbled nor wounded. He had contracted an early case of the Spanish influenza. He needed to bring his temperature down.

The flu was a disease that fed on conflict. In the spring of 1918, it had hitchhiked from Kansas to France in the lungs of American doughboys and made its way to outposts as distant as Samoa and sub-Saharan Africa. The mildest strains tended to stay in the field, while the deadliest sent their victims to crowded hospitals like Saint-Amand. The flu could find more carriers there, already weakened by injuries, poor rations, and relentless fighting. In just over a year, it would infect nearly a third of the world's population and leave some fifty million dead—more than the Great War itself.

Karl finally rejoined his company near Mourmelon-le-Grand, east of Reims, three weeks after he was hospitalized. His skin hung loose around his bony frame; his breath came in gasps when he had to heft his pack for any distance. The flu, at its most aggressive, wracked the body with fever, nausea, and diarrhea. It ravaged the lungs and inflamed the bronchi, filling the chest with a bloody froth. Some victims died of suffocation, turning blue as they drowned in the fluids from their own overreacting immune system. A full recovery could take weeks, but the Wehrmacht had no time for that: The Americans were on their way. A quarter of a million soldiers had shipped for Europe in May, and another 280,000 in June. Until they landed, the Germans still had the advantage in manpower along the Western Front. But not for long.

7

CASUALTY

IT WAS A STRANGE PLACE TO WAGE A WAR. THE FIELDS AND vineyards of Champagne lay in the northeast of France, about three hours from Paris by train or military transport. Driving from village to village a century after my grandfather was there, I kept thinking of what the French called this area: the Empty Diagonal. It was the tag end of a swath of sparsely populated land that spanned the country like a Legionnaire's sash. People had been abandoning the diagonal for cities and more fertile farmland for so long that only forty people remained, on average, per square mile. The weather in Champagne was windy, wet, and cold; the ground perpetually soggy. The meager topsoil lay over a deep stratum of white chalk—an ancient ocean bed, formed of the compacted bones of Cretaceous beasts. In the 1860s, Napoleon III tried turning the area into a giant woodlot, but the trees took grudgingly to the soil. The only things that seemed to love it were sheep. "Ninety-nine sheep and one Champenois," people liked to say. "That makes a hundred beasts."

And yet, twice in the past century, armies from across the globe had staked their lives on this forsaken spot. When the Germans first invaded, in September of 1914, they settled in as if they would never leave. Unlike the British and French, who had been forced to retreat and make do with shallow trenches on low ground, the Germans burrowed deep into hillsides and bluffs. They dug networks of trenches and tunnels like underground towns, complete with offices, sleeping quarters, infirmaries, and field kitchens. They built chapels, gymnasiums, libraries, and casinos behind the lines, and connected everything with light and heavy rail, branching across the landscape like arteries and capillaries. Between attacks, German civilians sometimes trucked in baked goods from across the border.

What remains is a vast ghost town. A boneyard above a labyrinth. An hour and a half east of Paris, the cemeteries and memorials rise from the roadside every few miles: Soissons, Château-Thierry, Montfaucon. Some four million men of more than a dozen nationalities died on the Western Front in the First World War. In the Battle of Verdun alone, between forty and sixty million shells were fired, till every square foot of ground seemed filled with shrapnel and lead. In Reims, where the kings and queens of France were crowned, German bombs shattered much of the cathedral's stained glass, and the façade is lined with faceless saints. In the country graveyards farther on, there are often no statues or monuments, just two plots carefully divided: the French beneath spindly white crosses; the Germans under crosses of coarse stone. At Auberive, where twelve thousand soldiers are buried, I found a notice pinned to the gate: "We have

been informed of the damage caused to this memorial by acts of
vandalism. The repair is in progress."

When I drove into the village of Sommepy-Tahure, forty-five
minutes east of Reims, the streets were deserted. No cafés spilling out
onto the sidewalk, no bustling marketplace or *centre commercial*. Just
some glum fieldstone buildings along an almost treeless street, with a
shuttered town hall at one end. For the French, the Battle of Sommepy was one of the pivot points of the Meuse-Argonne campaign.
In a postcard I had seen of the village in 1916, two years after the
Germans occupied it, all that was left were some crumbled walls and
the broken nave of a church. "*Je vous envoie des fleurs*," someone had
written on the back. I send you flowers. After the war, a French lieutenant from Sommepy toured the United States, raising funds for his
town's reconstruction. If not, Sommepy, like the five "lost villages"
just over the hill, might still be in ruins.

I walked up to the town hall and knocked on the door. The building was a near replica of the one that had stood there before the war,
with a pointy slate roof that hung low above the upper windows like
a pith helmet. A placard declared that it was open for only two hours
on Tuesdays and one hour on Thursdays, Fridays, and Saturdays.
This being Tuesday, I came back at the designated time and found
the office manager dutifully at work at her desk. She seemed startled
to see me. "*Mais vous devez parler à Brigitte et Jean-Pierre!*" she exclaimed,
when I explained why I had come. This is a job for the village historical society!

Within a few minutes, Brigitte Guyot, the society's secretary, was
on the line, and a frantic barking chain had commenced, from one
kitchen phone to the next across the village. I left after a while to get
dinner. But late that night, at an inn deep in the Argonne Forest, the
phone rang in my room. "Meet us at eight-thirty tomorrow morning," a gravelly voice directed. "We look forward to your visit with
great anticipation."

.   .   .

The Society for the Memory of the Wars and Sommepy's Past occupied a single room in a basement office a block behind the town hall. When I arrived the next morning and opened the door, I found seven members inside, seated around a long table, smiling up at me expectantly. In addition to Guyot—a small, bustling figure in owlish glasses—there was a former mayor among them, a retired car mechanic, a sheep farmer, and a PhD student who was writing his dissertation on trench warfare. Every available surface was papered with photographs, postcards, topographical maps, and portraits of *poilus*—"hairy ones," as French infantrymen were affectionately known. One wall was covered with a map of the battle lines in Champagne in 1918, crosshatched with roads, tunnels, railroads, and trenches—blue for German, red for French.

Jean-Pierre Thirion, the vice president of the association, stood up and made the introductions. His was the low voice I had heard on the phone the night before. He had a long, jowly face, balding on top, and sly, alert eyes. A retired plumber and electrician, Thirion had built a company with twenty-five employees and served five terms as village councilman. He ran the meeting with jovial disputatiousness—especially toward his friend Daniel Jacquart, the mechanic. Jacquart stood in the corner in a blue smock and black watch cap, a wary, hangdog look on his face. "Your grandfathers made war, one against the other!" Thirion said, pointing at the two of us and smacking his hands in the air. "Now here you are, reconnected by their history!"

Thirion had never known a time not defined by war and its stories. He was born in 1944, when Sommepy was again under German occupation. His father hid American and British pilots in their house during the Second World War, in a secret compartment he had built behind an armoire. But the locals didn't like to talk about that war. "The mayor was for Pétain," Thirion said. It was the First World War, with its endless trench battles, that still occupied their minds as well as the landscape.

When Thirion and Jacquart were boys, in the 1950s, they liked to play in the German tunnels beneath the church, or in the trenches around town. The soil still made for poor farming then, so it was decades before the trenches were filled. Scampering through them after school, they found old rifles, bayonets, human skulls, and un-exploded shells. Some they kept as mementos; others they sold as scrap. The buyers in town sent railcars full to the smelters in the north. "The bags of black powder we just blew up," Thirion said. What couldn't be sold or exploded was repurposed by local farmers—swords into plowshares. Old tanks became truck chassis, bayonets became screwdrivers, rifle barrels became garden stakes for tomato plants. Some farmers took German helmets and turned them into flowerpots or roosts for nesting chickens.

As they got older, Thirion and Jacquart ranged farther afield. On Saturday mornings, they would jump on their bikes and head for the military camp a few miles south of town. The area had been set aside after the First World War for army training and target practice. It encompassed some thirty-three thousand acres of the most devas-tated land on the front, including the ruins of the five lost villages. The boys would crawl under the fence and search for tins of military rations, hoping to find a plug of tobacco or bottle of wine. They col-lected snails to sell in town and hunted for mushrooms where the military had exploded live shells left over from the First World War. Morels and truffles grow best after a thermal shock, like a sudden freeze or thaw.

The military camp was a time capsule, but all around it the land-scape slowly transformed. The soil began to yield to modern fertil-izers. The chalk beneath it turned out to be a natural irrigation system, absorbing water in the rainy season and releasing it in times of drought. Beets, barley, rapeseed, flax, hemp, potatoes, wheat, and Champagne grapes came to cover every spare acre. Yields increased as much as threefold after the 1950s. Yet the more the land was reclaimed, the more its history was destroyed. At Blanc Mont, a ridge three miles north of Sommepy, a bunker full of German drawings and graffiti was pried apart and bulldozed flat. "The Great War was considered banal," Thirion said. Locals had lived with its remains so long that they took its astonishing history for granted. "So we erased it for . . ." He rubbed his fingers together.

It wasn't until 1970, when a young priest, newly arrived in Sommepy, became fascinated by the town's experiences in the First World War, that people began to understand what they had lost. "We knew nothing," Thirion said. In 1974, the priest organized a *son et lumière* about the destruction and reconstruction of the church. A year later, the Society for the Memory of the Wars and Sommepy's Past was born. "The more you learn, the more you civilize yourself," Marie-Josèphe Guyot, a former mayor and now president of the Society, told me.

Pierre Taborelli, the PhD student, stood up and led me over to an enormous map of the battle lines in 1918. The trenches were at their most sprawling and elaborate then, he said—as many as ninety kilometers of them for every kilometer of front line. But as terrible as trench warfare was, the real horrors often occurred when the soldiers were out in the open. "If you look at the number of deaths in the war, year by year, the peak was in 1918," Thirion said. "It was when the soldiers weren't just in their trenches. They were charging between them and exposed to gunfire." *C'était une guerre de mouvement,* he said. That was when the real dying began.

·   ·   ·

By late September, when Karl arrived in the Py River Valley, the German army was in retreat, its trenches in shambles. They had lost a million men between March and July. Karl's battalion was flu-ridden, half starved, cut off from supplies. The days of civilian pastry deliveries behind the lines were long gone. The German people, like their soldiers, were famished and weary of war, worn down by years of inflation and war taxes. Bread rations were down to five and a half ounces in some parts of Germany, supplemented by horse sausage, acorn coffee, and beech-leaf tobacco. The country was on the verge of revolution. The British were advancing on Damascus, the Hindenburg Line was nearly broken, and the Bulgarian Army would soon pack up its arms in Greece and go home.

Crouched over his mess kit on many mornings, Karl would get word of the latest deserters. Men who had slipped past the guards that night and were slinking across the countryside, scavenging food and sleeping in ditches, heading for the border. In the early days of the war, German soldiers would hitch a ride to the edge of town on fine summer afternoons, and bathe in the meandering currents of the Py River. Now propaganda flyers came fluttering down from British balloons: "For what are you fighting? . . . They promise you victory and peace. You poor fools! It was promised your comrades for more than three years. They have indeed found peace, deep in the grave, but victory did not come!"

The Allies weren't much better off. The healthiest and best-equipped troops, the most eager volunteers, were dead or exhausted, leaving the green and grizzled to man the trenches. In Champagne, as on battlefields throughout Europe and Africa, the infantry was often stocked with soldiers from colonized countries—the armies' preferred cannon fodder. The great majority were British soldiers from India and French soldiers from Algeria, Morocco, Tunisia, West Africa, the Somali Coast, and Madagascar. But others were recruited or forced into service in Belgian Congo and German East

and Southwest Africa. In all, some two and a half million Africans
and a million and a half Indians served as soldiers or noncombatants
in the war. Their gravestones, onion-domed and inscribed in Arabic
for the Muslims, were scattered amid the crosses and Stars of David
in the cemeteries around Sommepy.

Among the American troops in Champagne was the all-Black
369th Regiment, known as the Harlem Hellfighters. In training,
their mere presence had almost caused a riot in Spartanburg, South
Carolina—it was like "waving a red flag in the face of a bull," the
mayor told *The New York Times*. Once on the Western Front, the Hellfighters were among the few Americans that General John "Black-
jack" Pershing was willing to put under French command. But first
his headquarters circulated a memo among French officers, entitled
"Secret Information Concerning Black American Troops." "It is important for French officers who have been called upon to exercise
command over black American troops, or to live in close contact
with them, to have an exact idea of the position occupied by Negroes
in the United States," it began.

> The increasing number of Negroes in the United States (about
> 15,000,000) would create for the white race in the Republic a
> menace of degeneracy were it not that an impassable gulf has
> been made between them.
>
> As this danger does not exist for the French race, the French
> public has become accustomed to treating the Negro with famil-
> iarity and indulgence. This indulgence and this familiarity are
> matters of grievous concern to the Americans. They consider
> them an affront to their national policy. They are afraid that con-
> tact with the French will inspire in black Americans aspirations
> which to them (the whites) appear intolerable. It is of the utmost
> importance that every effort be made to avoid profoundly es-
> tranging American opinion.

Although a citizen of the United States, the black man is regarded by the white American as an inferior being with whom relations of business or service only are possible. The black is constantly being censured for his want of intelligence and discretion, his lack of civic and professional conscience, and for his tendency toward undue familiarity. The vices of the Negro are a constant menace to the American who has to repress them sternly.

The French ministry ordered the memos gathered and burned. The Harlem Hellfighters went on to distinguish themselves in battle, earning two Medals of Honor and 171 French *Croix de Guerre*. Yet the message had been made clear to them: You are an army of the unwanted, a weapon of last resort. Now go and sacrifice yourselves for your country. Even more than the men on the other side, beyond the barbed wire and poison gas, they must have asked themselves why they were there. FOR WHAT ARE YOU FIGHTING?

· · ·

The last American offensive of the war began on September 26, 1918, at 2:30 in the morning. After an hours-long bombardment of mustard and phosgene gas, thirty-seven Allied divisions surged north along the front, from west of the Argonne Forest to the Meuse River near Verdun. They were backed by more than seven hundred tanks and five hundred planes—the fearsome yet clumsy machines of modern war. The French advanced to the west, the Americans to the east, leaping from their trenches and across the blasted ground, through the smoke and sulfur of exploded ordnance. In the first three hours, the Allied forces alone fired more ammunition than was used in all of the American Civil War.

The Germans, apprised of the Allied attack, had fortified their lines with extra divisions. But the attack was too swift and furious, the enemy too numerous. Under General Henri Gouraud, who had lost an arm and broken both legs in the Battle of Gallipoli in western Turkey, the French advanced three miles by noon in some places. By day's end, they had retaken Sommepy and a nearby mound known as the Butte de Tahure—a strategic overlook that had changed hands three times already. They had more than seven thousand German prisoners, to go with the sixteen thousand already taken by the Americans. That was day one.

For the Allies, this was something of a disappointment—they had expected more prisoners, greater advances. For Karl and his comrades, it was a nightmare long expected: There were now 1.3 million Americans on the Western Front—nearly as many as British and French. "They looked like Tommies in Heaven," a British army nurse who had served in northern France later wrote. "So splendidly unimpaired in comparison with the tired, nerve-wracked men of the British Army." The Americans were visibly larger than the Europeans, and clearly better fed. "There is no necessity for an American soldier out in the trenches to get wet or even to get cold feet," Paul Coelestin Ettighoffer, an Alsatian who fought for the Germans at Verdun and became a bestselling novelist under the Nazis, complained. "No, his health and comfort are catered for in the best way. When he comes back from his sentinel task, he could wrap himself in one of his two camel hair blankets and profit from hot wine punch coming from the field kitchen. His haversack holds every time good tobacco, sweets, and tinned food. . . . The German soldier looks at all this deliciousness with only reverential amazement. And one or the other musketeer supposes, shaking his head: 'Oh yes, it is easy to go to war with all this stuff.'"

Still, the American soldiers were raw and untested. They had never been in a war and had been tossed into this one with only months to prepare. General Pershing was skeptical of artillery. He believed in the rifle and bayonet, in soldiers rushing headlong across open ground to overwhelm the enemy, not crouching in trenches lobbing mortars and grenades. Rather than wait for the big guns to clear their way, his troops often raced ahead and got mowed down by machine-gun fire. At Soissons, in July, some units had lost as many as half their men and all their officers as the Germans fired on them from three sides. "The combat method of the Americans above all lacks war experience," one German clerk observed, in a regimental log later captured by American troops:

> This lack is so conspicuous that it is noticed even by the German privates. As soon as the attacking infantry received artillery or machine-gun fire, it scattered. At first, the men threw themselves to the ground, a few ran around in circles not knowing what to do and soon they broke for the rear and finally pulled all the others back with them. . . . The American has not the slightest idea how to make use of the terrain. . . . The uniform of the Americans is too light in color and is conspicuous especially against a green background. Skirmish lines lying on the ground offer an easy target. In all of these cases, the American suffers heavy losses.

Like the other German recruits, Karl must have clung to such reports with a mixture of hope and commiseration, knowing that he could be just as clueless in the field. The daily logs from German battalions in the offensive, written in the raging cacophony of battle, carry a tremor of repressed panic: "A runner was hurriedly sent with the information to Blanc Mont. Whether he managed to get through could not be determined. However, for the regimental staff it was high time to dodge the enemy."

After the fighting, the logbooks were sent to headquarters or stripped from the bodies of enemy soldiers, to be scoured for clues to their movements and strategy. They would eventually make their way to the state archive in Karlsruhe, or to the U.S. War College in Carlisle, Pennsylvania, where they would be translated, bound, and left to molder on library shelves. When I leafed through the logbooks in Karlsruhe, the pages still bore traces of mud from the trenches. The bindings had been roughly stitched together in the field, and the entries were written by hand, in *Sütterlinschrift*. In the front, neat columns of notes and numbers marked the date, place, and martial activity; in the back, they listed the dead, wounded, and missing.

The logs were supplemented by typed orders, mimeographed sheets, and handwritten notes. Their tone tended toward the coolly didactic at first, as if composed over a glass of claret in the commander's tent. But by late September, the penmanship had grown ragged, frantic. Instructions on hygiene and the barracking of soldiers of different religions gave way to diagrams of British gas mines and notes on targeting enemy zeppelins and planes. I pictured Karl's company hunkered beneath a broken wall, trying to make sense of the following as the bombers approached: "The plane moves 40–50 meters forward per second. The vulnerable parts of the aircraft thus cross the bullet's path in 1/10 second. At this rate, the plane can be hit by at best one projectile, if it passes through the middle of the target and the machine gun fires 600 shots per minute."

Later, in the New York Public Library, I read through some of the captured German logs from the U.S. War College. Their entries read like a steampunk nightmare: horses and tanks, bayonets and machine guns, oxcarts and flamethrowers. A war of lethal anachronisms. The regiments had wireless radios, but reception was so spotty that they often used carrier pigeons instead. A thousand years of hand-to-hand combat had collided head-on with mechanized warfare, and a generation had leapt into the crossfire—taught too late that the weapons of one age are unequal to those of another. As the historian Edward Lengel put it: "The armed forces of the United States entered the modern era on 26 September, 1918."

.   .   .

Just after dawn on September 27, a line of trucks rattled into Karl's camp. For three months, his battalion had been marching back and forth across the deserted farms around Reims, shoring up this position or attacking that, never knowing where they would collapse to the ground at night. They had no time to bathe or mend their uniforms, write letters or pick the lice from one another's hair. The entire battalion smelled of rancid meat.

Karl had made a good friend, by then, who stuck by him like the runt in a pack of young hounds. I've never managed to learn the soldier's name, but he always figured in the few stories that Karl told my mother about the war. I imagine him as an earnest country kid like Karl, but shyer and not so serious-minded. Someone to instruct and protect. Their division had lost eighty officers and twenty-six hundred men since early August, and the survivors were spent beyond exhaustion. To recover any semblance of combat strength, one of their officers wrote, they needed at least eight days of shelter and rest. Instead, they were sent to the heart of the battle.

The trucks took them east to Juniville, then south to a camp near Bétheniville, where they were provisioned and loaded up again the next morning. They were headed to Blanc Mont, where French and American tanks and troops would batter the Germans in coming days, storming through their lines and taking hundreds of prisoners. Karl could see the flicker of explosions and hear the bellow of the cannons rolling over the hill, but his battalion never joined the battle. Instead, they were ordered to march southeast toward Sommepy, where the seventh Bavarian infantry was dug in. The men were glad for the reprieve, at first, but soon found themselves in the thick of the fighting, trying to move laterally into position in broad daylight. In the hollows beyond Blanc Mont, the ground was littered with twisted bodies, poisoned by gas. Karl was too tired to care. He dropped his pack amid the slaughter and fell into a fitful sleep.

By morning, it was drizzling rain. The battalion had been ordered to head for the village of Orfeuil, three miles to the northeast, so they slogged through the muddy hollows, dodging potshots from the French artillery. There was chaos to every side. On the open ground north of Aure, the last survivors of the Third Guards Infantry Division were strung along a trench, shooting at shadows, their defensive line long since shattered. Karl staggered over to fill in a gap, knowing the French could overrun them at any moment. That night, he and his friend crept into position along the ridge southwest of Liry. They were scanning the sky when the battle erupted.

First came the shuddering retort and hammer blast of artillery. Then the enemy bombers, blackening the stars in their squadrons. Then the strafing fighters, swooping down with a scream and chatter of machine-gun fire. Then, at last, the Algerian light infantry hurtled at them in wave after wave, ripping through the exhausted German line. The front was collapsing, the grenadiers hurled back in retreat, when Karl's leaders threw themselves forward to meet the enemy. "So great was their combat fury that it was hard for the battalion leaders to hold back their reserves," veterans of the battle later wrote. "Here exploits of rare and magnificent heroism were accomplished. It would take too long to describe them all."

The Algerian attack collapsed on the flanks of the ridge. But Karl and his friend weren't among the magnificent victors. When the attack came, they barely had time to scramble for cover. In the mayhem that followed, when everything was heaving and splintering and crashing around them, Karl's friend flew into a panic. It was all he could do to keep from leaping into the firestorm. Karl was trying to calm him down, cradling his friend in his arms and rocking back and forth, when the blast hit them. A land mine had blown nearby, knocking them down the ridge in a cloud of smoke and soil.

When Karl came to, his ears were bleeding and he could barely see—a piece of shrapnel had pierced his right eye. Other pieces were lodged in his right arm and right upper thigh. But the most lethal fragment—the one aimed at his heart—never reached him. It struck his friend in the back, killing him instantly, but stopped inches short of Karl's chest. "For a long time after the war, in both my waking life and my dreams, I was homesick for a hole in the ground somewhere in France," Karl later wrote. "Did his soul take me there?"

.   .   .

One winter morning, sixty-five years after the war ended, a dog fell into a hole in Orfeuil. Its owner, Jean-Luc Evrard, didn't notice the absence until later that day, when he was parking his car in his garage. He had driven halfway in when he saw that the concrete floor had collapsed ahead. When he stepped out to inspect the hole, he heard a muffled whimper and found his dog trapped inside.

Evrard rescued the dog and left the hole where it was. But a few weeks later, on the Monday after Easter, he and his wife's uncle went back to the garage with shovels. The soil had begun to thaw by then, so it was easier to excavate, but the hole kept getting larger and deeper. Soon they were using a tractor and pulleys to drag buckets of gravel and caved-in timbers out of the ground. The tunnel plunged straight down at first, around a set of stairs that had been hacked into the hard chalk underground. You could still see the pickaxe marks in the white walls. When the passageway finally leveled off, forty feet below, it widened into a corridor. A series of vestibules opened to either side, some with hospital beds in them and bottles of medicine nearby.

It was here that Karl was most likely taken on the night of September 30, 1918, broken in body and spirit. The clerk who filled out his service record noted only that he was wounded near Liry on that date. But Karl's regimental history places his battalion southwest of the village, within a mile or two of Orfeuil. The infirmary that Evrard found underground was the closest one in the area, along a well-established road. It was well hidden from the enemy, with three escape tunnels snaking in different directions. One came up into the house and another into the courtyard next door. The third led to what is now the garage, where it later collapsed beneath Evrard's dog.

The infirmary was designed, in part, as a shelter for the officers in the house, so it ran especially deep: More than thirty feet of solid chalk lay above it—enough to repel even a bunker-busting shell. It had no natural light and little ventilation. The temperature stayed around fifty-three degrees year-round, but felt much colder. The rain that seeped into the chalk from above kept the air damp and conductive. The cold reached up through the soles of your feet, till you began to feel like a cadaver on ice.

"We tried keeping wine down here, but it was too chilly," Evrard told me, when I went to see the infirmary with Thirion and Jacquart. "The wine wouldn't age. But for Champagne? Perfect!" A jovial, square-built man with a thick beard and rectangular glasses, Evrard had on an army surplus jacket and an olive watch cap pulled over his ears. He led us down into the gloom, along a string of yellow carbide lamps, past mounds of beets and potatoes and niches full of war relics: splints, disinfectants, flasks of beer and flat soda, jars of opium and hundred-year-old toothpaste. One ledge held a rusty caltrop— a seven-pointed star designed to hobble horses that stepped on it. Another held a screw picket: a thin steel spike that could be twisted into the ground to hold barbed wire, or sharpened to pierce a soldier's boot or slice his belly as he crawled over it.

The war raged on above ground as the soldiers' wounds were tended forty feet below. Orfeuil lay along *la route Boche,* as some people called it—the main transport road for the German army. From the farmhouses on top of the ridge, row after row of trenches fell away to the south toward Sommepy: the area's last great line of German defense. If the Allies could breach it, their path to the north was clear. Five days after Karl was wounded, the French reached Orfeuil. Another month and the war was over.

Had Karl chosen a different foxhole—had he managed to keep out of the line of fire for just a little longer—he might have made it back unscathed. Instead, he came home hobbled and half blind, with a sense that never left him that the world was a shattered thing, in need of radical repair. Climbing back to the surface, I tried to imagine how he must have felt, reemerging to the light after days underground. Outside, the sky was clear, but an icy wind blew across the frozen fields. Jacquart stuck his hands in his pockets and hunched his shoulders. "*C'est un vent prussien,*" he said, smirking. A wind out of Prussia.

What was left of Orfeuil lay around us: a handful of farmhouses built over the ruins of those laid waste by the war, and the few keepsakes that Evrard had found. Fragments shored against our ruins. I thought of something Thirion had shown me the night before at his house: a small stone flower, carved from the chalk of a trench wall. It had been made by a soldier waiting for the battle to pass on above him. "This is what they did when they had nothing to do," Thirion said. "This is what they did when they weren't being shot at."

8

GHOST

THE VILLAGERS IN HERZOGENWEILER STILL TELL A STORY about Karl's return from the Western Front. He was on a transport train heading across northern France when he noticed a young soldier sitting a few rows up. He recognized the face immediately—it was one of his bunkmates from his infantry battalion. But that couldn't be true: That soldier had died months ago.

Karl was staring at him, confused and a little frightened, when the soldier stood up and smiled, then gestured for Karl to join him. Karl followed him down the aisle and through the door of the compartment. He had just stepped into the next railway car when the air detonated behind him, heaving the compartment sideways and hurling him into the seats. The car he had left had been hit by mortar fire, Karl later learned, and he had escaped it just in time.

The soldier never appeared to him again, but the vision saved Karl's life. His older brother, Josef, wasn't as fortunate. While Karl was posted to France, his brother was sent to Belgium, site of some of the war's most sustained and brutal fighting. After the Germans launched the *Kaiserschlacht* in the spring of 1918, more than three dozen divisions joined the battle against Allied forces in Flanders, hoping to push through to the English Channel and cut off the British from their supply lines. They never made it. The Allies, reinforced by French troops under Maréchal Foch, held their ground. More than two hundred thousand soldiers were killed or wounded in that part of the offensive alone.

One night that spring, in Herzogenweiler, Karl and Josef's mother, Luise, woke up to the sound of footsteps on the road outside her farmhouse. The village was deserted at that hour, her daughter and husband asleep. But she knew that shuffling gait and heavy footfall. It could only be Josef, home at last from the war. She lurched up in bed to greet him, then stopped and listened again, more intently. No. It wasn't him after all. It was just his spirit, come to pay them a last visit. She lay down and shook her husband by the shoulder. "*Jetzt isch de Josef gschtorbe,*" she said, in her soft Black Forest dialect. "Now Josef has died." Two weeks later, they received word that he had fallen at Flanders—on the same day that his ghost had passed by.

For my mother, that story was proof, of a sort, that there was more to Luise's visions than superstition or mental illness. That the ties between loved ones can stretch beyond death. She and my eldest daughter owe Luise their middle name—a keepsake of the old country, like a lock of hair or a finger bone. Although they've never been known to socialize with the dead, a strain of second sight is said to run in the family. My great-aunt Regina, who was born in Romania, worked as a fortune-teller in Herzogenweiler during the Second World War, scanning coffee grounds and tarot cards for news of fallen soldiers. My mother, too, has had her share of strange premonitions: accidents foretold, telephones answered before the first ring. She's a historian by training and a sober thinker by nature, but she has never quite shaken her belief in ghosts.

It's an old German habit of mind, this mixing of the mystical and the scientific. You can see it in medieval sages like Meister Eckhart and Hildegard von Bingen, and in the aisles of any German drugstore, where modern pharmaceuticals sit side by side with homeopathic tinctures. "To our modern way of thinking, this all sounds quite insane," Rudolf Steiner, the patron saint of organic agriculture and alternative schooling, declared in 1924. He had just urged an audience of Silesian farmers to fertilize their fields with cow intestines stuffed with chamomile blossoms, and stag bladders filled with yarrow root (stag bladders being "almost an image of the cosmos"). Steiner claimed that he, too, could see spirits in his waking life. "Just as in the body, eye and ear develop as organs of perception," he wrote, "so does a man develop in himself spiritual organs of perception through which the soul and spiritual worlds are opened to him."

.   .   .

I thought of those stories one morning in Berlin, in the heart of the old western zone. I was sitting in the drawing room of an ornate prewar building, on a leafy side street off Neue Kantstrasse. The room was bare of furniture aside from a dozen mismatched chairs and a dresser of figured maple. One tall window let in a wintry light. The chairs were occupied by a circle of silent, seemingly spellbound men and women, their eyes pinned on a woman at the center of the room. Her name was Gabriele Baring, and she was there to help us make peace with our dead.

A man across the room was telling Baring about his family history. He was a therapist like her and a veteran of this type of gathering, known as a *Familienaufstellung*, or family constellation. Ulf, as I'll call him, was a bearish man in a lumpy burgundy sweater. He wore suede sandals with dark socks and had a child's bright, confiding eyes—a face not made for sadness, somehow, though he couldn't seem to escape it. Ulf had twice been hospitalized for depression and panic attacks in recent years. "I'm wondering if this has something to do with my parents' history as refugees during the war," he said.

Ulf's paternal grandfather died in a Russian prison camp in the First World War. His father enlisted at seventeen, in 1939, was sent to a boarding school for elite Nazi officers in training, and wound up in a Russian prison camp as well. By the time he got out, in 1946, his family had been driven from East Germany. Ulf's mother was also a refugee, from Kiel, on the Baltic Sea. It was a lovely city before the war, Ulf said, crisscrossed by canals and bridges. But it had a naval base and a submarine factory, so Allied bombers reduced it to rubble. His mother was nine when her family fled.

Baring jotted down some lines in a black Moleskine notebook, then looked up and held Ulf's eyes for a moment. At sixty-two, Baring still had the wholesome, high-spirited look of the German poster girls of the 1930s—apple cheeks and white-blond hair. But her voice had a smoky, conspiratorial warmth. Her own father had lost a leg on the Russian front in the Second World War, and her hometown of Hanover was nearly as devastated as Kiel. "This country had fourteen million refugees in 1945," she said. "The fact that we were able to absorb them has been called one of the great accomplishments of postwar Germany. There were all sorts of problems—prejudice, ostracism—but there was no civil war."

Her listeners shifted in their seats. Most were middle-aged Germans like her, unaccustomed to self-pity and allergic to national pride. Theirs was a country responsible for history's bloodiest war and most efficient mass murder. They were here to wrestle with that guilt, not to make excuses for it. Yet Baring believed that there had been more than enough suffering to go around, and not nearly enough compassion. Of those fourteen million German refugees, some were colonists in Nazi-occupied territories. But the great majority were civilians fleeing bombed-out cities, or ethnic Germans who had settled abroad long before the war. They and their children had the same psychological issues as the refugees who had flooded into Germany from Syria and other war-ravaged countries: depression, alienation, no sense of place. "I've led whole sessions filled with nothing but people like you," Baring said.

She asked Ulf if he was ready to start, and he nodded, gathering himself. What happened next was hard to categorize. It was part theater, part therapy, part séance—a measure of just how far Germans will go to come to terms with their past. It was reminiscent of a type of group therapy called family sculpting, in which patients take turns posing one another in groups to depict key moments in their lives. How and where people stand—whether a wife faces her husband or has her back to him, for instance—embodies their relationship. Sometimes it helps people see it clearly for the first time.

A *Familienaufstellung* is both more impersonal and more weirdly intimate. The people in our group would take turns posing one another, as in family sculpting, but none of us had met before that weekend. We were complete strangers, yet somehow we would try to intuit Ulf's deepest feelings and personal relations. "There is a kind of family consciousness we share," Baring told me later. "Why does a mother go walking along a beach and suddenly know that her daughter in Canada or Asia just had an accident? Why does a dog know that his master is coming home? They have information we don't have. That's what we're trying to uncover—the family secrets that lie hidden in our cells."

Ulf stood up and looked around the room. His eyes paused on each of us in turn, as if tapping a tuning fork and assessing the pitch. When he had gone the full round, he pointed at a tall, wiry man with a penetrating gaze. "Will you be me?" he said. He asked another man to be his uncle and a woman nearby, with birdlike features, to be Fear. Each time he chose a stand-in, Ulf walked around behind them and laid his hands on their shoulders. Then he closed his eyes and slowly pushed forward. "Just stop when you feel like they're in the right spot," Baring said. Soon the room was filled with people frozen in place, like statues in a war memorial. For the next hour or so, they would try to channel the person or emotion they had been asked to represent. To let their spirits speak.

Ulf was about to sit down when his eyes lit on me and he did a double take, as if we had met somewhere before. "Will you be my father?" he said.

•   •   •

Like the others in the room, I was there to untangle a knot in my mind. I had come to Germany to research my grandfather's life, yet the more I learned about him, the more I wanted to know—and realized I never could. I had grown used to a certain kind of omniscience as a journalist. If an online search or database couldn't answer a question, an expert source was moments away by phone or email. It didn't matter if I was writing about bull breeders in Texas or sapphire miners in Madagascar. And now here was my grandfather, a man closer to me than anyone I had ever written about. I wanted nothing more than to sit in a room with him and have a conversation—to ask him all the questions I was too young to ask as a boy. Yet he was impossible to reach.

Germany was full of such spectral figures. Hardly a family I knew wasn't haunted by them. There was no lack of information about Karl's generation, but it was scattered across the Continent like so much shrapnel, lodged in bookcases and file cabinets in hundreds of archives in Germany alone. When I first arrived in 2014, the sheer quantity of research material—the inexhaustibility of the past—had

seemed overwhelming. There were seventy miles of files and micro-
fiche in Berlin's Bundesarchiv; eighty miles in the Stasi archives
across town; thirty million documents in the Holocaust archives in
Bad Arolsen. There were letters, diaries, and reams of statistics,
maps, blueprints, and bills of lading. I felt as if I had stumbled into
Borges's Library of Babel, its shelves stretching infinitely in every
direction.

Wherever I went, the archives were full of people. They tottered
past in reading rooms, arms laden with leather-bound volumes, or
sat hunched over handwritten documents, the pages yellowed by the
acid in their fibers. Berlin was home not only to the Bundesarchiv,
and the assiduous, half-mad files of the Nazi Party leadership, but
also to the Deutsche Dienststelle, where many of the German military's records were kept. At the latter, the wait time for visitors had
grown from six months to fifteen months within two years. "We've
just been flooded with inquiries," one archivist told me. "War veterans and their wives have priority—they're often dying. But even their
children aren't so young anymore. After that, who's to decide who
comes first?"

They rarely liked what they found: an uncle in the Gestapo, another in the Waffen-SS, a family fortune built on confiscated goods.
I spoke to Matthias Neukirch, a successful actor in Berlin, who had
spent years researching his mother's father, Hans Schleif. A noted
architect and archaeologist, Schleif had tried to steer clear of politics
at first. But then he came under the patronage of Heinrich Himmler,
the supreme mythmaker of the Nazi Party. Soon Schleif was exca-
vating ancient Germanic sites in Poland, to help justify Hitler's invasion there, and overseeing the looting of the State Archaeological
Museum in Warsaw. When Neukirch requested Schleif's files at the
Bundesarchiv, the cart came back with folders stacked two feet high.
Buried inside were architectural drawings for underground munitions plants, to be built by concentration camp inmates.

"I went through a phase where I just wanted it all to go away," my cousin Karin told me, when I visited her in Bavaria. "I hated that whole wartime generation." Karin was my uncle Gernot's first child. Born in 1957, she grew up in the wake of the '68ers—the generation of Germans who had rebelled against their parents' willful amnesia about the war. For Karin, that meant school field trips to Verdun and Dachau. It meant hour after hour in darkened classrooms with clattering projectors, watching cities burn and gravesites heaped with corpses. "Three times a week, we had Guilt," as the German comedian Michael Mittermeier put it. "On Fridays, we had Shame."

When Karin visited Dachau, at sixteen, and the guide wrenched open the oven door in the crematorium, she fainted. "I just wanted all those old soldiers to go ahead and die," she told me. "When the last one is dead, I thought, I won't have to feel guilty anymore." And, of course, they did die, in time. But then a strange thing happened. As the generations turned and the war loosened its grip, people began to realize how little they knew about their parents' and grandparents' lives, and how much that silence had shaped their lives. They needed to hear those terrible stories after all, and the last eyewitnesses were passing away. Germans of the *Tätergeneration,* or generation of perpetrators, were nearly gone. But their children were still alive by the millions. They were too young to have fought or to understand the fighting, but old enough to have been traumatized by it. *Kriegskinder,* they called themselves: children of war.

·   ·   ·

A few weeks before the *Familienaufstellung,* I went to Cologne for a national congress of *Kriegskinder.* It was held in a Lutheran church not far from the city's Gothic cathedral—one of Germany's oldest pilgrimage sites, where the bones of the Three Wise Men were said to lie. More than twice as many people had requested tickets as the number available, and the church was packed to a third over capacity. "We had to turn so many away," the organizer, Curt Hondrich, told us in his opening talk. But the tight quarters and meager rations would help set the mood, he said. "It will remind us of our theme."

Hondrich was one of the founders of the *Kriegskinder* movement. Red-faced and roundly built, with a bald pate fringed with gray, he looked like Freud's jolly younger brother. He had worked as a student pastor and journalist before becoming interested in psychoanalysis. Born in 1939, Hondrich spent his early childhood in an atmosphere of constant alarm. His mother was Jewish by Nazi standards (one of her grandparents was a Jew). His father was a party member. He manufactured munitions cases for the Wehrmacht in Cologne and used his work and political connections to hide his wife's background. "It was like living in a family with a time bomb sitting inside it," Hondrich told me. "My mother knew that at any moment she could be taken away."

The memories sometimes came back to him in flashes: Cowering in a concrete bunker with other neighborhood kids, their parents too hysterical to pay them any mind. The ground above them shaking from phosphorus bombs. The sky flaming red afterward, flecked with white as British bombers bailed from stricken planes and drifted down to the burning city. The bodies splayed like black puppets on the sidewalks. Later, after the family fled to northern Germany, Hondrich was bathing in the Weser River one summer afternoon when enemy fighters appeared above the trees. They turned and dived and strafed him as he scrambled for cover, the sand flying up to either side where the bullets struck. "It stayed with me," he told me, "that deep experience of fear."

What to do with memories like that? Tamp them down in your chest. Bury them so deep that you forget they're there, betrayed only by your hammering pulse. Hondrich was always afraid to swim after that, but he never connected that fear to his experience on the Weser.

Then one day in 1990, when he was working as a culture editor for Westdeutscher Rundfunk in Cologne—the West German NPR—he saw a report on television about the Gulf War in Kuwait. Ever since the fighting began, elderly Germans had been hoarding food and water, as if preparing for an attack. The war was five thousand miles away, yet they could already hear boot steps approaching. What are they thinking? Hondrich wondered as he watched the footage. It was a while before he realized that he was crying.

Hondrich went on to assign a story on *Kriegskinder* to Sabine Bode, a reporter in Cologne who had been investigating her own family history. Germany still had more than fifteen million inhabitants born between 1930 and 1945 (they're now dying at the rate of a third of a million a year), but Bode had trouble finding any who would talk about the trauma they had experienced. "If I was on a train to Hamburg and saw a person with gray hair sitting alone, I would ask if I could take a seat beside them," she told me. "It wasn't hard to get them to tell stories about the war. That was very easy. But when I asked how it affected their lives—they couldn't answer this question. 'No, no, no. It didn't do us any harm,' they said. 'We were just children—it was normal for us.'"

The *Kriegskinder* belong to a generation raised with *Schwarze Pädagogik*, the German version of "Spare the rod, spoil the child." Bedwetting, stuttering, slumping your shoulders: Any deviance was swiftly corrected, any whining dismissed as weakness. (In *Der Struwwelpeter*, perhaps the most famous German children's book, a character's thumbs are chopped off because he won't stop sucking them.) One of Bode's respondents remembered her mother scolding her after a bombing raid: "Why can't you be happy for once? Just be glad you're alive." So she took the lesson to heart. The war wasn't so very terrible, she told herself; it was an adventure, really. "Children are little masters of self-comforting," Bode told me.

It took Bode ten years to gather and prepare the stories for her first book, *The Forgotten Generation*. Published in 2004, it sold poorly at first. To speak openly of German war trauma—to play the victim in a country that had victimized so many—was still taboo. "*O, das biss-chen Krieg! Andere hatten es viel schlimmer,*" Bode's respondents would tell her. "Oh, that bit of war! Others had it much worse." But then, slowly, word of the book began to spread, and the *Kriegskinder* grew older and lost their compunctions. Their stories multiplied and with them their audience. By the time I met Bode, her book was in its tenth hardcover printing and had launched *Kriegskinder* groups across the country. "The ghost is coming out of the bottle," she said.

.   .   .

Late one night at my cousin Karin's house, we went down to the basement to look through some bins of old photographs. Karin had known Karl much longer and better than I had. She was the oldest of my cousins and had lived in the same town as my grandparents for much of her childhood. While my uncles could be tight-lipped or forgetful where family stories were concerned, Karin had never been afraid to speak her mind. Tall and tightly wound, with bright, defiant eyes, she was the funniest and most combative of my relatives. She was a public-school teacher as my grandfather was, and a master of the withering retort and pungent dismissal. Part of her admired Karl's unwavering convictions, however misguided, his strict code of conduct. "No fear. No concern for anything but the truth. I hope we inherited some of that," she told me.

She and her little brother liked to call him Charlie. She couldn't recall why, but there was always a kind of suavity about him, a world-weary elegance. He was thin and refined with slender hips and shoulders, and always impeccably dressed in a three-piece suit. The first two fingers of his right hand were yellowed from the cigarettes he held loosely between them; his glass eye always fixed on some vague middle distance. "He wasn't the kind of grandfather who crawls around on the floor with the grandchildren," Karin said. "But I thought he was cool. I liked his sense of humor. His sarcasm. He was so quiet and then suddenly—boom!"

He and her parents often bickered, she said, needling one another even when they pretended to get along. Maybe it was because her father, Gernot, was the oldest child. When Karl was in prison, Gernot had to help take responsibility for the family, then step down again when his father came home. Maybe Karl envied Gernot's closeness to his mother, or Gernot envied Karl's closeness to my mother. But they never spoke about it. On Christmas Day, Karin remembered, the women would work furiously in the kitchen, fretting over the goose while the men smoked and talked in the living room, never lifting a finger to help. There was Karl with his glass eye, her uncle Sigmar with his shrapnel-twisted fingers, and Karin, not able to keep from staring, wanting to hear about the war but knowing it was taboo to ask. "It was too terrible, *zu schrecklich*," she told me. "He just wanted to forget. It was the same with others after the war. They were just as broken, as soul sick. I think they raised their kids without emotion to make them as tough as possible."

She picked through the bin for a while in silence, then stopped and fished out a faded black-and-white photograph. It was Karl in a field of wildflowers, giving the camera his cockeyed stare, like Samuel Beckett standing at the end of the world. She laughed. "Doesn't he look cool?" It was the only shot of him that she could find. The bin was full of pictures of her mother and brother, children, cousins, uncles, aunts, and in-laws. But not Karl. "You know, the more I look through these, the more I realize that in a strange way, I have no memory of him ever being in our house. I see everyone sitting at our table, but not Charlie." Like so many men of his generation, he registered mainly as an absence. A question mark where a person should have been.

· · ·

Almost exactly a year after my first *Familienaufstellung*, I found myself back at Gabriele Baring's studio in Berlin. The first time I came, I was merely an observer and stand-in for others—too skeptical and discomfited to talk about my own family. I still doubted that people could communicate with the dead, yet I couldn't get the last session out of my head. So many of its revelations had struck a chord with the people in the group. I knew that there was a great deal about my grandfather that I could never learn, but I wondered what a roomful of ordinary Germans would make of him.

The group in the drawing room this time included two doctors, a seminarian, a computer scientist, and a ponytailed art history student. Some were there to work through their family issues, others just to serve as stand-ins—*Familienaufstellung* junkies, people called them. The intensity of the sessions seemed to be addictive, and, according to a study at the University of Heidelberg, equally therapeutic for patients and stand-ins. The very act of empathizing so deeply could help people understand themselves.

Still, it was exhausting. Baring's sessions ran from nine in the morning until six at night. By the end of the second day, I had played a brother, a grandfather, Restlessness, and the country of Germany. I had watched people burst into tears, climb into one another's laps, and pretend to be God. I had heard a woman scream that she was bleeding from her vagina and that crows had eaten her baby. At times, the sobs and shouting rose to such a pitch that I worried the police might come. (Germans tend to be eerily quiet at home by American standards.) There were moments when I would rather have had all my molars pulled than be asked to play another Nazi war criminal. But if catharsis was what was required, then Baring surely provided it.

When my turn came, I felt a twinge of performance anxiety. All the others had ended their sessions in tears. Would I have to do the same? I imagined people circling the room for hours, telling dismal tales about my ancestors until I finally broke down. When I had placed my stand-ins around the room—one each for my mother, grandmother, and grandfather, and three for my uncles—they stood there for a moment in silence, as if humming to the same vibration. Then everyone seemed to move and talk at once. I remember my mother laying her forehead on the ground; my grandmother kneeling beside her and putting a hand on her shoulder; my grandfather saying, "You have to believe in something. If not God, then Hitler." But it's hard to recall how it all fit together. There is a dream logic to a *Familienaufstellung* that's lost in the retelling.

What stayed with me were quieter details. The mutual devotion of my mother and grandmother, for instance, and the eerie way that the stand-ins captured my three uncles. I had positioned my mother's two older brothers, Gernot and Sigmar, side by side, with their little brother Winfried behind them. And from that minimal geometry a familiar portrait emerged. Sigmar talked about his deep connection to his father, which I had learned about only recently from their letters. Winfried bemoaned his sense of disconnection, of being cast aside by his father: "Why can't he see me?" he said. Yet I never told the group that Winfried felt this way. Or that he was sent from home at age eight to live with relatives in the Black Forest, when the rest of the family was starving.

A lucky guess, you might say—the psychic's usual shot in the dark. But any good divination starts with a close study of the seeker. That's what I remember best from that day: the careful attention that people paid to one another—their hunger for stories and the ardor with which they abandoned themselves to them. The Germans I had known growing up were a stoic, thick-skinned lot. How reserved they were on the street! How cautious with their feelings compared with the average oversharing American. Yet here they were, sobbing in one another's arms, divided and united, accused and forgiven, reenacting their sorrows with people they had never met.

My session ended without undue drama. The others could tell that I was worn-out, I think, and unprepared for any more revelations. Or maybe they were just hoping for a happier ending. When they had fallen silent, Baring asked them to join me in the middle of the room. We stood there for a moment shoulder to shoulder, smiling as if for a camera: a family portrait. "I think it's good what you're doing," the ponytailed art history student told me. But I knew, by then, that the stories I needed to hear weren't in that room. They were in southern Germany, in the village where my grandfather first became a Nazi.

9

TEACHER

KARL PULLED THE LEAFLET FROM HIS POCKET AND STARED at the words again. He needed this job. The years since he had come home had been the hardest of his life. At least in the infantry he had always known where to go and what to do. But he had been wandering from village to village in the Black Forest for eleven years, and he still couldn't seem to find where he belonged. After he lost his eye in the Ardennes and was carried off to the infirmary; after they picked the shrapnel from his head and arm and upper thigh; after they cleaned and bandaged his wounds and soothed his shuddering mind with ether and morphine, they sent him back to Germany by truck and train and jolting transport. He arrived at the military hospital in Frankfurt on October 5, 1918. Two months later, he was finally whole enough to leave.

What then? Before he went to war, Karl had spent three years at the Lendersche Lehranstalt in Sasbach, a boarding school more than seven hours north of his village on horseback. He would later claim, when he petitioned the social welfare court to increase his veteran's pension, that he had planned to work in a technical field after he graduated. As proof, he pointed to the year he had spent as a mechanical engineer before going to boarding school. But this was a bit of strategic revisionism: By claiming that the war had derailed his career, he could ask for more compensation. The priesthood was his true goal in those years: The Lehranstalt was founded to train seminarians. Its motto, carved above the entrance, was INITIUM SAPIENTIAE TIMOR DOMINI. Fear of the Lord is the beginning of wisdom.

Karl had other things to fear by the time he returned from France. He had no money and no connections. The priesthood and engineering were now out of the question: His faith was too shaken, his vision too impaired. With only one eye, he had trouble seeing three-dimensionally or gauging distance accurately. If a shadow fell across the street, he would jump over it, my mother told me, thinking it was a ditch. Teaching seemed the next best option for a studious twenty-year-old. But when he took the entrance exam for the teacher's seminary in Meersburg, in 1919, his application was denied. The district physician in Villingen, a man by the name of Stöcker, had concluded that the rigors of graduate study were too much for Karl. He had passed the exam but failed the physical.

When Karl tried to have his veteran's pension increased a few years later, the claim was also denied. The social welfare office could find no evidence of Dr. Stöcker's exam. Nevertheless, he won his case on appeal. Whatever his career goals had been before the war, whatever discrimination he had faced since then, he had shown more than enough tenacity and willpower to become an engineer, the court ruled. "If only he had come home from the war with both his eyes," the judges added. Karl eventually had a doctor in Stuttgart issue him a clean bill of health, then reapplied to a teacher's college—this time at a seminary in Ettlingen, just south of Karlsruhe. On November 23, 1922, three years after the teacher's seminary first rejected him, Karl finally received his teaching certificate.

It was the worst time in modern German history to become a teacher. The economy was in free fall, its currency spiraling into hyperinflation. The year Karl graduated, a dollar was worth 320 Papiermarks, the currency of the Weimar Republic; the next year it was worth more than four trillion. Bank notes were worth less than butcher paper. Housewives used them for kitchen fires, children for making kites and paper dolls. By the end of 1923, a loaf of bread cost two hundred billion marks. A baker could always raise his prices, a waiter could stand on a table and announce that the *Eisbein mit Sauerkraut* now cost twice as much; but teachers were on fixed salaries. The best they could do was barter or hope for a raise—assuming they had work at all.

Less than two weeks after earning his degree, Karl took a job as a teaching assistant in his hometown. It may have been the only place that would have him. Herzogenweiler's one-room schoolhouse, built in 1874, had two mottos painted on its walls: *Der Geißt ist es der lebendig macht* (The spirit gives life) and *Gerechtigkeit erhöht ein Volk* (Righteousness exalts a nation). Karl hoped to live by the second. The school came with an apartment, a vegetable garden, and pigs, but those were for the head teacher. As his assistant, Karl earned just enough to pay for room and board in a neighbor's house.

Four months later, he was gone. He took another assistant's job in Schönwald, half an hour to the west, then moved on to schools in Linach, Volkertshausen, Emmingen, Anselfingen, Weiterdingen, and Oberschwandorf—eight positions in four years, in a weary circle through the Black Forest. He was moving around but getting nowhere.

.   .   .

Karl's war wounds had long since healed, if only physically. He bore himself with somber self-assurance now, almost a swagger. He was a fastidious dresser, always correct in his bearing: shoulders squared and a napkin on his knee at the table. Aside from smoking, which he loved for its elegance as much as for the nicotine, he had few vices or physical needs. Every Monday night at his bachelor's flat, he would roast a *Rinderbraten*, or a pork butt, and eat it for the rest of the week, with egg noodles and peas and carrots from a can. He fancied himself an intellectual, with his round spectacles and worldly mien, and the years in schoolrooms had amplified a natural didacticism in him—an urge to explain and define and solve. He had always been the smartest person he knew, whether in his village or seminary or infantry unit. But that soon changed.

He met Emma Egle in 1923. She was a teaching assistant at the elementary school in Volkertshausen, west of Lake Constance. He was a newly hired administrator. She was his opposite in almost every way: wistful, cultivated, undamaged by war. She was small and soft-featured where he was thin and knobby, she given to brooding while he was quick to ignite—the deep shade to his flickering sun. They both loved music and played the violin, but Karl's instrument was cheap and factory made. Emma had a beautiful old gypsy violin with a smooth, slender waist, herringbone purfling, and a lion's-head scroll. When they played together, the sound was rough and sweet in equal measure.

They seemed to come from different worlds. The daughter of a customs officer in Konstanz, Emma was comfortably middle-class. While Karl had spent his summers milking cows and harvesting hay, she had grown up in a city of art and music, where tourists strolled the shores in white linen and foreign dignitaries took the waters. Refinement came easily to her. In him, it could seem like pretense—like he was overplaying his role. He could be cutting when annoyed and given to sharp, peremptory outbursts. Farmer's talk. "If you were my wife," he once wrote to his sister-in-law, "I'd put you over my knee and the problem would be solved."

That sort of thing didn't fly with Emma. She would pin him with her quiet, appraising eyes and wait for his bluster to blow clear, his spirit to right itself. She loved his ardent mind and passionate sympathies, his mixture of high-mindedness and earthy humor—the Black Forest in him. But she was wary of his excesses, even then. He was itchy with promise and thwarted ambition. "I'm a person who sadly can't divide himself," as he later put it. "I can only do one thing wholeheartedly at a time." The country was broken, he said. Poverty and hunger might be new to Emma, or to the people pawning furs for loaves of bread in the cities, but not to him. He wanted to tear down and rebuild the world she found so comfortable. Yet he was powerless to do so.

Two and a half years after they met, Karl passed his second set of education boards. This qualified him to be a head teacher, but he couldn't seem to make the leap. He took another administrative job, then two low-level teaching posts, then went back to administrative work. Finally, on the first of December, 1926, in the village of Oberschwandorf, he was promoted to head teacher. By then, though, he had another problem. He and Emma were in love, but the closer they grew the more their work pulled them apart. Oberschwandorf was in the northern foothills of the Black Forest, a full day's ride from Emma's school in Ludwigshafen, on Lake Constance. Karl had made his leap, and it had carried him away from her.

•   •   •

My mother has a single letter from those years, dated January 25, 1926. When I found it one summer, in a zippered pouch full of documents stashed in the back of her closet, I had no idea what it said. There was no envelope with the letter, no indication of where it was composed. The handwriting was in *Sütterlinschrift*, elegant but hasty and nearly incomprehensible to me. All I could make out was the salutation—"*Liebster!*" (Dearest one)—and the signature: Emma.

My mother's eyesight was too poor by then to decipher the script, and her memory too porous to recall what it said. I tried scanning the pages and sending them to my cousin Susan in Germany, but she fared only a little better than I had. Then she told me about a group of elderly women in her hometown of Konstanz. They had formed what they called a *Sütterlin Schreibstube*—a kind of sewing circle crossed with a medieval scriptorium. Every weekend, they would gather at a senior center, and in exchange for a small gift to charity, transcribe the letters and diaries that people brought to them. Groups like this had sprung up all over the country. Countless Germans, apparently, were in the same predicament as I was: The *Schreibstube* in Konstanz had a four-month waiting list. But when Susan called to ask for their help, the group took pity on her. It was just the one letter. The woman who translated it was ninety years old, but still too young to have been alive when Emma wrote the words. And yet, when she read them aloud, their anxious longing must have carried through in her voice:

Dearest one,

See, I'm already back. Are you even a little pleased to hear it? I bet I've surprised you with this letter. Surely you didn't think I would be in a mood to write after that long train ride. You see, love is the mightiest power on earth. I feel that so firmly and deeply in my soul. Today, for instance, I went to Espasingen during the most beautiful sunset—I walked straight into its red embers. To the right lay the mountains, their snowy peaks lit with purest alpenglow, to the left the lake, glimmering with every hue. I was elated, of course, and my eyes drank soulfully of the beauty all around, but it filled only a small part of my being. I used to be able to stand still and calmly delight in all things, from the largest to the smallest. But today I was urged ever onward, wandering toward the west, and I searched with a deep yearning the heights that separated me from you. If I could, I would have gone all the way to your little room, and then I would have kissed you with all my heart and looked into your dear eyes and asked if you were still mad at me for my angry words. If you knew how I've hurt myself by everything I've done to you, I think you yourself would be in tears. Oh my treasure, isn't your soul filled with joy once again, knowing that I love you beyond words, as only a woman can?

They were married a year later, in the spring. Emma was twenty-eight—a little old to be single in that era, in those straitlaced southern German towns—and perhaps afraid that she would become a spinster, never have children. But that changed soon enough. She joined Karl in Oberschwandorf after the wedding, and Gernot was born the following May. Emma would always be the soul of the family, holding it together by sheer force of empathy. But she was also a teacher at heart, with a toughness and intellect that were more than a match for Karl's. She had been the top of her class in Basel, at the city's oldest school for girls, and was fluent in both French and English. But German law didn't allow women to teach once they were married. That was why Emma had put off getting married for so long. Sometimes when Karl was giving a lesson, my mother told me, her mother would sit on the steps outside the schoolhouse and listen, just to be close to a classroom again.

Oberschwandorf wasn't a bad place to land: a tidy little village tucked along the Waldach River, just twenty miles from the gracious old university town of Tübingen. But it was a full day's travel from their families in Herzogenweiler and Konstanz, and both Emma and Karl wanted more children. They needed help, and here was this leaflet announcing a job opening. It was for a head teacher in the village of Aulfingen, almost exactly halfway between their families' homes. An old handbook for job applicants described the position this way:

> Aulfingen, 470 inhabitants, 679 meters. . . . Railway town with freight traffic. . . . Electric lighting under consideration. Running water free of charge. 1 inn, 1 restaurant, 1 butcher and sausage maker, 1 dry goods store. . . . 75 students. 1 head teacher. . . . Teacher receives his wood allotment from the community, freely delivered (in exchange for 50 marks of his organist's pay). . . . Schoolhouse built in 1852, good two-story stone construction on local road in somewhat noisy surroundings, due to mill and pub nearby. Teacher's residence with 4 large, dry, sunny rooms on the second floor. Vaulted basement with occasional flooding. Stove for baking. Classroom on first floor, stable, woodshed, and poultry house. Indoor plumbing. . . . Organist's pay: 250 Marks cash. Yearly bonus: 10 Marks. Location suitable for beekeeping.

It was a bare-bones posting in a backward little town. The pay was low, the classes large, the basement damp. Four people were already in line for the position. This time, though, Karl was in luck. Two of the applicants, Hermann Huber and Hermann Müller, couldn't play the organ as the job required. The school board had proposed a third man, Artur Schaaf, but the local administrator didn't think much of him. "From my personal experience, there would be trouble from the outset," he wrote to the board on September 3, just before the school year began. "Besides, he's quite young." As for the fourth candidate, Alfons Knaupp, he was the son of a local teacher, well known to the community but not in a good way. "I share the concerns of the school board regarding his person," the administrator added.

That left Karl. He had eight years' experience and no marks against him. He was fluent in French and a passable organist—he had learned to play at boarding school. He could even carry a tune on the violin. On September 12, 1930, he was hired by the Ministry of Education and Cultural Affairs. Two days later, the Nazis received more than six million votes in the German federal election. Their party was now the second largest in the country behind the Social Democrats. Soon it would be the only one.

·   ·   ·

Karl stayed in Aulfingen for the next eight years, till the very eve of war. It was his family's first true home, where two of his children were born; where he honed his craft, became a community leader, and decided what lessons and values to pass on to his charges. Before Aulfingen, Karl was just another journeyman teacher, scrabbling to make a living. Afterward, he was a member of the Nazi Party, his pedagogy inseparable from his politics. It was the making of him and nearly the breaking.

That much I knew, but little else. Karl was too busy to send letters home in those years; too practical-minded for a diary. The story he told the welfare court about his life after the Great War ended before he got to Aulfingen. My mother and her brothers had few memories of the place—they were too young at the time—and they had rarely been back to visit. It was both the crux of Karl's early history and an enormous blank spot.

This presented a different problem from piecing together his wartime experiences. In that case, there had been less to go on but much more to find. Once I knew where Karl had fought and in what regiment, a flood of records and local memories welled up around those facts. His battles were cataclysmic events shared by tens of thousands of others. They had been picked over by historians and artists, and endlessly revisited by local people whose lives they still shaped. But who would remember a small-town teacher in a remote corner of Germany? The answer seemed to be no one.

I tried for weeks to contact the mayor of Aulfingen—a man by the name of Uwe Fröhlin—to no avail. The town hall was open for only a few hours a week, on Mondays and Thursdays, and Fröhlin never seemed to be in. There was no online archive to consult, no local historical society. When the mayor's assistant, Ilona Heizmann, finally returned my messages, she had bad news. The town had built a new school, she said, and there were no records from the old one, where my grandfather taught. In fact, Aulfingen had no archive at all. She promised to ask around town for me, to see if any of the older villagers could remember my grandfather. But that drew a blank as well. It was all such a long time ago, she said.

Over the next few months, I cast around for other sources, with a deepening sense of futility. I went to the German Diary Archive in Emmendingen, to the state archive in Freiburg, and to archives in Donaueschingen, Engen, Tuttlingen, and Villingen—the larger towns that encircled Aulfingen. I found no end of odd tales and vivid tangents, of teachers with paddles behind their backs and farm girls sent to the blackboard with knots in their stomach. I even learned a few lines of prewar bathroom graffiti (*Fünf Minuten wird geschissen, wer länger scheißt, wird rausgeschmissen:* Five minutes to take a crap, any longer and you're on your ass). But next to nothing about this particular teacher, in this particular village, in the tumultuous years before the war.

Then one morning in Tuttlingen, an archivist named Hans-Joachim Schuster—tall, stolid, blunt of speech—stopped at my desk. He had left me a pile of local history books to look through and a list of call numbers to research in Freiburg. But something still vexed him. "There must be at least *some* files for you to see in Aulfingen," he said.

These local archives were all the same, he went on: both meticulous and full of holes. Most places had at least some historical records: Of the fifty villages in this area, all but two had sorted and cataloged their archives. It was my peculiar bad luck that Aulfingen was one of the two. Anywhere else, I might have asked the villagers to show me their own letters and family albums. But I was interested in the Nazi years, and those records had almost all been destroyed. Some were obliterated by bomb raids and tank attacks, by the retreating German army, or by people who disavowed their Nazi past after the war. Some were confiscated by the French, others by the British, Americans, or Russians. Portions of those records were eventually returned and filed, scanned, and digitized. But many were still buried somewhere in Moscow or the Library of Congress—bureaucratic dross yet to be sifted for flecks of gold.

Schuster drummed his fingers on the table. "There should be some files in boxes on shelves," he said, frowning. "They won't be easy to sort, and you'll have to get them to let you do it. But they should be there." If he weren't going on vacation in two days, he said, he would drive to Aulfingen with me. But maybe he could give Uwe Fröhlin a call.

•   •   •

Aulfingen was twelve hundred years old when Karl and his family arrived, and it hadn't changed much by the time I visited. It had the same population of five hundred, the same stone buildings crowded beneath the bell tower of the church. Lake Constance glimmered to the southeast, beyond the hills blanketed in beech forest, drawing waves of Swiss tourists and bargain hunters across the border. But the area had kept its sense of serene isolation, its rural piety. At the entrance to town, a wooden bench sat along the shores of the Aitrach River, with Christ twisted on a crucifix beside it. A reminder to the indolent that all beauty is bought with pain.

On the June evening I arrived, the streets were deserted, the shops long since closed. Rows of locked doors and latched shutters ran from house to house, pale yellow, white, and bluish gray, like the darkened galleries in a de Chirico painting. I parked my car behind the Rathaus and stepped outside, not sure if I had come to the right place. Then the faint thump of a tuba reached me. I followed the sound around the corner and down an alley, and found myself in front of an enormous green tent strung with colored lights. When I stepped inside, I was hit by the double blast of an oom-pah band and a few hundred half-drunk Germans. It was the first night of the Pfarrbuckfest, Aulfingen's annual music and crafts fair. If the village was empty, it was because everyone was here.

I made my way to the concession stand across from the stage. The crowd was gathered at long tables beneath the wooden struts of the tent, eating *Grillwurst* and *Bratkartoffeln* with sour cream. There were groups of snowy-haired women and stooped older men, rows of stout burghers circling the perimeter, and in the corner, at a beer concession of their own, some rawboned teens smoking and horsing around. Every so often, one of them would peel off to sit beside their grandmother and see how she was doing. Even the band, dressed in velvet vests and dirndls, had as many young players as old. They were from a town just over the hill—one of more than a dozen villages whose ensembles played at one another's festivals, mixing polkas and waltzes with ABBA and the Beatles. To be asked to join the *Grosse Kapelle* was a great honor, the director told me. The village kids practiced for years to pass the audition.

To an outsider, the sight of an all-white German crowd in folk outfits was enough to set off alarms. But this crowd seemed happily unconcerned by history. In 1990, when the West German soccer team won the World Cup, most fans were still reluctant to fly the flag—much less drive through the streets bellowing fight songs. That began to change in 2006, when a unified Germany hosted the tournament and unexpectedly reached the semifinals. And the dam broke for good in 2014, when Germany won the World Cup outright. "That's not us," my cousin Karin in Bavaria told me when I visited her that year, not long after the final. A few nights earlier, she had called the police on a neighbor who had blasted soccer anthems from his window till two in the morning. "This group psychosis, this feeling that you have to belong to something or you're not strong. If that's how it is, I don't want to belong," she said.

Still, standing under the tent that night in Aulfingen, it was hard to see much cause for disquiet in the good-natured faces around me, or the teen musicians going cross-eyed as they blew their horns. That a village full of Germans should forget for a moment that Hitler and Goebbels reveled in the same country garb. That they should cheer the national soccer team without recalling that German athletics was once seen as proof of Aryan supremacy. That they should do this while quaffing a Fürstenberg or eating a slice of *Kirschtorte* seemed, in that moment at least, like a sign of psychological recovery, and not a slow backslide into fascism.

The man at the tap had been trying to catch my eye for a while. When I finally glanced his way, he nodded and gave me a knowing grin. "*Sie sind der Amerikaner,*" he said, then jerked his head toward some villagers standing to the left of the stage. A barrel-chested man in the middle was telling stories in a jovial bray. He was wearing a straw hat and glasses, striped shorts, and what looked like a bright-green bowling shirt. His features were as flushed and bulbous as a handful of radishes.

This was the elusive Uwe Fröhlin. His official title, I learned, was

Ortsvorsteher, or Village Representative—Aulfingen was too small to rate a mayor—but even that was largely honorary. Fröhlin's real job was as a chimney sweep. He was a popular figure in town—he had been elected four consecutive times, always with more votes than before. But neither he nor his assistant, Ilona Heizmann, were born in Aulfingen. "The truth is," he told me later, "local history never interested me all that much."

When the bartender introduced us, Fröhlin's bleary eyes went wide with delight. He grabbed me by the arm and pulled me to a quieter corner of the tent, stopping off at a table to grab a half-finished mug of beer. "It's important to keep well hydrated," he explained, dumping its contents into his own. Then he lifted his eyebrows conspiratorially and leaned forward to shout in my ear.

"I've found the archive," he said.

.   .   .

The next morning at ten, while most of the village was still recovering, I went back to the Rathaus. Fröhlin was waiting for me in the basement, looking rumpled and foggy. This was a punishingly early hour for him. Two older men, both named Manfred, were standing beside him and introduced as village historians. One was tall and taciturn with a thick gray mullet; the other short and bald with watery, mischievous eyes. This basement used to be the jail, the short Manfred told me. You could tell by the iron bars across the windows. But now the room was lined from floor to ceiling with leather-bound volumes, decomposing slowly in the dim, damp air.

Fröhlin plopped down onto a rickety chair and watched as I went through the books one by one. The Manfreds talked about the war. They told me about the forced laborers from Poland and Russia who were brought down here to be "disciplined" with a chain. The villager who was imprisoned for calling Hitler a *Scherenschleifer*—a knife-grinder, a peddler. (He was tried in the village square but released for lack of evidence.) In 1944, when the air-raid sirens would sound, children would scurry to the bunkers behind their mothers, carrying little *Köfferli* filled with their dearest possessions. The stories the Manfreds told were far more interesting than the archive. The books had been carefully assembled and bound, with handwritten notes in spidery nineteenth-century script. But their contents never varied: bills and receipts, bills and receipts, stretching back for two centuries or more. No letters, no diaries, no personal accounts. Another dead end.

Fröhlin stood up from his chair with a groan. "Well, that's it then," he said. "I'm going home to get some sleep—the Germans are playing in the World Cup tonight. But you can stay as long as you want." The Manfreds glanced over at the shelves full of books still to be gone through, and rose to join him. Nothing to see here. They were almost through the door when I remembered to ask Fröhlin about the restroom. He turned and sighed, his nap time once again deferred. "I'll need to unlock it for you," he said.

We were in a vestibule on the second floor, heading to his office to get the key, when I noticed the two enormous armoires. Fröhlin waved his hand at them as we passed. "Oh yes, you might want to look in those," he said. I walked over to the nearest one and swung open its wooden doors. Inside, a wall of documents reached to the top of the armoire. The files were bound in red cardboard covers and neatly organized on divided shelves: medicine, police, roadwork, schools. It was the archive I was looking for.

"*Ja, ja,*" Fröhlin muttered, when I turned to him, dumbstruck. "There could be something in there that interests you." He dropped the key to the restroom into my hand and headed for the door. "Just imagine that you're taking a walk in the woods."

.   .   .

I began in the corner and worked my way around the room. The second armoire was filled with leather-bound volumes from the nineteenth century. Then came a wall of open shelving lined with records from the 1950s and later, clamped in ring binders and tossed into cardboard boxes. When I had circled back to the first armoire I'd opened, I pulled down a pile of papers and sat on the floor to go through them. They were coated in a fine, viscous dust and stacked in rough chronological order, beginning around 1900—letters, circulars, diagrams, and official orders. Gathered loosely beneath their faded red covers, they traced an arc from depression to war, weakness to might and back again.

I separated out those from 1930 to 1938, when my grandfather was in Aulfingen. I focused on the signatures and datelines, and little by little his name began to drift to the surface. Flotsam in a storm gutter. There were letters to the mayor, village council, and school board, to the ministry of education and the local Nazi leadership. Karl sent notes about outbreaks of scabies, infestations of lice, and bouts of the grippe that kept half his students home in bed. Some were carefully typed and formatted, others scrawled in a hurried hand:

> The undersigned urges the Aulfingen village council to build him a ceramic stove with baking capability for the following reasons: the ceramic stove in the corner room along the street is dilapidated and not equipped for baking. In the middle room, there is a small iron stove whose heating power is insufficient for the room's size. . . . The fact that I, living in Aulfingen, am dependent on buying all my bread from a bakery in Leipferdingen compels me to make this request. In the long run, I cannot be expected to acquire my daily bread at such

great expense when its quality has given others cause for complaint. I am aware of the financial straits in which Aulfingen finds itself. But I also know from experience the good sense with which the Aulfingen town council provides for the community's needs. The construction of the stove would best take place between the harvest and the autumn holidays, when heating is not yet required.

Karl Gönner, head teacher
Aulfingen, the 25th of July, 1931

P.S. The latches on the windows of the old schoolroom have loosened, as they have on the apartment windows. A carpenter should be able to fix them.

That was after his first winter in the village, with a three-year-old and a newly pregnant wife in a house so cold that it fogged their breath. He did not want to live through another like it. He had arrived in Aulfingen just as his country, stumbling clear of hyperinflation, had toppled headfirst into a depression. The national debt, compounded by the war reparations imposed by the Treaty of Versailles, yawned so deep that the German government had raised taxes, lowered wages, and cut public spending to pay it off, further impoverishing an already destitute citizenry. Many teachers had to take second jobs or teach private lessons to stay afloat, yet they still couldn't afford meat more than once a week, much less coffee or cigarettes. Some couldn't even afford milk for their children.

Karl's family was never in danger of going hungry. That was one advantage of living in a farming community. Most weeks, some parent would send over a few eggs or a blood sausage to curry favor for their Gerlinde, who had nearly failed her geography test, or Dieter, who had poked Jürgen in the eye with a stick. "The best potatoes al-

ways went to the teacher and priest," one Aulfinger told me, still irritated at the memory eighty years later. But at Karl and Emma's
house, any extra food often went back out the door, to the beggars
who came knocking nearly as often as students.

By 1931, more than four and a half million Germans were out of
work, including some forty thousand teachers. "The fate of these
tens of thousands hangs like an avalanche over the otherwise peace-
ful valley of academic professions," Reinhold Schairer, the cofounder
and director of the German Association for Student Affairs, warned
in 1932. "Their masses grow and nobody sees a way out."

·   ·   ·

It was that poverty, and the class system that undergirded it, that
truly incensed Karl, Emma told my mother. Many of the local farmers had never been to school, and they came from generations of
menial laborers who regarded education as suspect. The school day
lasted only till lunchtime, but housework and chores, childcare and
church holidays still took precedence over it. To say nothing of the
harvest, when children were kept home for weeks. *Kartoffelferien*, they
called it: potato vacation.

For most Germans, education ended at fourteen when they left
Volksschule. Secondary school was strictly for the elite and gifted. The
middle-class and moderately ambitious might move on to *Realschule*
followed by an apprenticeship of some kind—in electrical work, say,
or masonry. But only a handful made it to a top-tier high school,
known as a *Gymnasium*, and fewer still to university. German education was a pyramid with steep sides, and *Volksschule* teachers like Karl
were at the bottom.

When Hitler came to power in 1933, he brought with him a lifetime's grievances against such classism. He had done well in elemen-

tary school, but then his father sent him to a private high school in Linz, where his grades were so poor that he was relegated to a state school in Steyr. He never graduated. "Our teachers were absolute tyrants," Hitler later recalled. "They had no sympathy for youth; their one object was to stuff our brains and turn us into erudite apes like them. If any pupil showed the slightest trace of originality, they persecuted him relentlessly." The contempt was mutual. "We pupils of the old Austria were brought up to respect old people and women. But for our professors we had no mercy," Hitler recalled. "They were our natural enemies."

Hitler was vindictive enough to nurse the grudge and clever enough to turn the tables on his old masters—to use their own schools against them. But the teachers who had tormented him weren't his true targets: He wanted to teach their students to be more like him. "In my great educational work, I am beginning with the young," he declared in 1934. "We older ones are used up. Yes, we are old already. We are rotten to the marrow. We have no unrestrained instincts left. We bear the burden of a humiliating past and have in our blood the dull recollection of serfdom and servility. But my magnificent youngsters! Are there finer ones anywhere in the world? Look at these young men and boys! What material! With them I can make a new world."

The source of that groundswell, its hidden epicenter, would be elementary-school teachers like Karl. Their colleagues in the higher grades were a recalcitrant lot—better organized and more reactionary. But elementary-school teachers were hungry for change. Like the peasants and laborers whose income theirs barely exceeded, they owed no fealty to the established order. It had done them no favors. And now here was this Austrian, this agitator, this fire hydrant of a man, promising to level the elites and bring dignity to all labor, to allow even ordinary workers to become homeowners. He was just what they were waiting for.

By 1938, nearly three hundred thousand teachers had joined the National Socialist Teachers League, 70 percent of them from elementary schools. "What is speed?" a joke among educators went at the time. "An instant so short that a grade-school teacher doesn't have time to change his politics."

10

BELIEVER

THERE IS A PHOTOGRAPH OF KARL FROM AULFINGEN THAT'S
unlike any other I've seen. In those from before and after that era, he
stares straight at the camera, his hair a stiff brush above a long, bony
skull. His eyes have a student's diffidence in early pictures; a war
veteran's haunted stoicism in later ones. But the picture from Aulfingen is taken in profile, from his good left side. His cheeks are full, his
hair swept across his forehead, his tweed jacket pressed and professo-
rial. A pipe juts from his mouth at a jaunty angle as he holds his baby
boy up for inspection. There is a self-satisfaction in his grin—an as-
surance that this one good moment must surely lead to others—that
he will never have again.

It was a common feeling in Germany then, if you were the right
sort of German. If you had the right ancestry, the right papers, the

right hair and skin color. If you could forget about those who didn't. In 1952, the American reporter and essayist Milton Mayer spent nine months in the town of Marburg, an hour north of Frankfurt, to try and understand how ordinary people came to allow such a catastrophe to happen. He chose ten townsfolk to interview extensively during those months. When he asked them how it felt to live under Nazi rule before the war, the answer was almost always the same: Those were the best years of their lives. "There were jobs and job security, summer camps for the children, and the Hitler Jugend to keep them off the streets," Mayer wrote in his book, *They Thought They Were Free*. "After '33, we had more children," one cabinetmaker told him. "A man saw a future. The difference between rich and poor grew smaller, one saw it everywhere."

One of the women that Mayer interviewed had been an anti-Nazi and was imprisoned for hiding Jews in 1943. She recalled standing on a street corner in Stuttgart five years earlier, during a Nazi festival. "The enthusiasm, the new hope of a good life, after so many years of hopelessness, the new belief, after so many years of disillusion, almost swept me, too, off my feet," she said. "Let me try to tell you what that time was like in Germany: I was sitting in a cinema with a Jewish friend and her daughter of thirteen, while a Nazi parade went across the screen, and the girl caught her mother's arm and whispered, 'Oh, Mother, Mother, if I weren't a Jew, I think I'd be a Nazi!'"

Mayer was raised Jewish and German American. When he thought about those interviews later, he found them both appalling and understandable. (He became a Quaker while in Germany and went on to popularize the phrase "speak truth to power" with fellow activist Bayard Rustin.) The Nazi Germany he had come to know as an outsider, living in America, was defined by its enemies and victims. It was a place of fear and suspicion, of hatred, defamation, and annihilating prejudice. These things were all true, he wrote. Undeniably so. But "there were two truths, and they were not contradictory: the truth that Nazis were happy and the truth that anti-Nazis were unhappy. . . . One man dreads the policeman on the beat and another waves 'Hello' to him, there are two countries in every country." Before he came to Germany, Mayer had assumed that Hitler ruled by force. "Now I see a little better how Nazism overcame Germany—not by attack from without or by subversion from within, but with a whoop and a holler."

In a city like Berlin, where Jews and Christians, Nazis and Communists, lived side by side, it could be hard to keep the two worlds apart—to live one truth without blinding yourself to the other. But how hard was it in a village like Aulfingen?

·   ·   ·

One Sunday morning before the church bell rang, I went to see Rita and Josef Gilli and their neighbor Edeltraut Burgert. They had offered to show me the old schoolhouse where my grandfather taught and my mother was born, and which was now their home. Built in 1852, at a cost of 5,004 gulden, it was a stout two-story building with a few flower boxes to soften its stern façade. Since the Gillis bought it forty years earlier, they had done their best to both modernize and preserve the place. They had pulled down walls and opened up the kitchen, put in new pipes, central heating, and double-glazed windows, and installed three balconies with walnut-stained railings. They had exposed the massive beams in the living room and attic—you could still see the ax marks gouged in the wood—and lined part of the stairwell with glass to show the gray-green moss stuffed in the wall for insulation. The floorboards were of old-growth German spruce, more than a foot wide and rubbed a glossy chestnut by generations of feet. A violin maker might have paid dearly to carve them. "In the old days there was a secret chamber up here," Edeltraut told me, "but they never let us go in." Josef grinned. "That's where they hid the gold."

Josef was short and gray-bearded with gnarled, capable hands—
he had done most of the renovations himself. Edeltraut had dove-
gray hair and delicate features. I had first met her at the Pfarrbuckfest,
after Uwe Fröhlin announced that there was an American journalist
in town looking for people who might have known Karl Gönner.
Within minutes, she had come and found me at the bar. Of course
she knew my family, she said. Her family used to live across the street
from the school, and the Gönners came over all the time. Her mother
was best friends with my uncles Gernot and Sigmar.

Although she never said it, I liked to imagine that Edeltraut was
named for my mother. She and Josef both went to school in the
1950s (Rita was from another village), and they shared the same stories. They remembered how the youngest kids always sat in the front
rows, the older ones in back. How they played Ping-Pong on picnic
tables and sang "Winde wehn, Schiffe gehn" in choir. How Edeltraut's mother would lean out from the window in her flour-dusted
apron, when the kids were playing tag in the street after school, and
shout for them to hurry home. Lunch was getting cold.

The schoolhouse had two classrooms on the ground floor: one for
grades one through four, and the other for grades five through eight.
The windows were set high on the walls, perhaps so that students
would concentrate on their books and not the birds outside. There
was a ceramic oven along one wall, a teacher's desk and blackboard
in front, and rows of double desks with built-in benches. But the
school outhouse was much more memorable to Edeltraut and Josef.
"It was *arschkalt* in the winter because it was open on top," she recalled. "For ventilation!" Josef said, and they laughed. On some of
the coldest days, his class would form a human chain to pass firewood from the storeroom on the second floor to the stove in the
classroom. "We were happy to do it," he said. "It meant we didn't
have homework that day."

What happened here wasn't so different, really, from what hap-

pened in country schools in Oklahoma and Finland, Newfoundland
and France: reading, writing, geography, and science, history, and
arithmetic. A gutful of learning before you went back to the fields,
like the dose of dewormer they gave to the goats. Elsewhere in Germany, education had grown less hidebound during the Weimar years.
There were schools for holistic, child-centered, art-centered, and
nature-centered learning, and youth programs for anarchists, communists, socialists, and vegetarians. In some places, students even
used their teachers' first names. But little of that reached Aulfingen.
The South was too buttoned-up for such shenanigans, too Catholic.
Life was lived too close to the bone. Most of the time, a teacher's real
job was just to keep the kids from killing one another.

·   ·   ·

"On December 8, 1938, the student Karl Amma threw a pine cone
that struck the pupil Oswald Gut on the lower left eyelid, causing an
injury to the tear duct," Karl reported to the school board one week.
"The student had to be brought to the hospital in Tuttlingen to be
treated by a doctor. He is there at this time. The students had been
expressly and repeatedly forbidden to throw pine cones. While most
were busy plucking blackthorn berries, the pupil Amma came up
with the idea of playing 'Little Hunters.' A classmate tried to prevent
the throw by shouting that throwing was forbidden. Nevertheless,
Amma threw and accidentally hit the pupil Gut. The teachers were
in close proximity to Amma at the time but could not prevent the
throw, as it was executed in a sudden and rash manner."

Karl had forty or fifty pupils in any given year, and he knew their
lives intimately. "Their shining little eyes, when they overcame their
first shyness, were like the little stars in the sky," he would later write,
perhaps forgetting the pinecone incident. "I always tried to make
sure that the little boys and girls kept that glow all year round." A

teacher was more than an instructor in these small towns. He was a moral and intellectual authority—the priest's worldly counterpart. He knew what parents did for a living and if their homes were tidy. He knew if they were widowed, remarried, or had children out of wedlock. He knew if they owed money or drank, skipped church or voted for the opposition.

Karl was careful never to play favorites: When his son Sigmar joined the class, he made him use the formal *Sie* in addressing him, and recite his name just like the other students. ("You know it already!" Sigmar shouted from the back row.) Yet even in country schoolhouses like this, in a sleepy southern backwater, parents and teachers were soon forced to take sides.

Before coming to Aulfingen, I had been to see my parents' best friend from childhood, Günter, who grew up in a village an hour to the west. White-maned and impossibly fit at eighty-four, Günter still swam two kilometers every morning and took long hikes in the woods near his house. When I asked him what he was taught as a boy, he bounded into the next room and returned with a small book with a faded orange cover in his hands: his elementary-school reader. Published in the Black Forest in 1942, the reader was filled with German fables and fairy tales, poems and songs, beautifully illustrated with black-and-white woodcuts. It had the timeless, folkloric look of many children's textbooks of that era. But in the last fifteen pages, the material began to change. There was an essay on camaraderie and a picture of a boy in uniform beating a drum, a crowd of men and women saluting with the flat of their hands, and a story that began: "This was in the fall, when the Brownshirts from all over Germany drove to the beautiful city of Nuremberg."

Near the end, across from a picture of a tank rampaging over barricades, came a story from the Führer's own childhood: "The boy learned well in school, but he preferred romping around the woods and fields with the other boys. They liked to follow him, and he was often the ringleader in their games. In history class, his eyes glowed with excitement. To hear about war and heroes, yes, that was for him! . . . One day, at home, he discovered a volume entitled, 'The Franco-German War.' He read it from cover to cover and was happy that he was a boy and could one day be a soldier. . . . In his young heart, a longing was awakened for a single, great empire that encompassed all Germans."

.   .   .

Karl wasn't one for hero worship. He had no patience for the *Alte Kämpfer*—the Old Fighters who strutted around at Nazi Party meetings, saying they had been with Hitler since the Beer Hall Putsch of 1923. Karl wasn't among the "Septemberlings" who rushed to join the party when it won 107 seats in the Reichstag in September of 1930. Nor did he join two years later, when the Nazis won the most seats in two consecutive elections. Many of the last holdouts gave in not long after Hitler was appointed chancellor of Germany, on January 30, 1933. *Die Märzgefallene*, they were called: the March Casualties. But Karl wasn't among them.

When he did join the party, it was through a side door. In 1933, local party leaders asked Karl to help out with the Winter Relief Agency. This was a charity that handed out food and clothing to the needy. The Nazis didn't approve of it at first: Hitler dismissed such programs as "welfare idiocy" that supported the sickly and weak at the expense of the healthy. But they were quite popular, and he soon saw their propaganda value. In May of 1933, five months after he became chancellor, Hitler folded the Winter Relief into the new National Socialist People's Welfare program. Henceforth, the party promised, "No one shall go hungry! No one shall freeze!"

Karl's party membership card is dated May 1, 1933. He later claimed that he didn't join the party until two years later—that a clerk backdated his card because the party was officially closed to new members by then. But he was a convert well before he joined. In the Aulfingen archive, I found a letter that Karl wrote to the mayor and the head of the Catholic parish. By the fall of 1932, he noted in the letter, he had an "open commitment to National Socialism."

Karl was always a political animal, my uncle Winfried told me. It was a natural extension of his teaching. His letters to his children were full of tips for self-improvement ("Get to work and your unnecessary fat will melt away!"), and that prescriptive urge carried over into his public life. He and Emma were intellectuals of the pre-Weimar variety, before Bauhaus and Expressionism and atonal music. Karl collected Goethe, Schiller, and other German classics; Emma read Shakespeare and Baudelaire in the original. The nuns who taught her in school had honed their English and French in convents abroad.

After the war, when my father would come to call on my mother before they were married, he found her parents rather intimidating. My father was an engineer, a builder of ham radios. He was not a literary man or music lover, and the Gönners seemed to care for nothing else. Once, in a fit of exasperation, my father asked my mother to name four famous physicists. She turned and pointed to portraits of Beethoven, Mozart, Schubert, and Wagner on the wall. "Can you name them?" And yet, he loved visiting her house. Emma and Karl were as lively and fractious as barristers, prepared to debate any point of doctrine or morality, no matter how obscure. "*Die Gönnerische Art*," my father called it: the Gönner way.

The Bilgers had no such pretensions. "I came from a potato-growing philosophy," my father liked to say. "The epitome of a man's duty to this world was to grow carrots and potatoes." His father grew up on a small farm near the Swiss border, one of twelve children, half of whom died young. He left school at fourteen, got a job in a factory building farm implements, then laid gravel in a railroad gang.

By the time my father was born, in 1935, his father had worked his way up to running the railway switches in Gottmadingen, half an hour south of Aulfingen. He and my grandmother, who worked as a secretary, lived above the train station. They were keen-minded, capable folks—Opa Bilger went on to become a stationmaster in Efringen-Kirchen, across the Rhine from Bartenheim, and then in Basel—and socially ambitious in their way. When my father was in high school, his mother made him leave soccer practice every day for a proper afternoon tea. But they couldn't be bothered with any bookish talk. "This intellectual stuff—it was for idiots," my father said.

Opa Bilger never joined the Nazi Party, though there were some fervent Hitler supporters on that side of the family. (One of my great-uncles was shot down in the street when he attacked a French tank with just a rifle.) While Karl spent his spare time at party meetings, Opa Bilger worked his garden and raised rabbits for meat. The Bilgers, unlike the Gönners, never went hungry during the war. One day in Efringen-Kirchen, while my grandfather was tending to his potatoes, the local party chief drove up to the house. This was strange—the two men hardly knew each other—but even stranger was what the party chief told him. It had come to his attention, he said, that Herr Bilger was partial to a certain breed of silver-haired rabbits, and that he raised only the finest bloodlines. In recognition of his efforts, the Nazi Party wished to present him with a certificate. It was a commendation for his experiments in racial purity.

My grandfather waited till the man drove off, then burst out laughing. It was still possible, in those early years, to dismiss the Nazis as blowhards—jumped-up thugs as absurd as they were self-important. Politics as usual. Few people in villages like Aulfingen had heard Hitler's speeches in the early 1930s. Most houses didn't have radios, and the radios that did exist weren't always equal to the purpose. "Radio is the mouthpiece of political and cultural life," a clerk in the town of Engen, just east of Aulfingen, complained in 1936, in a circular to

local mayors. "If the German *Volk* wishes to hear the voice of the
Führer and members of the government, a perfect transmission of
the speeches is absolutely required."

Karl had heard the speeches. He had been to two Nazi rallies in
Nuremberg. He knew that Hitler's nationalism was roiled by savage
prejudices. They may have echoed resentments of his own. I never
found any anti-Semitic comments in Karl's letters or personal documents. But I did find a description of a speech that he gave in 1940,
at a Nazi Party meeting in Alsace. According to a local newspaper,
Karl offered a short history of National Socialism and its roots in
Germany's economic collapse after the First World War. He blamed
the latter on the influence of "Jewish-plutocratic high finance."

How deep did his prejudice go? When I asked my mother that
question, I could see her wrestling with her memories and then re-
signing herself to them. Her father rarely made anti-Semitic comments at home, she said, but he did make them. Did he agree with
the Hitler of *Mein Kampf,* who described Jews as living personifica-
tions of the devil? No. He focused on the Nazis' economic program
and dismissed the rest as bombast. "Nothing's eaten as hot as it's
cooked," as an old German saying put it. Perhaps Karl convinced
himself that the Nazis might still build "a tolerable relation between
the German people and the Jews," as Hitler declared in Nuremberg,
in 1935. He should have paid more attention to Hitler's next words:
"If it fails, [the Jewish problem] must be handed over by law to the
Nazi Party for a final solution."

.   .   .

How could he have been so blind? That was the thought that would
always haunt my mother. She was born two years after her father
joined the Nazi Party, but she heard her mother complain bitterly
about it later. Emma had no tolerance for Hitler. All that talk of

motherhood and raising eight children—she had too much work
with four. And those brutish Brownshirts! They had no respect for
the law or property. Even worse, they glorified war. Nothing was
worth that risk. But Karl wouldn't listen. Emma's scruples were just
snobbery in disguise, he seemed to think. The Nazis' talk of blood
and soil might not speak to a city girl, but it must have reminded
Karl of the Black Forest. The farmers he had grown up with in
Herzogenweiler were bent and twisted by their labor. But in the
klieg light of Hitler's rhetoric, they loomed like heroic figures. *Blut
und Boden* were just words to Emma. To Karl, raised in the shadow
of his father's suicide, ashamed of his own history and bloodline,
they seemed to offer a kind of redemption.

It was a question of belief. Emma had never left the church. She
kept her religious teaching certificate, signed and stamped by the
archbishop of Freiburg, in a keepsake box beside her bed. All those
years in Catholic school, mumbling the catechism with rows of other
girls, knees sore against the oaken prayer bench, had only deepened
her faith. Religion was rooted in suffering, she believed, and pity for
those who bore it. But Karl had seen too much senseless pain to believe in God's mercy. All that was left of his faith, after the war, was
a hunger for order and justice. He still believed in the world's perfectibility, but he didn't need religion for that.

For a while, there was room for both beliefs in the new Germany.
Some Protestants recast Jesus as a holy warrior, going to battle
against the Jews. Or they joined the German Faith Movement,
which had the sun as its central symbol instead of the cross and rejected the idea of salvation and an afterlife. The summer after Hitler took power, his government signed a *Reichskonkordat* with Pope
Pius XI. It guaranteed the clergy's rights so long as they abstained
from politics and vowed loyalty to the regime. But the Nazis reneged
on the agreement almost immediately. Catholic organizations were
disbanded, church newspapers censored, priests and nuns arrested

on false charges. "Even amongst those who claim to be good Catholics, very few really believe in this humbug," Hitler would later say, although he was baptized Catholic.

Catholics were in the minority in Germany and used to keeping their own counsel in matters of politics. While many went on to support Hitler, fewer than 1 percent of Catholic priests joined the Nazi Party, compared to 20 percent of Protestant ministers. In Aulfingen, the archives were laced with signs of such resistance. "It is shocking to look into the situation of the rural areas, which still seem to be in the firm grip of the black-frocked teachers," a Nazi Party report from a district education office complained in 1938. "Bible quotes and church songs are what the pupils know best, while some of the ten-year-olds don't even know the name of the Führer." Another report, from the Reich Minister of Church Affairs in Berlin, complained of widespread reports that parishioners were taking party anthems like the SS "Song of the Faithful" and "I Am a Prussian" and replacing the words with religious lyrics. There was more than one way to keep your faith.

For most people, a day without church was still unthinkable. But for others, Hitler was the new God. "They took the cross from the living room and threw it in the street," a local historian told me. The archives were full of snippy letters between priests, teachers, and the school board, taking one side or the other. In Karl's case, the tone tended toward irritated rectitude, tinged less by lapsed faith or Nazi doctrine than his memories of the frozen chapel and intemperate priests in Herzogenweiler. "It was cold this morning; it may have been −19 degrees Celsius," he wrote in the winter of 1933. "The pastor sent a boy over to tell me that it was *not* cold in the church, and that the students should come there for their lesson. But I did not let the children go. I could not accept that responsibility. A survey of the third graders showed that all but two had cold feet during religious instruction."

Priests and teachers had always wrestled over their young charges in these villages. But a note of deepening suspicion had begun to wind through their relations. When the school hired a new priest from the nearby monastery at Beuron, the school board insisted that he profess his allegiance to the Führer. The priest duly obeyed. But his successor, Karl Bihler, was deemed insufficiently fervent. "For some time now," Karl's colleague, Heinrich Ganninger, wrote to the school board, "I have noticed that the local clergyman, Pastor Bihler, does not greet the classes with 'Heil Hitler' at the beginning and end of his lessons, but contents himself with 'Heil.'" In another era, the school board might have told Ganninger to mind his own business. But in this case, they welcomed the surveillance. "The official board will come to Aulfingen and investigate the matter," they responded, in a note typed on the back of the letter. "Teacher Ganninger is instructed to make further observations in the meantime and to report if necessary." Ganninger was delighted to comply.

Karl and Bihler seem to have understood each other—Bihler even wrote a testimonial for Karl after the war. But Ganninger could never abide the good pastor. Over the next eight months, he sent regular reports of Bihler's misdeeds to the district office. The pastor was using a new book of biblical history that had yet to be approved by the Reich. He was deliberately teaching choir in the church and not the school to avoid being monitored. He kept the students in class too late and blamed the church clock for their tardiness. He was faking a foot injury. When Bihler finally wrote to defend himself—he had been in a car accident and his foot was in great pain—the letter was a mess, by turns single- and double-spaced, its margins wavering badly. But he was careful to sign it "Heil Hitler!"

Karl, too, wasn't above Ganninger's suspicions. His son Gernot, when he was six years old, once asked him how the Russians greeted one another. What was their version of "Heil Hitler"? Karl told him, absent-mindedly, that they probably just replaced "Hitler" with

"Moscow." The next morning, when Gernot walked into Ganninger's class, he clicked his heels and shouted, "Heil Moscow!" That
took some explaining. It may even have contributed to Karl's falling-
out with party leaders. But early on, his problems came mostly from
the other side of the aisle, and he had only himself to blame.

As the town organist, Karl also directed the choir at the church.
He didn't mind the job—he still loved the somber uplift of the old
German hymns—but the atmosphere in the rehearsals soon began
to sour. Some of the singers were from families who had voted for
Hitler; others considered the Führer an enemy of the church. Karl
was caught in between. He was a party member but skeptical of the
Nazis' excesses; he had lost his faith but had not yet officially left the
church—he was raising his children as Catholics. Still, in the all-or-
nothing of village politics, his allegiance was clear. He had an "open
commitment to National Socialism," as he wrote in his letter to the
mayor of Aulfingen in 1934, and this led to "tensions and petty arguments" in the choir.

Soon the choir was split in two. When one group walked out,
Karl did his best to work with the rest of the singers to "provide a
worthy frame for the service," as he put it. Then another faction
emerged, driven by more "political machinations." Their spokes-
man, a singer named Hermann Biehler, was so insulting that Karl
threw him out of the choir. Afterward, Karl tried to merge his group
with the village singing club, which had previously formed in opposition to it, but to no avail. The church choir was hemorrhaging members, and Karl could not admit that his own politics were at fault. "If
I am to remain the conductor, it cannot be my job to resolve old
quarrels that date back to a time before I was here," he concluded, in
his letter to the mayor. "But if the troublemakers believe that they
can carry on their small-minded disputes at the expense of the fac-
ulty, they deceive themselves."

If the Catholic parish couldn't provide a choir of twenty to twenty-five singers, he concluded, he would have no choice but to resign. "On January 1, 1935, I will consider my activity as organist to be terminated. Heil Hitler!"

·   ·   ·

Sitting on the floor of the Rathaus, my grandfather's letter in my lap, I kept rereading the last two words, a hollow foreboding in my chest. "Heil Hitler" was the mandatory sign-off for civil servants by July 1933, but seeing it in Karl's script was still disconcerting. I had told myself that I could be a neutral observer of his life—a reporter first and a grandson second. But detachment was easy as long as he was an enigma. The more I knew about him—the more vividly I could picture him as a boy in the Black Forest, a frightened recruit on the Western Front, a broken and impoverished teacher in postwar Germany—the harder it was to keep my distance.

All around me in the dimming light, files and folders were piled on the floor in ragged stacks, sorted by year and topic. I had spent hours picking through them, scanning for Karl's familiar signature as the century-old dust flew off the pages and settled in my lungs. It was a fascination limned with dread. For long stretches, I would lose myself in the petty squabbles and resentments of village life, only to be brought up short by some brutal order from Berlin, some chilling notice from a regional propaganda minister. A reminder that all these minutiae were part of a darker pattern.

Near the bottom of the armoire, in a slot labeled *Polizei*, I had found a series of bulletins sent to Aulfingen by Nazi officials in Karlsruhe, the regional capital. "It goes without saying that the state sees no value in increasing its population of non-Aryans, and will refuse to accept them to prevent further racial mismanagement," the minister of the interior wrote on July 31, 1933. "Dissidents, nondenominationalists, and sundry atheists: Such individuals must always be suspected of supporting or having supported Marxism or Communism. Liberals also fall under this heading." Another bulletin, sent from Berlin on April 9, 1934, was headlined "Racial Research." It concerned the offspring of French colonial troops from Asia and Africa who were stationed in Germany after the First World War: "I have recently received numerous notes . . . demanding that measures be taken against the threat of these alien bastards mixing with pure German blood," it began. "I therefore request that police authorities, in cooperation with youth welfare offices, list the bastards in each community."

Jews were a recurring theme of these bulletins: a target of caustic asides at first, then obsessive headlines. Aulfingen had few if any Jewish families at the time. (Only one villager is listed in the online database of survivors and victims at the United States Holocaust Memorial Museum: August Berger, imprisoned in Dachau in 1938 for being "antisocial"—a category that comprised everything from criminality to pacifism, lesbianism, or simply being born Roma.) But there were large Jewish communities less than twenty miles to the south, in Randegg and Gailingen. Year by year the local authorities were told to step up their vigilance. Any immigrant who married a Jew would be denied citizenship, one letter noted in 1933. Two years later, another ordered the district offices to gather the names and locations of all Jews. Jewish families were prohibited from employing German housemaids, unless "the male Jews in the household, due to physical frailty, pose no threat to German or Aryan blood."

By September 1937, the net was nearly cinched shut. The mayors in the district were urged to report any Jew preparing to emigrate. The reason for the order, allegedly, was to prevent tax evasion, capital flight, and other actions detrimental to Reich finances. "Possible grounds for suspicion include: application for a passport, liquidation of a business, abandonment of a dwelling, sale of land, permits, and so on." The following March, the village received a copy of a confi-

dential letter from Berlin, addressed to state police departments and
the office of the SS. When prisoners were taken into custody, it noted,
the leaders of the SS Death's Head units and concentration camps
had been instructed to send a form letter to each prisoner's wife and
relatives. This would allow them to confirm that the family—
"especially the children"—was being properly cared for.

Karl's letters in the archive made no mention of all this. Whether
the mayor told him about the race ordinances, kept them secret, or
deemed them irrelevant to a small town like Aulfingen was hard to
tell. The archive was full of cross talk between administrators—notes
scribbled over letters or hastily typed on the back—but mostly about
mundane village affairs: roadwork, plumbing, outbreaks of the flu.
The one area where politics intruded was in discussions of after-
school activities. As the head teacher and a party member, Karl was
in charge of the local Hitler Youth. "In the winter, the lads are introduced to the principles of National Socialism in weekly study sessions at home in the evenings," he explained in a letter to the mayor.
"In the summer, athletics and military drill allow for the necessary
physical fitness." Like the choir, the Hitler Youth deeply divided the
town: Only half the teenagers came, and the creation of a new soccer club threatened to scuttle the program. "In my observation,"
Karl complained, "the boys who play soccer are precisely those who
have been forbidden to join the Hitler Youth by their parents, and
they don't have enough pluck to go where they belong."

Karl was still a political animal. But his principles were increas-
ingly untethered from Nazi policies, if not completely at odds with
them. Charities like the Winter Relief Agency that had brought him
into the party were giving way to race ordinances and munitions
factories. And no number of study sessions on winter evenings could
rationalize the change. Soon, Karl would be fighting a battle on two
fronts, as alienated from his party as he was from his faith.

•   •   •

One October morning in 1934, in the second-floor study of his schoolhouse, Karl sat down to write a letter on behalf of a friend. It had been less than two years since Hitler was appointed chancellor. In that time, he had banned trade unions, formed the Gestapo, and withdrawn Germany from the League of Nations. He had claimed the right to pass laws unilaterally and banned all political parties aside from his own. The Nazis had yet to reoccupy the Rhineland or pass the Nuremberg Race Laws, but they had long since insinuated themselves into every tendril of the nation's consciousness.

And yet, those years had been good to Karl. For the first time in his life, he had a lot to lose. He had steady work, a position of respect in the village, and a spacious apartment with bright windows overlooking the main square. He had two boys, ages six and almost three, and a girl on the way—my mother, born eight months later. He could imagine his life going along this way indefinitely, rolling toward a hazy blue horizon like the hills around Lake Constance. And yet, lately, he had begun to have his doubts. First his politics had torn the church choir apart, and now the party had turned against his friend Hans Müller. If they could ruin a good man like him, what could they do to Karl?

Müller was a head teacher in Kirchen-Hausen, the next village over. It was only two miles north of Aulfingen, but a different world politically. The divisions in Karl's town stayed mostly beneath the surface, or bubbled up through their children's spats. In Kirchen-Hausen everyone was at one another's throat. The local party chief and agricultural director couldn't stand each other; the mayor didn't get on with either one; and the priest detested all three. Even among the Nazi faithful, rancorous disputes erupted over issues like *Schwarzschlachten*—black-market butchering—or whether to hang the

Christian cross in your living room. When Müller declined to join
the party, an assistant teacher by the name of Mühlheisen began to
spread rumors that Müller was disloyal, and the school board was
soon informed. Within a year, Müller was transferred to another
town against his will.

To Karl, this was more than an intramural tiff, as his letter made
clear. It was a sign of deep rot within his party. The old Nazis in these
villages had become impetuous and power hungry. They bent their
politics toward personal gain, regardless of what was right. Overt
resistance was nearly impossible for teachers by then. Jews and left-
ists had been purged from academia, and nonconformists were
"spied upon, censored, demoted, or fired," as the historian Konrad
Jarausch put it in his book *Broken Lives*. By 1937, all but 3 percent of
public-school teachers would belong to the National Socialist Teachers League. To speak out against the Nazis—not in some smoky corner of a village *Kneipe,* but in a letter to the local leaders, and in the
most unsparing terms—was career suicide or worse.

Karl wasted no time on niceties. His letter to the leaders of the
National Socialist Teachers League had the blunt, combative tone of
a man accosting a neighbor on the street. "Today Head Teacher
Müller received his transfer orders over the phone. Four days ago,
Müller was told that he had until Easter. . . . This sudden transfer, for
no apparent reason, has had a devastating effect. It banishes all belief in justice and reason. If teachers are to be fair game, if they are
to be made the playthings of megalomaniac colleagues and incom-
petent party members, better for the ministry to throw open the
doors of the insane asylums and have their patients teach the people.
It cannot be that party membership has become a free pass for
scoundrels. . . . Mühlheisen and the local party leader are liars. . . .
Any punishment for Müller is an injustice. This most recent decision
is a monstrosity."

Years later, Müller would describe the letter as an act of fearlessness. Karl himself had twice been denounced by Mühlheisen for petty party infractions. Defending Müller made him even more suspect. And yet, incendiary as it was, Karl's letter wasn't the work of a whistleblower or resistance fighter. It was the work of a former believer, an aggrieved follower, a man who couldn't accept that the party in power—the one that he had joined—was full of madmen.

·   ·   ·

What finally made him write? Müller's transfer was a trivial punishment by Nazi standards, but it was close to home: A fellow teacher was being targeted, and sinister rumors of other Nazi programs may have started to circulate by then—some of which pertained to Karl's students. Among the letters in the Aulfingen archive, a number were filed in a slot labeled *Medizinalwesen*—medical matters. They included a series of orders from the minister of the interior under the heading "Custody and Sterilization." The first was dated June 8, 1934—a year after the German government had passed a Law for the Prevention of Offspring with Hereditary Diseases.

"It has come to our attention that some district welfare organizations believe that people, especially females, who have been institutionalized for imbecility or other mental defects, no longer require such custody after they have been sterilized," it began. "It must be emphasized that although sterilization spares the cost of caring for the offspring of the feeble-minded, infertility has no influence on the patients' mental or physical condition." Other documents noted that doctors and midwives were failing to report abortions induced by the procedure after the thirty-second week of pregnancy. Word of the sterilization campaign was spreading despite strict orders of confidentiality, they added, "with the consequence that the genetically diseased are not only being mocked, teased, and poorly judged, but also that the procedure is considerably more difficult to implement."

Forced sterilization was nothing new. In the United States, eu-
genicists like Charles Davenport and John Harvey Kellogg—
inventor of the corn flake—had been promoting it since the early
1900s. Their goal was to protect the population from undesirable
traits, at least by their racist standards. Blacks, Jews, immigrants,
and indigenous peoples were deemed genetically inferior, as were
the poor, criminal, and disabled. Their genes had to be kept separate or removed from white, Nordic, and Anglo-Saxon stock. By
1937, forced sterilization was legal in thirty-two states. Davenport
set up a laboratory at the Carnegie Institution that kept index cards
on nearly a million ordinary citizens and advocated for strict immigration laws and sterilization of the unfit. When the first German
eugenics research was done in the 1920s, the Rockefeller Foundation helped fund it. Josef Mengele, later known as the Angel of
Death for his medical experiments on prisoners at Auschwitz, was
among those Rockefeller supported.

The Nazis went on to forcibly sterilize nearly four hundred thousand people. Then they went much further. When I was in Kirchen-
Hausen looking into the Hans Müller affair, I asked a local historian
named Friedbert Trendle about the sterilization letters I had found
in Aulfingen. Tall and lean, with a closely shaven head and raked
eyebrows, Trendle fixed me with a flat, unwavering gaze. Then he
leaned back in his chair and took a long drag on his cigarette. "Nasty
things were done here," he said.

He beckoned me into his office and logged on to a military records site called Fold3. A few years earlier, he said, he had spent six
weeks in the National Archives in Washington, D.C., trying to track
down stories like these. He pulled up a series of documents seized by
the American military in 1945 and later submitted as evidence of
crimes against humanity. The pages bore the letterhead of the minister of the interior in Karlsruhe, in elaborate Gothic print. They

were stamped *Geheim,* or confidential, sometimes with an exclamation mark:

February 24, 1940

To the Wiesloch nursing home and care facility
Attn: Mr. Möckel
Re: Relocation of patients in accordance with special
administrative measures

With reference to my decree of November 28, 1939, No. 87386, I order the transfer of the patients listed in the attached list from your institution. The sick are to be picked up on my behalf by the public patient transport GmbH. which will contact you. . . . Restless patients are to be pretreated with appropriate means for a trip of several hours. As far as possible, the sick should be conveyed in their own underwear and clothing. . . . Medical records and personal files with details on next of kin are to be handed over to the transport manager.

Wiesloch was no ordinary nursing home. It was an extermination center. Located just south of Heidelberg, two hours north of Aulfingen, it was part of a network of facilities used to kill nearly a third of a million physically and mentally disabled Germans between 1939 and 1945. Some were injected with phenobarbital or morphine-scopolamine; others were placed in specially designed gas chambers or simply starved to death. Two weeks later, the families of the victims would receive a forged death certificate and letter of consolation: "To our regret we must inform you that [. . .], who had to be moved to our institution following a ministerial order, unexpectedly died of [. . .]. Considering his/her severe incurable illness, his/her death comes to him/her as a relief."

The patients listed in the seized documents came from villages all over the region, including Geisingen, just a mile and a half west of Kirchen-Hausen. They were of all ages—the youngest was fifteen, the oldest eighty-one. Some of the disorders listed for them were psychological (idiocy, dementia, schizophrenia, exhibitionism); some physical (epilepsy, encephalitis, blindness, progressive paralysis); and some behavioral (theft, fraud, alcoholism, sodomy, homosexuality, pedophilia, and other sexual offenses). One patient, it was noted, "killed his wife and children while in a twilight state," but he was a "first-class saddlemaker." At the same time as these patients were being loaded into trucks in Geisingen and other villages, a special children's ward was established at Wiesloch, supervised by a Dr. Josef Artur Schreck. Parents were either assured that their child would receive the best possible care or told that their child had an incurable condition and would be euthanized for his or her own good. By the end of the war, an estimated five thousand children had died in such facilities.

Trendle's great-aunt worked in a nursing home half an hour south of Kirchen-Hausen. "She told us that one day, in 1938, a dark bus came through the village and these children were brought out to it," Trendle told me. "They held on to the worker's hands as they stepped on board. Then they were driven north to Württemberg, where they were gassed or injected." The same was done to the mentally ill. "We knew that here in Kirchen-Hausen," Trendle went on. "Just a hundred meters from this house, there was a young woman, Fräulein Hamburger, who liked to look at the birds all day. She disappeared from one day to the next." He shook his head. "My mother wouldn't believe it. She used to say, '*So etwas könnte im Land der Dichter und Denker niemals passieren.*'" Such a thing could never happen in the land of poets and thinkers.

·   ·   ·

Late that evening, after the sun had dropped behind the hills, I drove back to Aulfingen through deepening shadows. It was the culminating night of the Pfarrbuckfest. The village's only restaurant, Gasthaus Adler, had spent two days cooking dozens of whole beef tongues in Madeira and mushroom sauce. Under the festival tent, an enormous screen now hung above the stage. Germany was playing Mexico in their opening match of the World Cup, and the crowd was full of adults and children—it was hard to tell the difference on game day—in their idols' jerseys. It would prove a frustrating night for them. The projector kept freezing at key moments, with the strikers in midflight, and the opponent looked disconcertingly skilled. "*Sie sind eifrig diese Mexikaner,*" the old woman next to me muttered. They're lively, these Mexicans. When Lozano darted forward to score on the Germans in the thirty-fifth minute, the announcer tried gamely to rally the fans at home, but the players looked as listless as sleepwalkers. "When will Germany wake up?" he said.

The less there is to cheer, it seems, the more patriotic people become. Looking out over the crowd with Trendle's stories still in my ears, the flags and folk outfits seemed less innocuous than they had before. The Germany that had greeted me when I first moved to Berlin in 2014 had lost some of its glow in the intervening years. Far right and nativist groups were on the rise across Europe, as they were in the United States. In Germany, the anti-immigrant party *Alternative für Deutschland* had claimed 13 percent of the national vote in 2017, nearly triple the number in the previous election.

The far right was weaker here than in much of Europe, but it felt more sinister. In its rage against the "Islamization" of Germany, its pledge to ban mosques, burkas, and Muslim calls to prayer, its rhetoric could sound unsettlingly close to Hitler's. Some politicians had even tried to rehabilitate the word *völkisch*, which the Nazis used to glorify the Germanic race. Modern Germany, the country that had taken in a million refugees in just two years, the country whose stodgy, stoical leader had said, "We can do this," then nearly lost her governing coalition when the immigrants came—that country could never truly shake free of its past.

Milton Mayer believed that most Germans, by the early 1940s, knew that terrible crimes were being committed. But few had what he called binding knowledge—information so irrefutable that it left them no choice but to act. "Anti-Nazis no less than Nazis let the rumors pass—if not rejecting them, certainly not accepting them," he wrote. "Either they were enemy propaganda or they *sounded* like enemy propaganda, and with one's country fighting for its life and one's sons and brothers dying in war, who wants to hear, still less repeat, even what *sounds* like enemy propaganda? Who wants to investigate the reports? Who is 'looking for trouble'? . . . There was *nichts dagegen zu machen*." Nothing to be done about it.

Mayer likened this attitude to that of Americans who turned a blind eye to lynchings in the South in the same era. Or who had watched more than a hundred thousand Japanese Americans incarcerated in camps in California and elsewhere during World War II. But there was no need to go back so far for disturbing parallels. In Oklahoma, where I grew up, twenty-first-century politics could be just as reactionary as it was in Germany. Oklahoma had always been conservative, but in a more reticent, plainspoken way. Texas without the swagger. Now it was riven by conspiracy theories and religious fundamentalism, voter suppression and anti-immigration bills. "What happened here was the gradual habituation of the people, little by little, to being governed by surprise," a German philologist told Milton Mayer in Marburg. "Each act, each occasion, is worse than the last, but only a little worse. You would wait for one great shocking occasion, thinking that others, when such a shock comes, will join with you in resisting somehow. But the one great shocking occasion, when tens or hundreds of thousands will join with you, never comes."

．　　　．　　　．

One of the last things I found in the Aulfingen archive was a file full of report cards that Karl had written. Among the students he taught was a boy named Franz Josef Baldus, born July 18, 1923. Baldus was a first-grader when Karl arrived in the village, and school was already a struggle for him. Two years later, he could still only count to the number five, and he hardly advanced after that. "Franz Baldus is in the second grade," Karl wrote in 1934. "He belongs in the fifth. Unknown reading material causes him great difficulty. He can't grasp the meaning of what he has read. . . . In arithmetic, no progress has been noticeable for years. It seems that the numbers below 20 are gradually being forgotten." By the age of twelve, Baldus was still in the third grade and could only add single digits with great effort.

The doctors in the euthanasia program had no tolerance for such incapacity. Boys like Baldus were deemed "life unworthy of life"— "useless eaters," unfit for productive labor. Yet Karl stuck by him. Six years after coming to Aulfingen, he still had Baldus in his class. Rather than declare the boy a lost cause or send him on to be another teacher's problem, Karl filled out his report card year after year, his tone softening as he realized that Baldus was doing his best. In 1934, he rated the boy's effort and attentiveness just "sufficient," but added that with a little help from his parents, Baldus might grasp his German lessons. Two years later, Karl gave him top marks for effort and behavior.

I thought of Karl's letter defending his friend Hans Müller in 1934. Better to throw open the asylum doors and let the inmates teach the students, he wrote. The *Alte Kämpfer* in the party—the Old Fighters who had been with Hitler from the beginning—never forgave him. "They tried to silence this vexatious man at first," Müller later wrote, in a letter to Karl's lawyer after the war. "And when that didn't work, to drive him away. The superintendent in Villingen tried to buy him off with some headmaster positions in 1937, but Gönner refused." Finally, in 1938, when Karl was once again denounced by the *Alte Kämpfer*, he requested a transfer and was sent to Weil am Rhein.

In Müller's telling, Karl's resistance was heroic. Yet for all Karl's protests, he never left the Nazi Party nor truly risked his life to fight it. When Milton Mayer was in Marburg, he wished, above all, that the townsfolk he had come to know—his "Nazi friends," as he put it—could go back and relive their lives. Find the courage that so few people find. "What I really want . . . is for each of them to have cared enough at the time to have thrown himself under the iron chariot of the State," he wrote. "This none of my friends did, and this I cannot forgive them. They did not care enough."

By the fall of 1938, when Trendle's aunt saw the dark buses carrying children away to Württemberg, Karl had left Aulfingen. What would he have done had he known the children's fate? Would that terrible knowledge have been binding enough to make him act? I still wasn't sure. Was my grandfather the man who stood by Baldus when the regime deemed such boys useless? Or was he the avid leader of the Hitler Youth? Was he the man who called party membership "a free pass for scoundrels"? Or the one who sent a letter to the school board in Villingen in gratitude for his new position in Weil? "Let my thanks be my promise," he wrote, "that I shall continue to promote the National Socialist worldview with all my strength."

11

INVADER

MY MOTHER'S EARLIEST MEMORIES OF THE WAR—HER FIRST
memories of any kind, really—are of a lost paradise. In the spring of
1938, when her family moved to Weil am Rhein from Aulfingen, she
was a month shy of her third birthday, her mind still surfacing into
consciousness. She could see the linden trees but not the darkening
forest around them. Weil was a town of nine thousand huddled along
the shores of the Rhine. A former Roman outpost, it lay at the extreme southwestern tip of Germany, wedged between the Swiss and
French borders and the foothills of the Black Forest. Karl and Emma
still couldn't afford to buy a house—few teachers could—but they
found something nearly as good: some rooms for rent in an old
grange. The property dated back to the fourteenth century and had
been rebuilt by the Benedictine monks of St. Blasien in 1571. It had

an orchard of cherry, plum, apple, and pear trees and a sunlit courtyard surrounded by a high stone wall—a hidden world. It was known
as the Bläserhof.

"This was, to me, the most beautiful spot in the world," my
mother said when we passed through the gate one July afternoon. I
had asked her to join me in Germany that summer to show me some
of the places where she and her father had spent the war. What had
started out as a little research into our family history had turned
into something more pressing for her: a struggle to rekindle her
memories—to hold on to the past she already knew. She longed to
come to Germany, but was barely strong enough to travel. I had to
roll her through the Chicago and Zurich airports in a wheelchair,
and the train connections in Germany were a challenge. I would
grab all her bags and mine, strap the dog carrier across my shoulders
(my shih tzu, Alfonso, was mercifully portable), and waddle down the
steps to the platform. Then I would drop the bags and the dog, run
back up the steps, take hold of my mother's hand, and slowly guide
her down as the train pulled up and commuters jostled past. Later, I
wondered why I was in such a hurry. We could have just taken the
next train. But everything seemed urgent then.

The Bläserhof was an oasis of quiet after that. My mother hadn't
been there in more than twenty years, but it seemed unchanged to
her. A chestnut tree loomed over the center of the courtyard. A
swaybacked carriage house stood to one side and a rambling, three-
story manse to the other. Someone had set a vase full of lemons in an
open window, above a flower box overflowing with lavender and saffron blossoms, and their scent drifted toward us as we walked. After
a while, an elderly man emerged from the house. Tall and stooped
with a mop of white hair and thick black glasses, he had a slow, rolling gait that listed precariously to one side. My mother pointed her
walker at him, like a sailor steering for a distant atoll, and shuffled
forward, watching her feet on the cobbles. When they finally reached

each other, after what felt like an hour, she let go of the walker and clasped his forearms tight. "*Grüss Gott,* Karl-Frieder!" she said, beaming up at him. He looked down and shook his head with a shy, befuddled smile. "*Jesses Gott!*" he said. "*Die Edeltraut gibts auch noch.*" Dear God! Edeltraut is still around, too.

Karl-Frieder had lived in the Bläserhof all his life. His family had inherited the property and lived above my mother's family in the manse. The two of them were inseparable when they were four and five; now they were in their early eighties and living on different continents. She was blind in one eye and prone to dizzy spells; his cheeks were spidered with burst capillaries, his eyes bulbous behind thick lenses. He and his wife used to perform together at town festivals, he said—she sang and he played accordion. But his back was a little balky these days, so he rarely left the Bläserhof. My mother nodded: "I can't drive anymore—not since a long time." She looked around as if trying to fix the courtyard in her mind one last time. "In four days, I'll be back in America."

"But that's your home now."

"*Ja, scho, aber vergesse tut ma nit.*" Yes, of course. But you never forget.

When the monks of St. Blasien built the Bläserhof, they were granted the right of sanctuary: They could offer asylum to any convict or criminal for up to six weeks and three days. Seven centuries later, the place still felt like a refuge. In the first months of the war, when concrete bunkers were going up along the Rhine, my mother and Karl-Frieder were learning to roller-skate in the courtyard. When the French were dismantling their pontoon bridges to prevent a crossing, she was hanging from the wooden arms of the wine press in the carriage house, spinning round and round as the press screwed down. When local lorries and factories were being requisitioned for the war effort, and the Wehrmacht was patrolling the Swiss border, she and Karl-Frieder were leaping from the swing on the linden tree and digging tunnels and forts in the fields behind the orchard. The vineyards were in full leaf that spring and summer of 1938, all the way up to the Feldberg, and the air was filled with the lazy buzzing of her father's bees. "We were shielded a little behind these walls," Karl-Frieder said.

A year later, Germany was at war. My mother didn't see much of her father after that. On Sunday evenings, he might lead a hymn around the harmonium in the living room, or he and Emma would play together on their violins—"*Bist du bei mir*," "*So nimm denn meine Hände*." But most of the time, he was hunched over his desk in the office next door, grading papers or working on party matters. After Hitler invaded Poland in September of 1939, Karl was called to Lake Constance for two months of military training. Forty years old, with a missing eye and four children at home—Winfried had been born a year earlier—Karl wasn't promising military material. But the implication was clear: He could be drafted at any time.

My mother's stories from that time have a quality of barely averted disaster, as if she could sense what was coming: the time she and Karl-Frieder took shelter in the doghouse during a storm; the time she hid under the living-room table to escape Sigmar and the plaster ceiling collapsed on top when he slammed the door. Whenever the Führer gave a speech, her family crowded around the big console radio in Karl-Frieder's family's living room, along with neighbors and children and a woman who ran a marionette theater. The news from the front was always good in those days, but Emma knew it couldn't last. Later, when she thought my mother was asleep in the bed beside her, she turned on Karl, her voice bitter and scared. *Blood and honor! The thousand-year reich!* Hadn't they heard the same puffed-up talk before the Great War? What had Karl's party brought them, for all its grand promises? Another war.

Twice in the next year, Weil was evacuated for fear of French attacks. The first time, Karl was away in military training and some farmers took in the rest of the family. They let them stay for four months and even found a crib in the attic for Winfried. (The father was later killed by the Gestapo when he was overheard saying that the Germans would lose the war.) When the evacuation was called off in December 1939—the French attack had never come—disaster struck from an unexpected quarter. Just before Christmas, a train full of townsfolk was returning to Weil one night, in heavy fog, when another train collided with it. Ninety-nine people died in the crash, and forty-seven were seriously injured: the town's first casualties of war.

The second evacuation came the following spring, when the German army crossed the Maginot Line into France. This time, the French did attack, sending a barrage of shells across the Rhine on May 26, hitting factories and railroad facilities in Weil. But my mother and her family had long since fled to the Black Forest, and the town was empty. Come September, the Battle for France had been won. The Germans were in Alsace and Karl had joined them.

Weil and its environs were once again "the very picture of peace," a local historian later wrote. *"Der Krieg tobte weitab."* The war raged far away.

· · ·

Across the river in Alsace, a boy named Georges Baumann had just turned nine when he heard that the Nazis were coming. His family lived in the village of Bartenheim, eight miles from my mother as the crow flies. (He was no relation to the Georges Baumann who was later killed in the village: Alsatians tend to pass around the same small assortment of names, like treats from a chocolate sampler.) If Weil was a town that felt like a village, Bartenheim was a village that was beginning to feel like a suburb. Its unpaved main street had given way to a major through road. Its fields, once a patchwork of medieval crops like spelt and madder (a root used to make a red dye), now had uniform rows of oats and rye. The townsfolk still liked to call themselves *Kuhbür* and *Rossbür*—cow farmers and horse farmers—though only about half of them farmed full-time. The rest worked in local shops or commuted to the textile mills and chemical plants of Saint-Louis and Mulhouse, the "city of a hundred chimneys."

"The world has changed a lot," Georges's wife, Marie-Rose, told me when I visited them one afternoon. Georges nodded. *"Was damals zu viel war ist jetzt zu wenig."* What was once too much is now too little. Like many of the older villagers, Georges and Marie-Rose preferred to speak German. He was eighty-five and she eighty-three, though they looked as if they might live to 150. He was red-cheeked and round as an acorn, bobbing at the edge of his seat as he told stories, grabbing my arm at the punch lines. She was small, tightly wound, and more talkative still—she had run a produce stand for decades in Mulhouse. When I asked a question, she would glare at me for a moment as if outraged at my effrontery. She would screw up her eyes and furrow her brow with the effort of remembering, then laugh and tell another story.

Their lives before the war could seem, in retrospect, like idyllic tales from a schoolhouse primer. "We were always happy with what we had," Marie-Rose said. "We had rabbits and hens and pigs and flowers. We had currants and mirabelles, plums, cherries, leeks, potatoes, and Brussels sprouts. And there was a stream in front of the house where we washed the vegetables. My mother said, 'If you plant an onion patch, you can keep what you grow.' So I started very young." Georges's family had two horses and eight cows on fifty acres. Every morning, he would lurch awake to the sound of his uncle bellowing from the courtyard—*"Hop! Isch Zeit!"*—then spend the day milking cows and scything hayfields. School was almost an afterthought, at least until the invasion.

It began as a false alarm. When the Germans overran Poland on

September 1, 1939, the French assumed that they were next in line. Within a week, they had evacuated 417 communities along the German border in Alsace and Lorraine. The evacuees were allowed thirty kilograms of luggage each, including a blanket, four days' worth of food, and a spoon, fork, and knife. The roads to the transport points were marked by arrows, but it was easier to follow the crowds: farmers on tractors and old bachelors on bicycles, gangly young men on foot and families in horse-drawn carts, their children sprawled among the sacks and boxes. Sheep scampered across the road and cattle blocked the intersections, as farmers herded them into holding pens and communal barns. When they were done, the men hurried to join their families on trains and buses headed south and west, to the Haute-Pyrénées, Dordogne, Haute-Vienne, Charente, and the Landes. More than 600,000 Alsatians and Lorrainians were evacuated in all, including 250,000 from Strasbourg alone. Within days, the empty city was overrun by stray cats.

The passenger trains were all full when Georges's family reached the station. They could only squat on the muddy floor of a boxcar. "For us, this was fun," he told me, though he was surely speaking for himself as a nine-year-old. Three days later, when the boxcar door rolled open and his family staggered into the sunlight, they were six hundred miles from home, in the town of Dax, along the Atlantic coast of France. They joined the crowd of bedraggled evacuees in the station and watched as people were divided up and shuttled by bus and motorcar to villages throughout the area. The Baumanns and four other families were sent to Siest, a village of ninety souls fifteen minutes to the southwest. Four years later, the director Pierre Prévert would film his crime caper *Adieu Leonard* in Siest, with Charles Trenet, Simone Signoret, and assorted local villagers playing themselves. But in the fall of 1939, the place felt like the end of the world: Siest had lost a third of its population since the turn of the century. "There was nothing there," Baumann said.

Most of the evacuees spoke German at home, and the elderly had no French at all. This was a source of some confusion, if not mistrust, among the locals—who were these Germans fleeing other Germans? "The French kids would say, 'Do you hear those *Bosches?*' Then we'd slap them good," Baumann told me. But the townsfolk were mostly kind to them. The alderman invited the evacuees to lunch that first afternoon, and the mayor had them to dinner that night. Each family was assigned a host family and an empty house—there were so many in town—and the children were registered in a Catholic school. Then everyone settled in to wait for the war to begin.

·   ·   ·

Back home, in the emptied villages and abandoned fields of Alsace, the last preparations were in place. The French Second and Third Armies were dug in along the Rhine. The villages were surrounded by barbed wire, antitank trenches, and machine-gun nests; the roads were blocked by overturned cars. In Bartenheim, as in other towns along the main artery, explosive charges had been buried beneath the crossroads and central square—a final booby trap to greet the enemy.

And then . . . nothing. For the next eight months, Alsace lay in a sinister suspension, like a vase hovering in the air before it crashes to the ground. French soldiers lounged in cafés or sunbathed outside their bunkers, sipping espresso or *bidons* of red wine. They sang themselves hoarse at night in the bars and sent romantic postcards home, showing debonair officers in movie-star poses. "*J'attendrai / le jour et la nuit, j'attendrai toujours / ton retour,*" a radio crooner promised. I shall wait, by day and by night, I shall still await your return. The same song, in translation, went on to be a hit in Czechoslovakia, Denmark, Germany, Lithuania, Norway, Poland, and Sweden.

Une drôle de guerre, the French called it. A funny sort of war. Some British officers went so far as to try to import beagles and foxhounds to their French postings, hoping to do some hunting in their idle hours. "Nothing could have led people to believe that they were on the front lines," a villager from Rosenau, just east of Bartenheim, later wrote. "Often at dinnertime, you could hear the Krauts from across the river, on the hill in Istein, beating their bowls in a deafening din, crying, 'Come and eat! Come and eat!'"

The reason for the stalemate seemed clear. To reach Alsace, the Germans first had to cross one of the most formidable defenses in human history: the Maginot Line. Built by the French in the 1930s at a cost of more than three billion francs, this was a string of forts, bunkers, and gun emplacements that ran for nearly three hundred miles along the German border, connected by telephone lines, high-voltage wires, and underground rail. The largest forts were like subterranean cities, with levels upon levels of barracks, infirmaries, workshops, barbershops, kitchens, mess halls, and elaborate systems of tunnels and elevators. They had control towers, periscopes, and heavy guns on retractable turrets. They had heating, air conditioning, indoor plumbing, and walls up to eleven feet thick, proof against any tank or aircraft. All told, the Maginot Line contained more than fifty million cubic feet of concrete and three hundred million pounds of steel. It was, as General George Patton said of all fixed fortifications, a monument to man's stupidity.

The Germans, when they finally came, simply went around it.

.   .   .

The first soldier of the German Reich entered the city of Mulhouse at seven in the morning on June 18, 1940. He was riding a bicycle, as were the others in his squadron. They had left the nearby village of Ensisheim at dawn and in some haste, apparently—a few of them were riding women's cycles, requisitioned from the local populace. When they arrived at the city hall in Mulhouse, they parked their bicycles in formation in front of the steps. One soldier positioned himself in the antechamber of the mayor's office, another stood next to the staircase, and a functionary was sent to fetch the mayor at his house. "I don't want to leave Mulhouse," the mayor complained. "I'm too old for that. I've always done my duty. I don't give a fig for the rest."

The invaders had a hard glow of manifest destiny about them, their rides notwithstanding. They had stormed through Belgium, across the French defenses in the Ardennes that General Pétain had declared impenetrable. They had marched west to Paris and south into Alsace. By the time they reached Strasbourg, other German troops had crossed the Rhine from the east on inflatable boats, easily overcoming the skeletal French forces left along the Maginot Line. In Mulhouse, when the bicycle squadron had secured the city hall and hung the Nazi flag from its roof, two French bureaucrats emerged from the building and handed out cigars and chocolates to the invaders. A few onlookers, gathered on the sidewalk, began to applaud. Others wept or muttered under their breath, though no one could hear them by then. The streets were shaking from the hobnailed boots of German infantry, row upon relentless row, singing "Das Engellandlied" at the top of their lungs:

> Give me your hand, your white hand,
> Farewell, my darling, farewell my darling, farewell, farewell
> For we're going, for we're going,
> For we're going to England
>
> Should you hear that I have fallen,
> That I sleep in the sea tide
> Don't cry for me, my darling, but think:
> He shed his blood for the Fatherland

Ten years later, when the war was over but its memory still harsh and bright, the French government sent a questionnaire to correspondents in dozens of towns and cities across the country. Entitled "An Investigation into the History of the Occupation and Liberation of France in the Department of the Haut-Rhine," it covered everything from kindergarten and village festivals to death camps and forced abortions. The answers, typed and formatted in the punctilious French manner, ran up to a hundred pages, with appendices for the exiled, the conscripted, the court-martialed, and the condemned. When I stumbled upon the questionnaires one afternoon in Colmar, in an unmarked box in the Archives du Haut-Rhin, I felt as if I had opened a door onto a crowded auditorium: a thousand voices speaking at once, each with a story to tell.

In Pfastatt, a suburb of Mulhouse, trucks began to line up in front of the town hall at eight one morning. "By four o'clock, the operation was complete," Eugène Dessoud, a local reservist, later recalled. "The suspects, designated in lists beforehand, had been searched at home by armed police and taken to the town hall, where they were assembled in the corridor. Their houses, furniture, and possessions were all confiscated. Several collaborators profited from the occasion to settle in among their neighbors' goods. (After the Liberation, they left the premises only grudgingly.) Of the twenty-seven families arrested—some seventy people in all—60 percent were given the choice of remaining in Alsace if they signed a declaration of loyalty, or if the women sued for divorce. All refused. It was one of the war's most striking acts of resistance."

In Lutterbach, a mile to the west, villagers lined the road to offer bread, drinks, and canned goods to the French prisoners as they were led away: "Nearly everyone wept to see them leave in such a state. They were guarded by members of the SS who were true brutes. Some knocked away the prisoners' buckets as they drank; others beat them with whips. The population stood by, helpless and indignant, unable to do anything. There were often family members among the prisoners, but we had no right to speak to them. The colonial soldiers [many of them from Algeria, Morocco, and Tunisia] were treated even more harshly. The Germans gave them nothing to eat or drink." In Rosenau, three miles east of Bartenheim, French troops left piles of weapons and ammunition behind as they fled. In Galfingue, fifteen miles to the west, three French soldiers hid from German troops until June 19, then disguised themselves in civilian clothes and fled for the Swiss border.

"We're not bad people," a German infantryman was heard to remark in Pfastatt. "We're just soldiers. But watch out for those who come after us." He and his messmates hoped to be home again by Christmas, they said, with London safely in German hands. In Mulhouse on the morning of the occupation, when the German infantry marched past the Banque de France, they passed a banner hung from the façade by some of their own: "You never learned to love us," it said in German. "But you shall learn to fear us."

·   ·   ·

That September, when the Baumanns finally returned home to Alsace, a surreal welcoming party awaited them. There were brass bands and children's choirs as they stepped off the train in Mulhouse, cheering crowds and speeches by Nazi dignitaries. Black-and-red bunting adorned the public squares, and parades led the evacuees home. "We young people all got a flag to wave with a swastika on it," Georges Baumann told me. "We didn't know any better." It was not an offer that was easily refused.

Gauleiter Robert Wagner, the governor of Alsace during the war, was one of Hitler's most fanatical followers. *Der Schlächter vom Elsaß,* they called him: the Butcher of Alsace. Short and clean-shaven, with sharp, ferrety features and a flair for the hunt, Wagner was a master of propaganda and a decorated veteran of Verdun and the Somme. (His original surname, Backfisch, was slang for teenage girl, so he took his mother's maiden name while in the army.) "If an Alsatian comes to me and says, 'I'm not German but French,' I can only tell him, 'You aren't French, you're a German traitor,'" Wagner declared. "'You're a traitor to your name, to your tongue, to your nationality, to your blood—in short, to your very nature and destiny. Therefore, you should understand that we'll dispose of you quickly, as traitors are disposed of all over the world these days.'"

France signed the armistice on June 22, 1940. Its northern and western territories were relinquished to German occupation, while the puppet Vichy regime took over the "Free Zone" to the southeast. But Alsace was a separate case: It became a de facto part of the Greater German Reich, merged with the state of Baden across the Rhine. Within a month of the signing, Wagner ordered all French civil servants to be laid off and replaced with Germans. French soldiers from Alsace were welcomed home, so long as they signed a certificate attesting to their German-Alsatian origins. French loyalists and those with honorific titles were summarily expelled. In all, some fifty thousand Alsatians were deported. The rest, like Georges Baumann and his family, were forced to return to their villages.

To the Baumanns, Bartenheim was now occupied territory. To the Nazis, it had been German all along. Torn from the bosom of the Reich by the Treaty of Versailles, Alsace had finally returned to its rightful owners. Yet it felt like a foreign country. On the ride back from Siest, the Baumanns had watched the train stations roll past one by one, the signs changing languages as the train entered Alsace. The French announcements gave way to German, but this wasn't the earthy Alsatian spoken around their dinner table. It was the stern High German of the politician and headmaster: the language of authority.

In Bartenheim, deeper shocks awaited them. In the months after the evacuation, the town had been fortified as a base of French resis-

tance, but its machine-gun nests and antitank guns were now manned
by German soldiers. The fields around the village, unplowed for
nearly a year, were covered in nettles and noxious weeds, their crops
long since gone to seed. The dynamite beneath the town square had
been set off by the villagers. It hardly slowed the Germans down but
left a yawning crater surrounded by demolished houses. Their owners had no choice but to live in barracks erected among the rubble.
In Ranspach-le-Bas, four miles to the south, houses were ransacked,
their drawers left hanging open, their furniture misplaced or stolen
or broken apart for firewood. In Mulhouse, the first German signs
were already propped in the windows, targeting their new clientele:
WOHNUNG ZU VERMIETEN. Apartment for rent. "*C'était le commencement
d'une misère,*" a villager from neighboring Magstatt-le-Bas later wrote.
The misery had begun.

·   ·   ·

When I was a boy, my family lived for a year in Karlsruhe, across the
river from Alsace. Sometimes in the evening, my mother stood by
the open window of our second-floor apartment and listened for the
bells of the Strasbourg Cathedral, fifty miles away. It was a magnificent building, she told me, with sandstone walls and a soaring, fili-
greed tower—once the tallest structure in the world. The city around
it, laced with canals and footbridges, was nearly as beautiful. Once a
day, at half past noon, when the sun was at its apex, the great astro-
nomical clock in the cathedral creaked into motion. A mechanical
cock crowed, and a procession of wooden apostles passed before
Jesus, who gave them his blessing. On the track below, a child trundled by, then an adolescent, a soldier, and an old dotard with a cane,
while death rang his bell again and again—a cycle as relentless as the
city's political history.

Strasbourg was like a child of divorced parents, my mother said.

For centuries, the French and Germans took turns lavishing the city with gifts whenever they had custody of it—museums, churches, libraries, grand public squares—and shielding its monuments from the worst of the bombing when they were at war. Each side wanted to prove that it was the more generous, more loving parent. And with each occupation, the new leaders were more unshakably convinced that Strasbourg was theirs alone. That it was only natural for Alsatians to change their names and learn a new language and salute a new flag. For they would always and forever belong to only one country—the one that happened to be in power that day.

"This war has put us in a strange position," Philippe Husser, a schoolteacher from Colmar, wrote in his diary in 1914. "It induces in the Alsatian a moral and physical suffering. He loves Germany and cannot hate France. He feels like a child who adores both his parents and suffers to see that they don't get along; not only that, they beat each other and decide to separate. The father, a severe, regal, authoritarian man, is given custody. The son takes him as a role model and does very well. He loves and respects his father, but can't forget his pretty mother, that charming woman. The father knows that she's making every effort to get her son back. So he scrutinizes her every maneuver, and his son's every gesture, with suspicion and jealousy. When she manages to obtain a visit, and her son greets her with all-too-obvious joy, the father punishes him severely."

After the First World War, when the French reclaimed Alsace, they were welcomed as liberators. The Prussian army had treated local people like enemy agents rather than fellow Germans, executing suspected collaborators and setting a village on fire when some soldiers were shot there. (The shooters were later said to be drunk German soldiers.) Alsatians had spent four years crouched in cellars as the walls quaked above them. Four years making porridge from crop gleanings and melting down church bells for munitions. They had seen deserters shot and traitors hanged and young men marched off to Russia. They were sick of war and sick of the Prussians and more than willing to wave a flag for those who had chased them away. But that did not yet make them French. They had been German citizens for more than forty years, and even the Francophiles among them spoke German at home. An independence movement had been gaining momentum, and some Alsatians hoped that the new regime would put the question to rest with a referendum on statehood. But the French, like the Germans before them, dismissed the idea out of hand. Alsace was theirs by historical right, they insisted. They had just given it back to its people.

Some of them, anyway. Less than a month after the liberation, some two thousand Alsatians were sent packing across the Rhine for insufficient loyalty, including policemen, functionaries, and *vieux allemands*. The rest were issued identity cards of varying types, depending on their ancestry: A. for Alsatians whose parents were both born in Alsace, B. for those with one parent born in Germany, C. for those with parents from Allied or neutral countries, and D. for those with two German parents. Alsatians were once again second-class citizens, as distrusted by the French as they had been by the Germans. As Husser put it: "The French yoke is starting to weigh more heavily than the Prussian boot."

Twenty years later, he would have to do it all over again. "So here I am, German once more," Husser wrote on New Year's Day 1941. "French from 1862 to 1870, German from 1870 to 1918, French from 1918 to 1940, and now German again. No doubt this will be my last change of nationality."

He was wrong, of course.

·   ·   ·

Changing nationalities was more than a matter of swapping street signs. It reached down into society's smallest gears. Sermons had to be rewritten, labels reprinted, and anthems relearned. Farmers had to change their crops (out with grapes, in with hops), restaurants re-work their menus (in with wurst, out with foie gras). For an Alsatian, it was the familiar turned foreign, the trusted turned threatening—an uncanny valley of shadows. Flags were replaced and statues taken down, portraits swapped and busts exchanged—Hitler for Napo-leon, Goethe for Voltaire. Gravestones were tossed out or recarved in German, berets declared illegal. The Nazis called the latter *Gehirnver-dunkelungskappe*, brain-darkening caps, and gave out fines and jail time to those who wore them. "More than one Alsatian had his beret ripped from his head by a Nazi, then summoned by the village party chief to explain himself," a villager in Lutterbach wrote. Some par-ents responded by clothing their children in ever more ridiculous headgear: cowboy hats, perhaps, or Viking horns.

"For me, what were the Germans?" the children's book author and illustrator Tomi Ungerer later wrote in his memoir, *Tomi*. He was eight years old when the Germans marched into his hometown. The Ungerers lived on the grounds of a textile mill in Logelbach, an in-dustrial suburb of Colmar. Like most Alsatians of patrician stock, they were Francophiles, but they had fallen on hard times when To-mi's father died. "I had been completely brainwashed in school and at home," Ungerer wrote. "I was blinded with patriotism, filled with the sparkling deeds of French heroes. And, of course, the French were all good, the Germans all bad. . . . I remember that I was wor-ried about my hands—I had heard in school that the Germans would come and chop off the hands of all the children. This fabrication went back to World War I, when some children in Belgium were maimed playing with hand grenades."

Ungerer had learned his fear of the Germans, in part, from Al-sace's other great illustrator, Jean-Jacques Waltz, better known as Hansi. Born in 1873, just two years after Alsace was annexed by Germany after the Franco-Prussian war, Waltz belonged to a family of fervent Francophiles. The Prussians had given the people of Alsace a choice: They could become German subjects and keep their homes and property, or they could stay French and pack their bags. Waltz's family was among the grudging holdovers. "When the history teacher had insulted our fathers and all French people going back to the time of Charlemagne," Waltz later recalled of his schooling, "and I had come home sad and discouraged, it was then, to console me, that my father would talk about how beautiful our city had been in the time of the French."

Waltz went on to become the most famous satirist in France. Nostalgia and sentiment became his stock-in-trade as an illustrator, but the bitter memory of his years in German school never left him. So he took his revenge with a children's book. Published in 1912, when Alsace was still German, *The History of Alsace as Told to Young Children* is first of all a ravishing work of art. Waltz poured the sum of his talent into its delicately tinted drawings of village life—as intimate and obsessively detailed as embroidered pillows. The book takes the reader on a chronological tour of Alsace, from the first cave dwellers to the Prussian occupation, showing how its noble French origins were undercut, at every turn, by the *barbares* from the other side of the Rhine.

"If you were to chat with some Alsatian farmers," the book begins, "you would notice that all of them, every one, carries in the depths of his heart an instinctive, ferocious hatred toward the people of Baden and all others who come from the other side of the Rhine. This hatred is so great that even the atrocities of the last war can't suffice to explain it. To understand the feeling, you have to know that it has been transmitted from father to son across countless generations of descendants, from before the era of recorded history."

Reading Waltz is like listening to a family argument gone terribly wrong. You can hear the familiar jibes turn corrosive and unforgiving. A border dispute becomes a blood feud. German and French are like different species in his telling—Caesar's stereotypes twisted into grotesques. (The same is often true in German accounts. As Goethe wrote in *Faust:* "A Frenchman is a thing no German man can stand, and yet we like to drink their wine.") In olden times, the French were "tall, upright, and very courageous," Waltz writes. "Their wives were pretty and liked brightly colored clothes and beautiful jewelry." As for the Germans: "They were savages. . . . They covered themselves in animal skins bristling with quills. When they gathered in numbers, you would have thought you were seeing bears or a pack of wolves." Everything sad and terrible and ugly that has come to Alsace, Waltz concludes, "has always come from across the Rhine."

.   .   .

When the invasion finally came, the German soldiers were almost a disappointment to the young Tomi Ungerer. Their first act was to set up a horse-drawn field kitchen in the courtyard of the factory and serve lunch. One of them offered him a taste of his soup. "They were not the hordes of Huns I had so vividly imagined," Ungerer wrote. "What's more, they seemed nice, even cordial." Yet even for a boy like him, bedazzled by guns and gleaming uniforms, the occupation quickly soured. Not long after the Armistice was signed, posters began to appear on shop windows and streetlamps throughout Alsace. They showed a broom sweeping away a pile of French books, a crowing cock, and a miniature Eiffel Tower. "*Hinaus mit dem welschen Plunder,*" the slogan declared. Out with the Gallic trash.

The Germanification of Alsace proceeded "*mit Stumpf und Stiel,*" as Hitler was fond of saying: from root to branch. Two months after the Armistice, Robert Wagner signed a public order entitled, "Toward the Reinstatement of the Mother Tongue." French was henceforth a forbidden language in Alsace. Saying *bonjour* on the street could earn you a fine; longer phrases were punishable by a

year in a reeducation camp. Even German words of French
origin—*friseur, restaurant*—were worthy of a scolding to schoolchildren. So intent was the new regime on uprooting the culture's Gallic overgrowth that Alsatians had to change their own names. In
Mulhouse alone, three thousand birth certificates were modified.
In the back pages of the postwar reports, lists of French street
names and family names appear in endless columns, flanked by
their German doppelgängers:

Rue des Chèvres	Ziegenstrasse
Place Communale	Hermann Goering Platz
Rue Eugène	Jakob Grimm Strasse
Rue du Progrès	Kaiserstuhlstrasse
Rue Jeanne d'Arc	Kantstrasse
Belmontet	Schönberg
Blanchegorge	Schermesser
Boulanger	Becker-Bäcker
Cordonnier	Schuhmacher
Dumoulin	Vondermühl
Meunier	Müller-Möhner

"The whole Nazi mechanism, with its well-oiled grinding cog
wheels, was now in place," Ungerer later recalled. "With Germanic
thoroughness, this perfectly efficient meat grinder took control of the
smallest details of your life." In Colmar, where he went to school,
only High German was allowed in class, and the mayor forbade the
use of dialect by public officials. Ungerer spoke Alsatian anyway—if
only for its many creative expressions for drunkenness (186 of them,
by a friend's count). Like Alsatians for centuries before him, Ungerer
became a master at code-switching: "German in school, French at
home, and Alsatian with my friends. To survive in this huge spider's
web, new standards were applied to morality—cheating, double

standards, deception, faking, and lying to the enemy were all considered virtues."

It was a dangerous game, even for a child. One summer, after Ungerer had spent his vacation on a farm owned by some family friends in Regisheim, he sent a postcard to thank them. One of his favorite memories was of the family pig, which they had jokingly named after the founder of the Gestapo. "I cannot wait to visit you again once you've slaughtered Hermann Goering," he wrote, "and to enjoy a good hunk of the Fieldmarshal's ham." He realized only later how close he had come to disaster. Had the postcard been intercepted by Nazi censors, both his family and their friends would have been deported.

· · ·

The Jews were already gone by then. Alsace-Lorraine was home to some twenty thousand Jews before the war, many of them descended from refugees of Russian and Polish pogroms. Unlike the more assimilated Jews in Paris and cities like Strasbourg and Mulhouse, those in Alsatian villages tended to live in tight-knit communities. They maintained Jewish customs and spoke Yiddish with a little Alsatian mixed in. *Unseri Jüdde,* other Alsatians called them: Our Jews. But that familiarity didn't spare them from discrimination. When Alfred Dreyfus, the French military officer at the heart of the Dreyfus Affair, was falsely convicted of treason for passing military secrets to the Germans in 1894, he was doubly suspect as an Alsatian and a Jew. By 1938, acts of anti-Semitic vandalism, theft, and arson had become common in Alsace.

In September 1939, at the beginning of the Second World War, the French evacuated fourteen thousand Alsatian Jews to west-central France. Nine months later, when the Germans invaded, another five thousand Jews fled into southern France. The thousand or so who remained were given twenty-four hours to pack a suitcase. They could bring food for five days and no more than 2,000 francs, but had to leave their gold, jewelry, and wedding rings behind. Then they were loaded onto buses and deported to the French interior. Some would go on to serve in the Resistance, but most were rounded up again later by the Vichy regime. Some two thousand Jews from Alsace and Lorraine died in the Holocaust.

In Pfastatt, on the morning of July 17, 1940, a detachment of twenty police officers was sent to a Jewish hospice. Eugéne Dessoud, in his account of the occupation, described the police ordering the inhabitants to prepare for evacuation the next day, destination unknown. They confiscated the patients' files and any funds in the hospice safe and left ten men to stand guard. In the anguished hours that followed, one pensioner threw himself from a window and another drowned himself in his bathtub. Two days later, at seven in the morning, a convoy of green trucks with sideboards appeared—they would soon be notorious in the area—and thirty-five pensioners were thrown in back. Ten others, too weak or disabled to walk (including the man who had thrown himself from the window), were transferred to the hospital in Pfastatt, where three of them died. The thirty-five in the trucks were driven deep into the French countryside, a hundred miles to the west, and kicked out at the Pont de Parcey, which the Germans called the Jews' Bridge. "*So, jetzt seid Ihr in Frankreich und könnte verrecken wenn Ihr wollt!*" the head of the convoy told them. So now you're in France and can rot if you want! Eleven had died en route. Before the month was over, Alsace was declared free of Jews.

Thinking back on the Nazi occupiers half a century later, Ungerer was struck by their insouciance, their clear-eyed depravity. When they first came to his hometown, some officers were quartered in the apartment downstairs from his family's place. One day, Ungerer's mother went to answer the door and found an officer standing outside. "He clicked his heels, took a bow, raised his arm, and said, 'Heil Hitler,'" Ungerer recalled. "He presented himself and, with the exaggerated smile of a fanatic, announced that he had three sons, two of them had already died for the Führer, and he hoped the third one might be up to his brothers' example for the eternal glory of the Third Reich." The officer paused and gazed out at a row of chestnut trees outside. Weren't they beautiful this time of year? "'One thing I promise you,'" he said. "'The day will come when you will see a Jew hanging from every branch.'" Then he handed Ungerer's mother a scrap of paper with some writing on it: his wife's recipe for carrot cake.

None of it made any sense to Tomi Ungerer. He was just eight years old. He wasn't sure what it meant to be Jewish, but there was no shortage of people to teach him. That fall, the Nazis began their massive *Umschulung* campaign. More than three thousand French teachers were sent to Baden to be retrained as Nazi educators, while more than seventeen hundred German teachers were sent to Alsace. On the September morning in 1940 when Karl first climbed onto his bicycle and pedaled across the river to Bartenheim, a schoolhouse full of French children awaited him. Georges Baumann and his future wife, Marie-Rose, were among them. It was Karl's job to turn them into good little Germans.

12

OCCUPIER

KARL FOUND A ONE-ROOM FLAT ON GARTENSTRASSE, AN eight-minute walk from the schoolhouse. He had wanted to move the whole family to Bartenheim—to enroll my mother in his elementary school and send his sons to *Oberschule* in Mulhouse. But Emma had no intention of moving to Alsace. The people there were more French than German, she said, no matter what Hitler and Gauleiter Wagner claimed. Why would she want to live among people who didn't want her? So Karl moved into the boardinghouse alone. For the rest of the war, he spent only weekends at home with his family.

Like so much of his life in France, it was an ordinary decision bristling with risk for those around him. Josephine Schöpfer, who owned the boardinghouse, was a young mother, recently divorced. She needed the extra income and wanted her children to learn German, so she gave Karl room and board in exchange for rent and weekly lessons. Karl was scrupulous in his dealings with her, even when eating the wartime rations she served—"I can have one egg, but not two," he would say. But a single woman inviting a German into her home inevitably gave rise to rumors that would come back to haunt her.

Karl would later tell French interrogators that he was sent to Bartenheim against his will, and that he had no political duties in Alsace. He was just a school administrator. But though the principal of his school in Weil confirmed that he never volunteered for the posting, Karl must have known that it was more than just a teaching job. Schools were crucial to the Nazi propaganda machine. Unlike high-school teachers, who taught only a quarter of the population, primary-school teachers taught everyone, and at the most impressionable age. With Karl's fluency in French, he was just the man to reeducate these Alsatians.

In Bartenheim, the Catholic girls' school was shut down, its nuns sent back to the convent or given office work or odd jobs in the parish. The preschool, or *école maternelle*, was replaced by a German kindergarten, overseen by the Nazi Women's League. The elementary school was restaffed. The principal before Karl arrived was an Alsatian man, Louis Obrecht, who had been in charge since 1937. Obrecht had joined the French army as soon as the war began but was captured almost immediately. When he returned to Bartenheim in 1940, he had to sign an oath of allegiance to Hitler before he could resume teaching. Even then, Karl replaced him as principal. Obrecht seems never to have forgiven him.

The schoolhouse in Bartenheim was quite grand in some ways, with its stepped gable and arched front windows, and preindustrial in others. "All classrooms are in good, friendly condition," Karl concluded, in a twenty-two-page report to German authorities in 1943. "Boys: 91, Girls: 92; Classrooms: 4, Gym: none, Laboratory: none,

Art room: none, Workshops: none; Bathrooms: none." There was an outhouse behind the playground, he noted, with five seats for girls and two for boys, along with a urinal.

In the one photograph that survives of his classroom, the light streams in from tall windows along one wall, illuminating rows of oak desks and benches rubbed smooth by fidgeting children. A podium stands at the front, flanked by a large abacus and posters of handwritten letters in *Deutsche Normalschrift*. (Hitler, whose portrait hangs above the podium next to a cross, had done away with *Sütterlinschrift* by then.) On a blackboard in the corner, propped on an easel, Karl has written "Bartenheim." And above it, *Die Vögelein singen im Wald*. The little birds sing in the forest.

·　　·　　·

"*Do isch mi Vater gsi*," my mother said. That's where my father was. We were sitting in a brasserie in Bartenheim called Le Gaulois, visiting the village together for the first time. Outside the window, across the street, the old schoolhouse looked just as it did in 1943, when my mother first visited it with her father. Her eyes welled up at the thought, and the memory that came flooding in behind it—of her encounter with Georges Tschill forty years later, on the sidewalk behind the building, when he told her that he had saved her father's life. "It was one of the few truly striking moments I've known," she said. "If I'd arrived just a moment later, or if Bapa had said, 'Come back in three minutes,' I would never have heard his story. It was as if someone in heaven had orchestrated everything down to the second."

She had nearly lost her belief in such things. The mystical strain that ran through her family—from her grandmother's visions of the dead to her father's dark premonitions—had flickered out when she came to America. She rarely missed a Sunday mass at first: The sight of seven Bilgers slumped in a row was a fixture of our church in Oklahoma. But a run of dull, reproving priests and guitar-strumming deacons—all the cheerful cant of seventies Catholicism—had doused her faith. By the time she met Georges Tschill, she hadn't been to church in ten years aside from Christmas and Easter. Then his words struck a flint in her mind.

It was his voice that she remembered best. His French was a little stiff and stilted, but then he switched to the easy stride of his Alsatian, as well grained as a walking stick. His words left her dumbstruck—"My heart was pounding all the way to Germany," she said—but it was the sound that stayed with her. "It was *wunderschön*," she said. "Alsatian can be a little crooked sometimes, and the vowels aren't always so nice. But his was just beautiful: rustic but not coarse. I could have listened to him for hours."

Everything that she had learned about her father since then—the stories I had brought from Alsace, the blank spaces I had filled—hadn't really changed how she felt about him. "Don't you have an interesting grandfather?" she would say, when I came back from the archives in Aulfingen or Colmar. It was as if all the misgivings that once weighed on her had been lifted off and given to me. She was tired of all that uncertainty. Her formidable mind had begun to falter lately—names forgotten, stories repeated—and to fall back, with a kind of relief, on first instinct. She loved her father.

Did I? The man I had gotten to know in Aulfingen wasn't easy to love. He was a zealot, a taskmaster, aflame with his own worldview and blind to its effect on others. I told myself that I would have done better. That I never would have joined the Nazi Party, never followed Hitler or left my family behind. But then everyone tells themselves that. The more I learned about life in occupied France, the more I could see the soft spots in my own character, the ethical give. Even in unthreatening times, I was liable to argue both sides of a point, to disguise self-interest as rationality. Would I have had the nerve to stand up to party leaders in Mulhouse? To risk my life for the people of Bartenheim? There was a mulishness in Karl, an unflinching conviction, that just wasn't in me—and that I might have needed. War finds our weaknesses even more than our strengths.

．　　．　　．

Georges Tschill died in 1999, but his son still lives in Bartenheim, as do his two grandsons—the boys he was pulling in the wagon on the day he first met my mother. With the strange and circuitous grace with which history sometimes moves, Tschill and my mother went on to become friends after that first encounter in 1983. They exchanged letters and Christmas cards and met on one side of the river or the other every few years. One summer, my mother even brought a video camera and taped Tschill telling stories about Karl and the German occupation. But she never asked anyone else in Bartenheim about her father. Maybe Tschill's testimony was enough for her. Or maybe she just needed someone else to do the asking.

When I was a junior in college in 1985, I spent a semester studying French and German in Strasbourg. That winter, my mother asked me again and again to visit Bartenheim. But my girlfriend, Jennifer, and I were living together for the first time (we got married three years later). We had a small apartment above a waterfall, in a neighborhood of canals and half-timbered houses close to the cathedral. And compared to their entrancing history, my family's past seemed both too personal and impossibly distant.

I never did meet Georges Tschill or get to hear his beautiful Alsatian. If there's any consolation for that great regret, it has been getting to know his son and daughter-in-law thirty years later. Just as Georges unlocked my grandfather's history for my mother, Jean-Georges and Monique Tschill have become my master keys to Bartenheim—my passe-partout to every closed door and reclusive source.

Whenever I come to Bartenheim, Monique starts by sitting me down in her kitchen. It's in a small, workaday room with bright yellow tiles and pine cabinets made by Jean-Georges and his uncle Paul. (All the Tschills seem to work with wood.) Round and quick with short blond hair and sly, gray-green eyes, Monique speaks in a fast, fluty Alsatian that can rise to a caw when she gets excited. While I tell her what I've found in the archives or heard in an interview, she bustles along the counter asking questions and deftly assembling dishes to set before me. One day it was a *pot au feu* with celery-root salad and *pâté en croûte*. The next it was a quiche Lorraine with a butternut soup that tasted faintly of chestnuts—the squash was grown in a chestnut grove, she said. If Jean-Georges is back from the shop, he'll sit beside me at the table, telling stories and eating methodically with his knife and thumb. Monique keeps an eye on his plate and an ear on his facts.

Jean-Georges has his father's face: lantern jaw and hair like steel wool, umber eyes and a frank yet forgiving gaze. He leans forward with his shoulders hunched, his corded forearms on his knees, telling stories with his hands and his unhurried Alsatian. He almost always wears blue canvas coveralls, ground with machine oil and sawdust. Now in his late seventies—born in the last year of the war—he still makes the rounds of the village almost every day, replacing this window or that door, fixing a cabinet or varnishing some wooden molding. His handiwork seems to keep the whole village standing, like a thousand tiny crutches. He knows everyone in Bartenheim and their houses even more intimately. Yet his wife has been my real connection.

Although she was raised in Rantzwiller, five miles to the west, Monique knows Bartenheim's history better than most locals—the tangled train of alliances and betrayals, love affairs and broken business deals that rattles through its past like tin cans behind a wedding car. "When there is something to know, she knows it before we do at the town hall," a local politician told me. "You think you're the first to hear, then you come to work and they've already heard it from her." Before I'm half done with dessert, Monique is back at the kitchen counter making calls and paging through the directory, launching phone trees in every direction, tracking down my grandfather's students, allies, and enemies.

In this way, a small, dauntingly traditional village, sealed tight as a walnut around its history, has been slowly opened to me. Barten-heim is full of Georges Tschills, as it turns out: people for whom those days of war are still more vivid than last week. They're all in their eighties now, suspicious of outsiders or disinclined to talk to them. But for Monique, or the memory of their old schoolmaster, they'll make an exception.

·   ·   ·

"Karl Gönner! *Da war ein Schulmeister!*" Georges Baumann shouted, when I asked him about my grandfather one afternoon. Now there was a schoolteacher! I was back in the Baumanns' living room, squeezed between Georges and his wife, Marie-Rose, on their green couch. "When he came to class in his uniform that first morning, we thought, 'Oh no, today is not a good day,'" Georges said. He leaned in close and wagged his forefinger at me. "He was a strict teacher!"

"But a good one!" Marie-Rose said.

"*Ja, da war ein guter Schulmeister,*" Georges said, nodding. "The whole town respected him. When he wanted something done, you did it his way."

"You didn't dare do otherwise!"

I hadn't expected to meet any of my grandfather's students when I began my research. Though my mother and her brothers were still alive, the idea that other, even older members of their generation might remember my grandfather seemed far-fetched. Yet wherever I went over the years, tracking his movements from Germany to France and back again, I found his old pupils waiting.

In Aulfingen one night, I talked to a group of elderly ladies who called themselves *Der Alter's Klub*. The Old Folks' Club. They grew up together in town and remembered my grandfather from elementary school. "Herr Gönner, when he left, all the kids were bawling," Edeltraut Burgert told me. Of course, this was in the days when Pastor Bihler would hold up a mirror to spy on students during mass, or yank them across the room by one ear. Other teachers spanked students or boxed their ears—"A man who is not beaten, is not educated," as an old Greek adage put it—or gave the best grades to those who brought them fresh eggs. So even a little kindness could go a long way. "*Ordnung hat er g'ha*," Mathilde Amma, a birdlike eighty-nine-year-old, told me when I asked about Karl. "*Aber böse war er nit.*" He kept order, but he wasn't mean.

But that was before the war. By 1939, two-thirds of German teachers had attended monthlong training camps run by the National Socialist Teachers League. By 1941, face slapping had been officially approved as a disciplinary measure, provided students were of an age when their vision and hearing would not get damaged. In most classrooms, a map of Europe now hung on the wall or stood on an easel. Stepping over to it with a wooden pointer, the teacher would trace its borders and tap its colored sections, offering a crisp report of news from the front: ships sunk, planes shot down, territory claimed. Afterward, the students would pass around a stack of German newspapers, heavily censored, and clip the best stories for their folders. The news changed every day, yet somehow not at all. The Führer's army was forever advancing, its setbacks gallantly withstood, its victory inevitable.

On the weekends, in some areas, the Hitler Youth received quasi-military training, crawling through freezing mud and clouds of tear gas, or learning to fire bazookas into haystacks. "The purpose of education is to create a political soldier," Hitler had declared. "The only difference between him and the active soldier is that he is less specially trained."

The public boarding schools for the Nazi elite were the purest expression of this philosophy. At the Adolf Hitler academies for twelve- to eighteen-year-olds, students were trained in Slavic languages, the better to subordinate future subjects in the eastern provinces. At Napola boarding schools, administered by the SS, they were put to work on farms and in factories to fortify their identification with the *Volk*, then given strenuous physical tests such as wrestling with Alsatian dogs. The most extreme were the four-year Ordensburgen finishing schools. Based in remote castles and rustic barracks, they were designed to train the ultra-elite alumni of the Adolf Hitler schools. Vogelsang in Westphalia, for instance, had the world's largest gymnasium, though it was never completed, with equipment that could retract into the floor and a pool with a thirty-foot springboard. The students used live ammunition in their war games and had to dig trenches in front of advancing tanks. Accidental deaths were common.

·   ·   ·

Karl must have known, by then, that there was a madness at the heart of his party. That Hitler's unhinged rhetoric was more than political theater: The man meant every word. Yet that madness had only glancingly affected Karl's life. He had lost his job to party politics only to be transferred to another. He had seen Nazi brutality but never participated in it. He had heard dark rumors about the camps and deportations, but his own work and home life went on as before.

That changed when he crossed the Rhine. It had been twenty years since he came to France and nearly lost his life there. He was just a foot soldier then, shooting at men who were shooting at him.

Now he was the principal of a school, responsible for the well-being of nearly two hundred students. It was his job to wake up every morning and don his uniform, square the imperial eagle on his cap, and march across the square to deliver war reports to children. It was his job to mold their minds for the new Reich.

The process was well under way before he arrived. It had begun with burning books. Children were given wagons with which to gather French books door-to-door. Some towns lost almost every volume in their library—some fifteen hundred in Lutterbach's case—leaving a tabula rasa for the German texts and propaganda to come. In others, the villagers handed over only worthless magazines and papers while hiding their books in cellars and cubbyholes. In Bartenheim, the books were burned in front of the town hall. In Pfastatt, they were piled in a field across from the school gymnasium and set on fire at dawn on the summer solstice. As they burned, some of the town's Hitler Youth led a mad dance around the flames. It was like "a pagan fire of a new sort," one observer wrote.

Four centuries of fighting over Alsace, each regime more bitter and self-righteous than the last, had come to this. Every lesson was an indoctrination, every field trip a political rally. It was a war fought with erasers and chalk, seating charts and vocabulary lists. Textbooks were revised, histories rewritten, instructors replaced with proper patriots. Some teachers wore Wehrmacht uniforms to class; others wore lederhosen. Some students had to say *"Heil Hitler!"* dozens of times a day; others muttered *"Drei Liter!"* (three liters) and got away with it. But the message was always the same: We're all Germans now.

War was the overriding theme, threaded through every subject. Math classes calculated bullet trajectories and bomb capacities. Chemistry classes memorized gas weapons, lung poisons, and throat irritants. Art classes drew searchlights and drifting paratroopers. (One textbook claimed that Leonardo da Vinci came from German stock: His original name was Leonhard von Wincke.) "Every day the state spends six marks on one cripple and four and a quarter marks on one feeble-minded person," one word problem for math classes began. "How much do the cripple and feeble-minded person cost in total, if each lives to the age of forty-five?"

Alsatian schoolchildren could be excused for being a little perplexed. Who was in power this time? Were they the good guys or the bad guys? The battle for children's hearts and minds had been going on for so long that it was hard to keep track. Most Alsatian parents had been born German and still spoke German at home. Yet they called themselves French and said the Germans were the enemy. Teachers said the opposite. They glorified the German people and hung illustrations of racial types on the wall: sporty Nordics next to crabbed Semites. Or they had students measure one another's skulls to determine their ancestry. What did it all mean? "One of my first homework assignments was to draw a Jew," Tomi Ungerer later recalled. "I came home and asked, 'Mama, what is a Jew?'"

·   ·   ·

Karl's classes began like most others. His students stood to say "Heil Hitler!" as he walked into the room. He led them through some songs, gave the news from the front, and had them cut clippings from newspapers. But then the real work began, his former students told me. As a school principal and party member, Karl could pass beneath the Gestapo's radar in a small town like Bartenheim, and he used that tenuous freedom to teach as he always had: reading, writing, science and math, history and languages.

"*Huit biens et trois passable!* Not bad!" Alphonse Huttenschmitt told me one afternoon. Huttenschmitt was one of my grandfather's students in eighth grade. He had brought his report card to show me. In the eleven subjects listed, Karl had graded him as "good" in eight and "satisfactory" in three—a commendable result for that era and that teacher. "The name Gönner I will never forget!" Huttenschmitt said. "He kept order in the school, but you learned something from him. This report card got me my first job!"

Huttenschmitt was eighty-eight, bald and bent-backed, his body clutched in on itself like a claw. But his eyes were sharp and clear, and he spoke with the stubborn certainty of a witness at a deposition. He was thirteen when the Germans came to Bartenheim in 1940, and he had already had a taste of war. He had helped plant the dynamite that blew up the town square to try to block the German advance. "We thought the attack would come from the east," he said. "But *manque de chance,* the Germans came from the west—from Belfort—so they caught us from behind." He showed me a picture of the blasted square, its half-timbered houses standing sawtoothed against the sky, their walls broken and roofs blown off. "*Es war ganz a weg,*" he said. It was all gone.

Alsace would be rebuilt in the Führer's image, the Nazis had promised, beginning with students like Huttenschmitt. The new curriculum wasn't hard to master. "The adolescent brain should not be burdened with subjects 95 percent of which it cannot use and hence forgets," Hitler had written in *Mein Kampf.* When students weren't doing sports or calisthenics, they were collecting rags, bones, scrap metal, and medicinal herbs for the war effort. (In the winter of 1942, Tomi Ungerer noted, Alsatians collected 3,963,699 old woolen scarves and 479,589 pairs of old socks.) On Saturdays, they headed into the fields to gather potato bugs. Known as Colorado beetles, the pests were rumored by the Germans to be a Negro-Judeo blight brought by the Americans.

The school in Bartenheim had two other German teachers: Fräulein Ruff and Herr Meyfarth. Ruff seems to have stuck to the prescribed curriculum. She may have assumed that she had no choice. Any break in protocol could be reported to the party—if not by colleagues or local collaborators, then by the children themselves. "Your

real father is the Führer," they were told. Self-censorship was the
most effective form of propaganda. But Meyfarth didn't have even
that excuse. He was a lazy sadist who delighted in following the Nazi
rulebook, his students told me. He liked to walk the streets of Bartenheim during blackouts and throw rocks through windows where
lights were still lit. In class, he would stroll up and down the rows of
students, rapping them at random with his wooden pointer. (When
Georges Tschill, who made the pointers for the teachers, heard what
Meyfarth was doing, he sawed thin notches into the wood so that it
would snap on impact.) The students called him "Monsieur
Maikäfer"—Mr. Junebug—because he liked to search them for lice
with a magnifying glass.

Karl's classes were different. "One learned with him," one of his
students told me. He was a strict taskmaster, making them copy out
"I shall speak German" if they used a word of French. But they were
used to that: Their French teachers had done the same when they
spoke Alsatian. He led the Hitler Youth in town and tried to badger
his students into joining—when one boy refused, Karl threatened to
stuff him into a sauerkraut barrel and set it in front of a Russian tank.
But his students must have known that he was bluffing: Only a handful came to meetings. In the rest of Alsace and neighboring Moselle,
the Hitler Youth had 130,000 members.

"One time, Herr Gönner asked some boys with whom they would
serve when they grew up," Huttenschmitt said. "Would they be in
the Luftwaffe or the Army or Navy? The first boy said the marines
and the second said the Luftwaffe. But the third boy said he would
serve nowhere, and then all ten or twelve boys who came after him
said nowhere, too. The first two boys were ashamed, but Herr Gönner said nothing more." Huttenschmitt took a long breath and bowed
his head. "I think he knew that we were French at heart," he said,
looking up and holding my eyes. "We weren't for the Germans, even

if we had to play along with them. He understood that. He was a Nazi, but a reasonable one."

.   .   .

A reasonable Nazi. I must have heard that phrase, or some variant of it, a dozen times in Bartenheim. What seemed an oxymoron to me was self-evident to the villagers. Raised in a divided culture, changing nationalities like others change houses, they knew how to keep two contradictory ideas in their heads at once. They were in their eighties now and beyond caring if anyone—even the grandson of a former enemy—should question their patriotism. They felt closer in spirit to the boys and girls they once were, amoral and wild, than the earnest adults they had become.

"I'll tell you a joke that we used to make," an elderly Bartenheimer named Félice Grienenberger told me one day. Then she launched into a story that only a bilingual Alsatian would find funny: "There was a man in a village whose name was Lagarde. When the Germans came, they changed his name to Wache, which also means watchman. Then the French came and changed it to Vache, which sounds the same but means cow. So the Germans, when they returned, changed his name to Kuh. Now the French are back again and his name is Cul, which means that he's an ass to everyone."

We were having Sunday dinner in the four-hundred-year-old mill where Félice and her ten siblings were raised. Four were still alive and at the table; all but one had had my grandfather as a teacher. The dining room had low white beams, faded floral wallpaper, and windows on two sides. As the Grienenbergers told their stories, bowls of potato-leek soup and plates of asparagus with homemade mayonnaise made the rounds. Schnitzel and new potatoes followed, and finally a huge pie that seemed to contain every fruit in their garden:

apples, pears, blueberries, and rhubarb, depending on where it was sliced. It reminded me of their conversation: everyone talking at once, correcting and repeating and interrupting one another. They seemed to quiet down only when François, the second youngest but most respected, took the floor. He was the village priest and rendered his final judgments in a deep basso.

The Grienenbergers had no illusions about war. It was neither glorious nor romantic nor meaningfully tragic in their telling—nothing but a terrible waste of life. A deep well of pain. In the childhood memories I had read from Alsace, war often seemed a kind of lark—a summer vacation, as Tomi Ungerer put it—full of adventure and hijinks and adults in funny costumes. You went barefoot when shoes were scarce, begged for rations from soldiers, and staged ambushes with paper helmets and rusty bayonets that you found in a field. "We weren't unhappy when the Germans were here," Marie-Rose Baumann told me. "We didn't know anything else."

But in the Grienenbergers' stories, the darkness was never far from the surface. "Those years were an eternity," Félice said. "We had nothing. We had potatoes. We had lard. I would fill my mouth with it and then go outside and spit it out for the cat." At the beginning of the occupation, she knitted herself a small pillow out of red, white, and blue yarn—the French colors—then spent months worrying that German soldiers would find it. By day, she could see spy planes high overhead, their wings glinting in the sky. By night, the windows had to be papered over, bicycle lights shrouded with a hood. "I was always afraid," Félice said. "Always." When the bombers came, she would hide under the kitchen table. As soon as the strafing began, the family would run to the basement and wait, listening to the falling bombs above ground. "You could feel the earth tremble as they fell on Mulhouse," Félice said. "*Ils ont sacrément bombardés!* That's when I would start to pray, Please God, stop the bombing and I will never talk in church again."

They were afraid of the Germans—"*C'est normale!*" But the line between them wasn't always easy to draw. One of Félice's sisters went to visit Karl's family in Weil during the war and always talked about it afterward. She liked them. And Herr Gönner was a good instructor, "rigorous in everything he did," François said. He showed them their first cartoons—"The Brave Little Tailor," "The Wishing Table"—and played along on his violin as they sang in class. Whenever he sang off pitch, Georges Baumann had told me, Karl would whack him with the hair on his bow. "*Baumann, Sie singen falsch!*"

In the archives in Strasbourg, I had come across a worn little volume entitled *Songbook for Alsatian Educators, 1940*. It had a drawing of the Strasbourg cathedral on the cover and a collection of tunes inside for children to sing in unison. Karl preferred the old folk songs, the Grienenbergers said—"*O Tannenbaum*," "*Tra-ri-ra Summer Is Here!*"—but those were in the minority in this book, and hidden in back. The first half was devoted to battle hymns and patriotic anthems, rife with every racist and imperialist trope the Nazis held dear. "*Volk* must to *Volk* as blood to blood and flame to flame," one of them began: "A stream of sacrifices shall unite all hearts." Another opened with Death riding a coal-black horse. "When our compatriots march to battle, Death gallops beside them. . . . When the girls stroll about, he leads them in a dance."

Joseph, eighty-seven years old and the most formidable of the Grienenbergers, set his hands flat on the table and drew himself erect. He squared his shoulders and lifted his chin and began to sing, though the sound was closer to a bellow: "*Panzer rollen in Afrika vor! Panzer rollen in Afrika vor!*" It was a song of Rommel's army, from the days when nothing could withstand his tanks in the desert. "Hot on the African earth the sun glows. Our engines sing their song!" With his white mane and clenched fists, Joseph looked like an Old Testament prophet, his eyes lit with memories. But then he shook his head and frowned. "And there was one against the Jews," he said. "*Krumme,*

krumme Juden!" he began. Crooked, crooked Jews, they move here, they move there, they move through the Red Sea, the waves strike and the world is at peace.

The room was quiet now except for the ticking of an old clock. "It was Meyfarth who made us sing those songs," Joseph said, settling back in his chair, his lips wrinkled in disgust. "We didn't learn anything with Meyfarth."

I thought of what Karl wrote on the blackboard in his classroom: "The little birds sing in the forest." He had never lost his love of music, though his own playing had more vigor than grace, yet his party had turned even that into a weapon. The Nazis knew that music was the quickest path to belief, so they wrapped their darkest themes in the sprightliest tunes. It was one of the cruelest parts of the occupation: the way it could bind ugliness to beauty, violence to joy. Karl had done so himself in those early, heady days in Aulfingen, when he thought nothing of teaching marching songs to a church choir.

"Was für Rindvieh waren wir," he would say, years later, when his former students came to visit him after the war. What cattle we were.

13

PARTY CHIEF

HE SHOULD HAVE SEEN IT COMING. THE SUPERINTENDENT
had assured him that he would be in Alsace for only three or four
weeks. Karl just had to help set up the new school system and organize the teachers' schedules and lesson plans. Bartenheim was an
easy bike ride from Weil, and there would be no *Alte Kämpfer* to watch
over him. No informants in the next room to make sure he said,
"Heil Hitler!" If Karl could just keep up appearances—wear the
uniform, go to party meetings, and refrain from chewing out Nazi
officials—he might make it through the war alive.

Now those three or four weeks had stretched to two years. In addition to running the school and teaching classes, Karl had to stay up
deep into the night doing official paperwork. In March of 1942, he
had been named *Ortsgruppenleiter,* or Nazi Party chief, of Bartenheim

and the surrounding area. Karl would later claim that he tried to refuse the position but the Nazi leadership gave him no choice. The previous party chief, Charles Reymann, had resigned almost a year earlier, and Karl was the only available replacement. "In war," he was told, "everyone must go where they are called."

As the school principal, Karl had always had some authority over the village. But he was now its de facto leader, more powerful than the mayor. He not only had to teach Bartenheim's children, he had to explain the Reich to their parents—and make sure they followed its rules. "*Mit der Bevölkerung fühlte ich mich verbunden,*" he would later write. I had grown attached to these people. The villagers had an acerbity to them, a sly humor that reminded him of his relatives in Herzogenweiler. But they could never truly relax around him. No matter what his sympathies, he was still their overseer—the official agent of a hostile force.

Alsace was meant to be a gleaming model of National Socialism, its *Volk* marching in lockstep with their Führer. But beneath its empty pomp and relentless propaganda was a place at war with itself. To survive, people had to play multiple parts: the good Nazi and the closet Francophile, the *Resistant* and the collaborator. They said "Heil Hitler!" on the street, then hurried home to listen to Charles de Gaulle on the shortwave. They flew the swastika from the front porch and hung the French *Tricolore* in the basement. There are two countries in every country, as Milton Mayer put it, but in Alsace yet another country lay beneath them: a place that was neither French nor German, but an intricate twining of the two.

The local papers, now in the hands of Nazi censors, did their best to ignore this. To convey a dogged sense of normalcy. There were ads for an embroidery and knitting exhibition, baking workshops, and birth announcements. ("The stork visited local families five times in the month of June!") There were reports on a speech entitled "A Wife's Duties in the House, Yard, and Garden" and a slideshow on the life of the Führer. One short "humorous" piece described Karl coming across a woman in Bartenheim feeding wheat to her chickens. This was a violation of wartime rationing—"He who wastes grain feeds England!"—and the woman was clearly flustered. "*Guten Tag*, Herr Hitler!" she blurted out. To which Karl grinned and replied, "My name is Gönner. I have no wish to be Herr Hitler, he has too great a responsibility!"

The occupation could seem like strained comic theater sometimes—amateur actors stumbling through their parts. But it was never that simple. A small minority of Alsatians welcomed the regime change, and Karl, at least in the early years, still believed in his role. Two months after he arrived in Alsace, he gave a speech at the town gym on the "Structure, Aim, and Purpose of the Nazi Party." All residents of Bartenheim were welcome, the paper noted— "especially the men"—in a tone only fractionally warmer than the warnings against listening to foreign radio broadcasts. Three weeks later, at a party meeting at a local pub, Karl went into even greater detail, describing the "wonderful organism" of the Nazi Party with its ingenious cells and blocks. "The headmaster's clear, straightforward presentation was met with great applause," a reporter concluded.

· · ·

It has been more than seventy-five years since the war ended. Time enough, one might think, to learn the truth behind such stories, to separate fact from propaganda. How popular were the Nazi gatherings in Alsace, really? And how enthusiastic the speakers? Were the lecture halls half empty, as some villagers later said? Or were they filled with eager converts? More than three hundred thousand people were charged as war criminals and collaborators in France after the war. But the records of those trials, and the evidence presented,

are still classified by the French government. To see the transcripts of
the police interrogations of my grandfather, I had to petition the
military justice archives in Le Blanc, France, then obtain special per-
mission from the attorney general.

Every occupied country has a secret history to tell. The problem
is knowing which version to believe. Was the mayor a Nazi sympathizer? Did the baker inform on his neighbor? Collaborators often
say they were resistance fighters in disguise. They may even believe
it. Whom to trust when the villagers themselves disagree—not just
about the enemy but about one another?

·   ·   ·

One July morning, I met Gabriel Arnold at the town hall in Bartenheim. Arnold was the deputy mayor and founding president of the
historical society. Slender and urbane, with thinning gray hair and
rimless rectangular glasses, he was the closest thing in Bartenheim to
an aristocrat. His French was precise, his demeanor unflappable, his
view of history rooted in human fallibility. He had a diplomat's love
of nuance. "You mustn't just believe the memories of people from
fifty years ago," he told me. "As long as there is emotion in it, it can't
be objective. You have to find the balance between viewpoints."

The Arnolds were Francophiles of long standing. Their history in
Bartenheim dated back to 1705, when they had financial ties to the
Habsburg dynasty. Gabriel's father was mayor of Bartenheim in the
early 1930s. He and one of his brothers fought with the French in
1939, while another brother was conscripted by the Germans and
sent to Russia. As in many Alsatian families, though, this was only
half the story. Gabriel's mother was a Grienenberger—the family I
had visited for Sunday lunch at the old mill—and his maternal
grandfather served in the Prussian navy. If Gabriel seemed unusually
refined, it was less by birth than act of will. He was raised on a farm

with five sisters and brothers, his hands as rough as his French. It was only later, at boarding school and the *école normale* for teachers in Strasbourg, that he polished his speech and manners.

"I was born in 1952," he told me. "When we talked about family history, it was mostly in terms of things that weren't allowed. And many things weren't allowed. You had to be quiet, couldn't speak against the Germans, because you risked deportation." Then, when Alsace became part of France again, it slowly lost another part of its identity. "If the Alsatians blame the French for anything, it's this: In both 1918 and 1944, they reclaimed Alsace as if nothing had been there before. As if it had never been German. The Alsatians were fine with becoming French, but they didn't want to forget everything that had happened here."

He beckoned me out of the office and down the hall, to the basement stairs that led to the archives. The town hall was built in 1881, he said. Its recent renovation—elevator, circular staircase, sleek new offices—was a testament to the town's prosperity. Bartenheim had fewer than eighteen hundred inhabitants at the end of the war. By the time I met Arnold, its population had more than doubled, and it was still growing. Along the way, a good deal of Alsatian history had been forgotten or deliberately redacted. "The generations change and the young people don't know the war," Arnold said.

He looked around the basement with its whitewashed cinder-block walls. To one side, four metal shelves were lined with large cardboard boxes. An archivist spent a day or two every year going through these files and sorting them by date, he said. "These used to be in the attic. Now they're in this climate-controlled space." He shook his head. "There's not much here, to be honest." The boxes were filled to the brim with brittle, yellowed documents—a treasure trove, one would have thought. But most of it was merely bureaucratic: lists of orphans and refugees, Alsatian men conscripted into the Wehrmacht and wounded veterans seeking disability compensation. There were stacks upon stacks of ration cards, as if these could still feed the hungry, but little else from the war. The dates on the boxes stopped at 1940 and picked up again in 1945.

"It's curious, don't you think," Arnold said. "It's as if the period in between didn't exist. After 1938, there are only administrative items—all the things that touch on people are gone. Were they taken out or sent to the departmental archives? We don't know. But if you want my opinion, a lot has been destroyed." I asked him about the postwar trials of collaborators—another glaring absence from the archives—but he shook his head. "I'm too young to talk about that. Either they didn't happen here, or people were afraid to mention them. We don't speak of *l'épuration*."

·   ·   ·

Bartenheim had always been a divided place. The war only widened the rift. "It was a simple thing, really," Arnold said. There were two factions, the Red and the Black, as in Stendhal's novel of the same name. The Blacks were named for the color of a priest's cassock and the Reds for the scarlet in a soldier's uniform. "The Blacks were on the side of the church; the Reds were more secular—we called them socialists but they weren't, really. *Pas du tout*—and they didn't like each other much." They were more like rival clans, fighting over turf, than political parties, he said. But their differences were all the more bitter for that.

For years, the Blacks ruled Bartenheim with an unchallenged hand. Both the mayor and the priest were members, so they controlled the village's cultural and political life. The Reds were perennial also-rans. While the Blacks met in the church, the Reds were relegated to the local gymnastics club. Then, in 1933, even that burned down. The fire was probably sparked by a crossed wire or tossed cigarette. Still, the Reds blamed the Blacks.

The following year, the church burned down in turn. This time, the cause was probably an overheated motor in the pipe organ. But of course the Blacks blamed the Reds. The village priest was among those who suspected arson, one villager told me, but he tried to turn the disaster to his advantage. The church stood on top of a hill west of town, but the priest and some congregation members wanted to relocate it to the center, closer to their houses. In the old days, when the priest was all-powerful in Bartenheim, this might have been easy. But the population was now polarized. When the Reds pushed for a town referendum, the priest's proposal was trounced. The church would be rebuilt on the hill.

Two years later, in 1936, Bartenheim elected its first Red mayor: René Kielwasser, the president of the gymnastics society. The town council was now split between Kielwasser on one side and the priest's cronies on the other. "If you look at the records in the town hall from those years, they're full of virulent arguments," Arnold said. "Just implacable opposition."

Then came war.

.   .   .

Kielwasser didn't have the look of a man to lead a village against the Nazis. He was born, in 1895, without a right ear and right eye, and he was congenitally undersized. His classmates called him "Little One Ear." Yet he was an excellent student and quick-witted enough to hold his own in the schoolyard. After graduation, Kielwasser went from working on the floor of a glue factory in Mulhouse, amid the stench of blood and boiling bones, to being its administrative director. He took night classes in French, after France reclaimed Alsace in 1918, and was soon nearly as fluent as he was in German. By the time he returned to Bartenheim, in 1927, he was a man of means. "Felt hat, buttoned waistcoat, black and white boots, cane in hand," as his eldest son, Marcel, later recalled in an unpublished memoir. "A real dandy!" He grew his mustache long and had German specialists in Pforzheim make him a new glass eye. In the right light, its gray-green iris, veined with scarlet, was a perfect match for his own.

On Sunday mornings, Marcel later recalled, his mother would stride down the aisle in church to claim the pew reserved for the biggest donors. But his father was a liberal at heart: He never forgot his time at the glue factory. When the village had to be evacuated in 1939, the ensuing chaos brought out Kielwasser's organizational savvy. Caught between hordes of panicked villagers and contradictory orders from Mulhouse, he requisitioned a fleet of vehicles to carry people west. Then he gathered the elderly and infirm that were left behind. Once at the Atlantic coast, Kielwasser scrambled to find food and housing for the evacuees. He made late-night runs to dairies and slaughterhouses, and set up medical care and supply chains. Still, in the end, opinions were sharply divided on the mayor's performance. Some villagers relied on his resourcefulness, while others accused him of favoring his family or even using the situation to line his own pockets. "Some felt supported, others abandoned," Arnold told me. But it was afterward, he said, that the mayor was truly caught "between two fires."

When the evacuees returned home the following September, Kielwasser tendered his resignation to the new German authorities. The Nazi Landkommissar wouldn't hear of it. It was Kielwasser's job to help revive Bartenheim's economic life under the Reich, he said, and Kielwasser reluctantly agreed. Like two-thirds of the mayors in Alsace-Lorraine, he stayed at his post. "Faced with a ferocious, sly, determined and brutal adversary, my father had to develop a simple and effective strategy," his son Marcel later wrote. "Pretend to agree with the party's decisions while torpedoing them." It was the only way to shield the village from its occupiers, Kielwasser said. But it put him in an impossible position. Some villagers would scorn him for collaborating; some Germans would suspect him of double-dealing; and the rest would never know for certain who was right.

·   ·   ·

Karl must not have known what to make of him. Was the mayor German or French? Nazi or Socialist? Did he keep his position in good faith, or just to subvert it? Kielwasser cut an odd figure in town, with his diminutive frame and lopsided features. But he and Karl were also eerily similar. They were both German at birth and spoke kindred dialects. Both came from humble stock—Kielwasser's father sold coal from a horse-drawn cart—and rose to authority by dint of their intelligence and drive. Both wore glasses and had no right eye. They looked nothing alike, yet when they ran into each other on the street, Karl must have had an uneasy feeling that he was looking in a mirror.

The stories the townspeople told about the mayor all seemed to contradict one another. Did he hide the town's most valuable French books to save them from the Nazi bonfires? Or did he toss them into the flames, shouting, "Out with this French filth, we're Germans and we'll stay that way"? Did he work the back channels to find extra funds for the villagers, or did he keep them for himself and his relatives? One minute, you would see Kielwasser hunkering down with local men at a café, muttering Alsatian jokes under his breath. The next, he was standing up at a party meeting, delivering a toast to National Socialism in impeccable German.

That first winter of the occupation, Kielwasser and his family would often listen to *Radio Londres,* as the BBC was known in France. They particularly liked a show called *Les Français parlent aux Français*—The French Speak to the French. It brought news from the front, speeches by Charles de Gaulle, and commentaries by Maurice Schumann, whose father hailed from Alsace—all of it punctuated by coded messages to the French Resistance. The Germans tried to jam these broadcasts by flooding the airwaves with signals on the same frequency. But reception was always good in Bartenheim: The Swiss transmitters were just across the border.

From time to time, other villagers would join the listening sessions. The group included Georges Kannengieser, a mason and restaurant owner who had helped rebuild the gym after it burned down, and Louis Obrecht, the teacher whom Karl had replaced as school principal. Kielwasser and Obrecht often met to discuss politics at the town hall, and pore over a pin map of the Allied and German positions. But Obrecht couldn't listen to the radio at home: His apartment was above the schoolhouse where Karl taught. So he would join the others at Kielwasser's house, sip a glass of kirsch or mirabelle, and settle in around the radio.

Karl knew what they were up to, more than one villager told me. It was hard to keep secrets in a town this small. In the spring of 1943, under direct orders from district command, he confiscated forty shortwave radios in Bartenheim. But until then, he feigned ignorance. If he did mention the broadcasts to Kielwasser, a familiar pantomime would ensue: a look of shock and affronted dignity from the mayor, followed by outraged denial. How could Herr Gönner accuse him of such a thing? It was the same with the black-market butchering that went on in town. On one occasion, a villager told me, Karl accosted Kielwasser with his eyebrows raised: "They've killed another pig illegally."

"No, no, Herr Gönner! That was a *Notschlachtung*—an emergency slaughter."

"There only seem to be *Notschlachtungen* around here."

If Nazi inspectors did happen to pay a visit, all evidence of wrongdoing would disappear. "The good thing about the Germans was that they always warned you that they were coming," Kielwasser's younger son, Gérard, told me, when I met him in Bartenheim.

Gérard was eighty-four. Small and self-contained like his father, he wore a white turtleneck sweater and gray vest and spoke in a low, creaking mumble. "The inspectors would say, 'Tomorrow we will come and take a look.' So the next day, when they arrived, the animals would all be there in good condition, and the inspectors would file a good report. My father and your grandfather knew the real story, but they didn't say anything."

Gérard's older brother, Marcel, thought of Karl and Kielwasser as implacable foes, engaged in a cat-and-mouse game. In his telling, Karl was like the sneering, unsuspecting Nazi commandants of American war movies, outmaneuvered at every turn. But to Gérard their relationship was more complicated than that. "Your grandfather was a National Socialist and my father was the opposite. They must have had some tense discussions, just for their ears," he said. "My father had a certain admiration for German order—*C'est clair, c'est nette*—but he didn't agree with Nazism at all. And your grandfather could have denounced my father a hundred times, and he never did."

It was a precarious pas de deux: each man both leading and following, accepting the other's lies while letting him know that he knew them to be false. When some local youths threw rocks at a portrait of Hitler in the gym, knocking it down and demolishing it, Kielwasser told Karl that it had fallen by accident. When Karl told Kielwasser that he had heard a villager got drunk and sang *La Marseillaise* in the street, Kielwasser asked him if he even knew the words to the song. One time, Gérard told me, Karl asked Kielwasser to move a bust of Hitler to the train station for a party meeting. Kielwasser complied but trundled it over in a manure cart. In each case, Karl never reported the incident. "They understood each other very well," Gérard said.

. . .

It couldn't last. Even the cleverest men couldn't survive for long playing both sides in a war. Their double game couldn't help but collapse
under its own contradictions. "During the occupation, administrators had the most to lose," Kielwasser would later say, in a speech to
the village on the occasion of his eightieth birthday. "To manage a
community under a hostile regime, to navigate between two oppos-
ing currents, to appear to observe regulations while acting against
them to protect local citizens—all this entailed a series of acts of
passive resistance, which caused ever greater difficulties for me."

Just how this happened wasn't clear to me until one afternoon in
Colmar, at the Archives du Haut-Rhin. My daughter Ruby was with
me that day. She had joined the rest of my family in Berlin that summer and had come to Alsace to help with my research. We had set up
a little assembly line at our table in the archive: While I pulled files
about the German occupation, she stood beside me and scanned
them with her phone. Ruby was a student of history like her
grandmother—she had just finished her sophomore year in college.
She loved leafing through the old letters and ration cards and faded
black-and-white photographs, but they didn't have the terrible po-
tency to her that they had to me. Ruby had spent her holidays surrounded by the babble of her relatives' Allemannisch. She had
walked the trenches in Champagne with me, read accounts of Nazi
atrocities, and heard her grandparents' memories of the war. But she
was too removed from all those events to feel directly implicated by
them. They were Germany's inheritance, not hers.

Ruby had her own history to grapple with, as a white American
coming of age during the Black Lives Matter movement. But I envied her detachment from our family's past. It made me realize
something about Kielwasser. Like most Alsatians, he had been forced
to think of nationality as a contingent thing: German today, French
tomorrow. He just took that knowledge much further. If the other
villagers were good at playing roles, Kielwasser was a master at it.

When Ruby and I had packed up and lugged the last box of files to the front desk, the young archivist looked up in surprise. "You're leaving?" she said. "But you have another box to go through!" I stared at her blankly. I hadn't ordered another box. "Yes, Monsieur Dreyer sent it up this morning," she said. "It's waiting for you."

Serendipity is the great redeemer of archival work—the flash of light after endless hours of murky slogging. It can seem inevitable in retrospect: the twist at the end of the story. But most of the time it never comes. In years of researching Karl's past, I had had one true stroke of luck: finding the archive in Aulfingen. This was my second.

At first glance, the files were more of the same: lists of taxes, road repairs, and indemnities for war damages, mostly from 1950 to 1962. But near the bottom of the box, I found a folder that seemed to be misplaced, stuffed with a thick sheaf of what looked like wartime correspondence. On closer inspection, it was a series of letters between the mayor's office in Bartenheim and the Nazi leadership in Mulhouse, and later between Kielwasser and the French military government. There were lists of the town council members during the war and those who were purged from the council afterward, descriptions of Nazi events that Kielwasser organized and grievances filed against him by both the Nazis and local villagers. As I laid the pages on the table and Ruby scanned them, the war years in Bartenheim slowly came into focus. It was as if a hidden camera had been placed in Kielwasser's office.

•   •   •

His opening strategy was simple enough. In his reports to Nazi authorities in 1940 and 1941, Kielwasser played the collaborator with unstinting conviction. He signed his letters *Ortspropagandaleiter,* or town propaganda leader, and did his best to make Bartenheim sound like a model Nazi village. He described a ceremony "glorifying the invincible power of today's National-Socialist Germany." He requested "a large number of swastika flags of various sizes for an upcoming event, and several pictures of the Führer" for Bartenheim's party headquarters. He noted that the villagers had been told to cut up their French flags and use them as dishrags, and complained bitterly when only three boys showed up for a Hitler Youth meeting, while dozens of others stood laughing to the side. "If more stringent action isn't taken, our once-proud Hitler Youth and League of German Girls, whose numbers have declined significantly of late, will disintegrate," Kielwasser wrote.

His son Marcel was the junior leader of the Hitler Youth, and Kielwasser's wife was the head of the National Socialist Women's League. This was purely for show, they later said. "It was a subtle yet risky game," as Marcel put it in his memoir. "It was called resistance." Yet Marcel, too, seems to have played his role with more zeal than strictly necessary. At one Hitler Youth meeting in 1941, he slapped two boys in the face when they failed to salute the Führer.

Marcel later denied this story. Even if it was true, the incident may have been just more misdirection—another diversion to help the village escape scrutiny. The folder in Colmar contained ample evidence for that view. For every letter that Kielwasser signed "Heil Hitler!" there was more than one from a villager attesting to the mayor's French patriotism, or to his good deeds on their behalf. "The man is a great friend to the French," an anonymous note to the Nazi authorities warned. "You need to throw him out."

In occupied France, every tale was double-sided, with a different ending depending on the teller. Yet the longer I looked at the files, the more a pattern seemed to emerge. Until 1942, Kielwasser's letters to Nazi authorities were enthusiastic, eager to please. Then his tone began to change. He grew defensive, self-justifying, theatrically aggrieved. "Yesterday, Saturday, I was called in to see District Propaganda Leader Rüger," Kielwasser wrote on December 20, 1942. "In his disclosures, I immediately recognized that a new attack had been launched against me. I stand accused of inactivity, as if it were my fault that Bartenheim no longer has a *Sturmabteilung*, Hitler Youth, or Women's League. . . . Such absurdities are hardly worth addressing."

Kielwasser went on to enumerate his efforts to build up the party and to recruit new donors and young followers. And then, with a mixture of self-pity and cunning, he resigned from his post. "You, Herr Landkommissar, know better than anyone how unenviable such a position is, especially in Bartenheim. You also know that I have no ambition to keep it. In order to eliminate all friction in the future, so as not to cause any harmful retroactive effects for the further expansion of the party, and to show that the mayor does not have his own party, I will withdraw completely from the administration and from politics. After careful consideration, I ask you to replace me as mayor."

The breaking point, Kielwasser's son Gérard believed, was when his father was told to wear a Nazi uniform. To Marcel, it was when he refused to sign an oath of loyalty to Hitler. Yet, from the evidence of his letters, the mayor had already begun to distance himself from the Nazis. The war was going badly for them. By late December 1942, the Battle of Stalingrad was almost lost. The Japanese had been defeated at Midway and Guadalcanal, and Kielwasser's zeal seemed to wane in direct relation with such defeats. "Kielwasser has lost his belief in the German victory," a local Nazi official later wrote.

This was the mayor's cleverest tactic, some villagers believed. He had always had a keen nose for politics. Now he knew just when and how to recalibrate his public image. He had to remind people that he was a French patriot.

·   ·   ·

Karl was being drawn in the opposite direction. As long as he was just the school principal, he could ignore Kielwasser's growing disdain for the party. But once he was appointed Bartenheim's party chief, in March of 1942, he answered directly to Nazi authorities in Mulhouse. It was no longer enough for him to give an occasional lecture on National Socialism. He had to oversee the party's activities in the village and carry out its orders.

As I was sifting through the archives in Colmar, I came upon some letters that Karl had written to his commanders in Mulhouse. Most were about ordinary bureaucratic matters, but one concerned Kielwasser. Dated January 30, 1943, it left no doubt about Karl's opinion of the mayor. The two may have come to an understanding on how and when to enforce the rules. But Karl couldn't abide Kielwasser's opportunism, his wavering allegiance.

"It's high time that we did some good work here," he wrote to Mulhouse. "The entire municipal administration should be removed from office. It is understandable that these men, who have made every effort to keep the French spirit alive in the community, were kept on by the German administration in 1940. . . . But they don't mean to be honest with us. They take advantage of their positions and play us for fools."

Had the war ended then—had the French liberated Bartenheim that winter, instead of a year later, and tied Karl to a tree to await execution—it's unlikely anyone would have vouched for him. He was a good teacher, by all accounts, but still led the Hitler Youth. He turned a blind eye to a few illegal activities, but let the villagers know he was watching. He was willing to overlook Kielwasser's double-dealing, but only to a point. He was still a loyal member of the Reich.

Four months after Karl sent his letter to Mulhouse, the mayor was relieved of his duties and sent to work in a factory in Weil. In his memoir, Marcel implied that this was hard labor: The factory machined parts for the war effort. But by his father's own account he was just an office worker there. Kielwasser went on to found a machining business of his own, which made his fortune. The man always landed on his feet.

Back in Bartenheim, a local farmer named Eugène Liebis was installed as the new mayor, but Karl now held most of the power in the village. The question was what he would do with it.

14

TRAITOR

IT WAS IN THE FALL OF 1943, BEFORE MY MOTHER'S WORLD collapsed around her, that she went to Alsace with her father for the first and only time. She had just turned eight that June but had known for a while that something wasn't right. She was used to her father being gone. Every Saturday morning for three years, she had waited for him to come home to their apartment in Weil. And every Sunday afternoon, she had watched him climb on his bicycle, strap his leather satchel across his shoulders, and pedal back across the river to Bartenheim. But now he was gone for weeks at a time, just when the family needed him most. Her mother always seemed so anxious, and there was less and less to eat—you had to have a special card just to get food. One morning, Gernot and Sigmar were bring-ing milk jugs back from the store, swinging them by their handles in big circles, when one of the lids popped off and the milk flew out. She would never forget her mother's face when Gernot told her— how she sat down on the steps and cried.

Their apartment in the old Bläserhof still seemed like paradise, with its musty barns and secret attics, its courtyard filled with clouds of red and white chestnut blossoms. Even the basement, where they hid when the sirens went off, was beautiful: cool and airy with high white Gothic arches. But she no longer believed it could protect her. Twice in the past four years she had been told to hurry up and pack her things; the enemy was coming. The last time, in May of 1940, it seemed like half of Germany was going with them. The Wehrmacht were invading France, people said, and the French might send bombs across the river in retaliation. Three months later, her family was back in the Bläserhof, but she never truly felt safe there again.

She knew things that she wasn't supposed to know. She was small and quiet, her nose always buried in a book. People sometimes forgot she was there. They were always saying that a new world was coming. That Germany was invincible. On parade days, all the houses flew flags and the streets were filled with people in uniform, marching around singing the Horst-Wessel Lied. But if the Germans were winning, why did her parents look so worried? Why were they fighting so much? She remembered one night when she was six, sitting with her father while he listened to the radio in the living room. When the announcer said that Hitler had invaded the Soviet Union, her father shook his head and turned off the dial. "*Jetzt hen mir de Krieg verlore,*" he said. Now we've lost the war.

Years later, when my mother remembered that terrible autumn, she wondered why her father chose that moment to take her to Alsace—to show her the life he left his family for every week. Why did he make her sit in that classroom in Bartenheim, surrounded by all those children she didn't know, and ask her a question she couldn't answer? Why did he make her fail him? She didn't know it then, but things were going from bad to worse in the war. A third of a million German soldiers had died in Stalingrad, and Axis forces had been routed in Egypt and Sicily. German U-boats were being sunk by the score in the Atlantic, and Allied air raids were battering Hamburg and Berlin. In the city of Kassel, in north-central Germany, the bombing would trigger a firestorm that would burn for seven days. The hinge of fate, as Churchill later wrote, had clearly turned.

Maybe Emma was sick that week and needed Karl to take my mother off her hands. Maybe Karl hoped that the villagers, seeing him with his daughter, would realize that he was more than an administrator. Or maybe he just needed some company. The two of them had always had an unspoken bond, a kinship of mind. In that final year of the occupation, when Karl's authority was slipping with each new report from the front, it must have been a comfort to feel her watchful eyes upon him as he taught. To know that at least one person saw him as a father and not just a Nazi.

·   ·   ·

The war was closing in. When Karl first came to Bartenheim in the fall of 1940, Alsace was hours from the front and Hitler's murderous obsessions were focused elsewhere. The minutes from town council meetings were yawningly mundane in those days, but they grew more unsettling by the year. "The undersigned, farmer Josef Keiflin in Bartenheim, asks that his son, Grenadier Kamill Keiflin, be granted agricultural leave to bring in the hay harvest," one petition read. "My farm is twenty-one acres in size and has been managed by my wife and me since my son was drafted. We have another twenty-two-year-old son, but an accident has made him a complete invalid and he must be cared for. I myself have had a bladder disease for several weeks and am unable to work."

Karl signed the request and stamped it. Early in the war, Bartenheim had been a place where minor requests could be granted and transgressions swept under the rug; where you could look the other way. But no longer. As Nazi Party chief, Karl reported directly to officials in Mulhouse. He was the local leader of the German war effort, even as that effort was starting to fall apart. In September of 1943, the Italians surrendered to the Allies. By June, the Americans would be in Normandy. The dictates of occupation—which words to use, books to read, hats to wear—were growing more ruthless, desperate. Women and children were being sent to dig trenches, young men of sixteen to fight on the Eastern Front. And the penalty for refusal was death.

·   ·   ·

Late one night, Karl was walking home from the school when a dark figure stepped out from the shadows. Karl couldn't see his face, but he recognized the tall, lanky shape. It was Georges Tschill, the wheelwright who lived behind the schoolhouse. He was getting ready to break the law. "I had a milk bottle in my pocket and was going to get a farmer I knew to fill it," Tschill told my mother, in the interview she videotaped in Bartenheim in 1992. Like meat and grain, milk was strictly rationed in wartime Alsace, and Tschill knew that he had been caught red-handed. "So I walked over and tapped him on the shoulder and said, 'Herr Gönner, if I were a bad person, I would have struck you dead with this bottle just now, and nobody would have been the wiser.'"

Karl took a long draw on his cigarette. He and Tschill hadn't spoken much before, but they often saw each other in the neighborhood and they knew each other by reputation. Tschill was the closest thing in Bartenheim to a neutral party. He was neither a Red nor a Black, Francophile nor Germanophile. But when he didn't agree with something, he said it, and his word carried weight. Before the

war, Tschill seemed to be everywhere at once, whether making sets
for the theater or rebuilding the gym and church when they burned
down. After the war, he was the villager most often cited as a character witness. Everyone seemed to want him on their side. While the
Germans had forced many Alsatians to change their names—René
Kielwasser went by Renatus—Tschill had stayed stubbornly the
same. "*Tschill isch Tschill*," his son, Jean-Georges, told me.

Karl didn't know Tschill well, but he had heard that the Alsatian
had done good work for the Wehrmacht when ordered. Tschill had
even taken one of Karl's German teachers, Frau Ruff, as a boarder.
"I'm just here to do my duty, Herr Tschill," Karl told him that night
on the street. "But it's true, I've been told a few times that you have
some anti-German attitudes." Tschill laughed and shook his head.
"I'm not anti-German. I have German blood and I speak the German language. Maybe not very well—I was only in school for three
years—but that doesn't matter. I'm German and I'll stay German. I
just can't stand the German system."

Karl turned to go. He had too much on his mind to worry about
a bottle of milk and a wheelwright's politics. But Tschill stopped
him. Something about the schoolteacher's expression—his weary
forbearance—must have encouraged him. "I want to tell you something," Tschill said. One of his most dependable carpenters, Henri
Schmitt, was being held at the internment camp in Schirmeck, in
northern Alsace, eighty miles from Bartenheim. It was Schmitt's
own fault, Tschill said. He was a good, dependable worker, but he'd
been mouthing off for weeks. Tschill had told him to hold his tongue,
but Schmitt couldn't help himself. One night, a few weeks earlier,
Schmitt was wandering around town half drunk when he started
shouting at the police on the street. He was loyal to France, he said,
and didn't mind if English planes were bombing Germany. Now
Schmitt was locked up at the camp, terrified he would never come
home.

Would Karl be willing to vouch for him in a letter? If he did, the commandant of the camp might let Schmitt go.

.   .   .

On a smoke-gray morning in late November, as banks of fog clawed up the slopes of the Vosges, I drove north along the Rhine to see the camps at Schirmeck and Natzweiler-Struthof. When I left Bartenheim, night still clung to the fields. Now the sun hung dim and woozy above the horizon, reluctant to get up. The road ran through rich bottomlands for the first hour, then veered west into the mountains, toward one of the loveliest landscapes in France.

It was a heartbreaking trip. Stands of spruce, pine, hemlock, and ash climbed up the passes, along the same path that tens of thousands of prisoners once took. It must have been a torture to them, peering through the slats of the trucks at this view: deep green valleys and tumbling river gorges, graceful bridges and houses perched above wooden waterwheels. One last look at all that was beautiful before it was snatched away.

Schirmeck was a reeducation camp. Located in a town of almost three thousand, it was where recalcitrants and loose talkers were sent to be remade into proper Germans. Natzweiler-Struthof had no such purpose. It was a death camp. Built in 1941, on a ridge high above Schirmeck, at twenty-six hundred feet, it was surrounded by two barbed-wire fences, one of them electrified. A garrison of SS Death's Head guards oversaw its prisoners as they chiseled granite from a nearby quarry or built munitions for the German war effort. In 1943, a gas chamber was added to one of the camp's dormitories.

In all, more than fifty-two thousand prisoners passed through Struthof, as Alsatians call it. Eighty-three of them were children, the youngest eleven years old. Some twenty thousand died. Many were members of the Resistance who were "disappeared" from French villages through Hitler's "Night and Fog" campaign. (The phrase came from Wagner's *Das Rheingold,* where it is muttered by the dwarf Alberich as he puts on a magic helmet to turn invisible.) Among the prisoners were a group of Roma transferred from Auschwitz and eighty Jews whose skeletons were sent to the University of Strasbourg after they were killed. The bones were supposed to demonstrate their racial inferiority. Other inmates were subjected to medical experiments with typhus, yellow fever, and phosgene gas.

Struthof was built to be inescapable. Stranded high on a mountain road, exposed to icy winds in the winter and relentless sun in the summer, it offered only one way in and one way out. The prisoners' barracks clung to the shoulder of a mountain, wreathed in mist, surrounded by forested slopes like palisades.

On the afternoon of August 4, 1942, an Alsatian named Martin Winterberger and four other prisoners, two of them dressed in stolen SS uniforms, commandeered a vehicle and drove through the camp gate under cover of a storm. With Winterberger as a guide, they abandoned the car and hiked deep into the Vosges, only to be stopped by a French patrol. Fortunately, one of the patrolmen recognized Winterberger as a local and let the runaways go. Four of them eventually made it to freedom; the fifth was caught, tortured, and hanged.

There would be no more escapes.

. . .

The Struthof gates still look as they once did: barbed wire and weathered timbers surmounted by a crude sign, stenciled in black and white: KONZENTRATIONSLAGER NATZWEILER-STRUTHOF. When I arrived at the camp, a line of cars and limousines was parked along the road and in a lot above the entrance. It was the seventy-fifth anniversary of Struthof's liberation, in November 1944, and a number of dignitaries were scheduled to speak, including the American ambassador to France. Rows of chairs had been set in front of the gate, facing a podium to the left and a military band to the right. A marble monument rose behind them, twisting into the sky like a white flame.

I took a seat behind an elderly man hunched over in a wheelchair in the front row. He was wearing a woolen cap and a striped scarf and had a gray blanket draped over his knees—the damp cold sank into your bones up here. I watched as a stream of guests came over to pay their respects, then I leaned over and asked what had brought him to the ceremony. His name was Pierre Rolinet, he said. He was ninety-seven years old and had first seen the camp on April 14, 1944. He was one of its last living survivors.

During the war, Rolinet belonged to a Resistance group in the village of Glay, an hour west of Bartenheim on the Swiss border. In the fall of 1943, he and seven comrades were captured by the Germans while transporting arms. Rolinet was imprisoned in Montbéliard and Besançon and condemned to death that winter, only to be sent to Struthof instead. He was twenty-one years old. "The camp we had entered was a kind of hell, punctuated by beatings and curses," Rolinet told us, in a raspy but still strong voice, when he came to the podium. "To obey without reacting, to be reduced to the level of beasts through torture, hunger, and disease, to have your name replaced by a number and exist at the mercy of SS and capos. . . . As prisoners, we glimpsed man in all his suffering, but also in all his dignity."

The American ambassador, Jamie McCourt, strode to the podium next, her angular frame wrapped in a puffy black overcoat. She peered at the crowd with a coiled impatience, as if waiting for her prey to be flushed from cover, then dove into her speech. When she was a girl, she said, her family lived in a neighborhood of Jewish immigrants in Baltimore. Her parents, too, were Jewish (her maiden name was Luskin), and her father used to always tell her to take time to speak with anyone who had numbers tattooed on their arm. She talked about the attack on the Tree of Life synagogue in Pittsburgh a year earlier, in which eleven worshippers were killed during Shab-bat morning services. "The question is not how can this happen, but how can we prevent it from happening again?" she said.

Afterward, a bugler played taps, and a children's choir sang a glum, half-hearted version of *Le Chant des Partisans:* "Friend, do you hear the black flight of crows over our plains?" Then the crowd hur-ried off to the museum for cake and tea. Along the way, I was intro-duced to Robert Steegmann, the foremost historian of the camp. He smiled thinly when he heard that I wrote for *The New Yorker.* "It's readable," he allowed, "unlike most American publications." The ambassador's speech had gotten on his nerves, he said. Her accent was terrible, her words full of paranoia and self-interest—"*cet esprit Trumpiste.*" Listening to her was like having a choker tightened around his neck, he said, then swept off to the museum with his entourage.

I turned for a last look at the camp gates. Pierre Rolinet was nearby, making his way through the crowd in his wheelchair. Noth-ing could detract from the mere sight of him there, alive, in this place that had killed so many. When he first arrived at Struthof seventy-five years earlier, the SS guards told him, "You came in through the gate, but you'll leave by the chimney." Yet here he was. "That was the one flaw in the concentration camp system," he had said in his speech, "the only unforeseen element in this hyperorganized world: that people could stay human in the midst of this degradation. And that some of them could survive."

·   ·   ·

Three days after Karl first met Georges Tschill, Henri Schmitt was released from Schirmeck. Karl had sent a note to the camp's com-mandant, as Tschill requested. Something about Tschill's blunt, un-apologetic manner—the simple humanity of his appeal—must have cut through all the role-playing and double-dealing of those years. He and Tschill weren't so different after all. From then on, the two men formed a tacit alliance, picking up where Karl and Mayor Kielwasser had left off. While Tschill worked behind the scenes, knowing that Karl wouldn't expose him—at one point, Tschill hid a fugitive in his house half a block from the schoolhouse—Karl appealed to party officials on the villagers' behalf. He sent letters for those who had been arrested for anti-German sentiment or for trying to evade the draft through self-mutilation. He wrote for those who had had their businesses closed or apartments sealed for political reasons, and for a barber and his wife who had been caught fleeing for Switzerland.

The more Karl wrote, the more he came to think of himself as the village intercessor—interpreting the commandments sent down from Mulhouse and trying to deflect their harsher judgments. "For two and a half years, I was responsible for two thousand people," he would later recall. "That was my happiest, if also most difficult time." He was like a sleepwalker, he wrote, letting his own family fade into the background as he tried to follow "the hard path of duty"—to carry out his orders without violating his conscience. Emma came to resent it, but he felt that he had no choice. "Those people over there were lost between fronts. They needed support."

Most of what Karl could offer were small mercies: fines avoided, loose talk ignored. Bartenheim was just a small village, far from the war's great calamities. Yet lives were at stake even here. In four years of German occupation, no one from Bartenheim was sent to Struthof, nor to Buchenwald or any other death camp. No families were deported, no political prisoners executed. (The one villager who was sent to Germany, because her husband had tried to escape the draft, was brought back with Karl and Kielwasser's help.) In the postwar reports from some nearby towns that I found in Colmar, the appendices were filled with grim accounting: numbers exiled, numbers imprisoned, numbers gassed, disappeared, or shot by a firing squad. But in a region crosshatched by cruelty, Bartenheim was a blank spot. A hole in the fabric.

Size and isolation had something to do with this. The largest towns in occupied Alsace—those closest to Nazi headquarters or military targets—often suffered most. In Lutterbach, three miles west of Mulhouse, thirty-four people were exiled and thirty-six sent to concentration camps. In Bourtzwiller, less than two miles to the north, nine were executed and twenty-six drafted into the SS. Meanwhile, in the tiny village of Magstatt-le-bas, four miles west of Bartenheim, only a few families were deported to Germany after their sons escaped to Switzerland to evade the draft. "The War ended without notable incidents," the mayor reported. "The occupation passed quietly and everyone did their work."

But isolation can also bring out the worst in people. Party chiefs like Karl were often petty tyrants. They were so low in the Nazi hierarchy that they drew only part-time pay for their work. Yet they had the power of life and death over villagers. "They had a bad reputation, those party chiefs," Karl's nephew, Gerhard Blessing, told me. "If someone didn't show up for a work detail, they could put them on a train to a camp the next day." When Karl came to the Black Forest to see relatives, Gerhard recalled, he kept his distance from those men. "They would all go drinking together, but he would eat by himself. He didn't want to identify with them."

The village of Rosenau, three miles east of Bartenheim, was a good example of how such men could subjugate a town. According to the postwar report from the village, the mayor, Auguste Waltzer, was an Alsatian Autonomist turned fanatical collaborator. Within days of the German occupation, he had his nephew appointed party chief, his brother-in-law director of human services, and his wife a schoolteacher, though she hadn't taught in twenty years. In this way, the report noted, "the Waltzer family took all the cogs of municipal administration in hand, and used them to destroy all French sentiment in the population and to exert a tyrannical pressure and terror on the inhabitants."

Rosenau went on to be named a model Nazi community ("Sad title!" the report writer noted). Every so often, the mayor and Ortsgruppenleiter would make the rounds of the village to see which families were flying swastikas. Those who didn't, or who refused to join the party or participate in its meetings, were fined or denied welfare or fertilizer allotments. "*Du machst nicht mit, es kann Dir nicht geholfen werden,*" they were told. You don't join in, so you can't be helped. In December 1940, the Goetschy family, with seven children and an eighth on the way, was expelled from the village, their furniture confiscated and sold. The following year, the Ortsgruppenleiter denounced the brothers Emile and Oscar Biry for anti-Nazi sentiments and they were sent to the camp at Schirmeck. By 1943, a long list of local families had been drawn up for deportation. Only the liberation of Alsace saved them.

The occupation in Bartenheim had all the same trappings—parades and swastikas and party meetings—but with fewer consequences. In Bartenheim, a handful of boys joined the Hitler Youth while the rest made catcalls from the sidelines; in Rosenau, the group's ranks were almost full. While villagers in Rosenau were being exiled or sent to Schirmeck, Karl was writing letters to have villagers released.

All told, five men from Bartenheim were interned at the camp, and one of them also at Dachau. All five came home. Even in Nazi territory, Karl could still walk back a few villagers' words or minor transgressions. What he couldn't do was shield them from war.

•   •   •

A hundred and thirty thousand men from Alsace and neighboring Moselle were drafted into the German army in the Second World War. Strictly speaking, this was illegal: The Hague Convention forbade armies from conscripting civilians from occupied territories. But of course, to Hitler's mind, Alsace wasn't occupied territory. It was and always had been part of Germany. The Nazis knew that Alsatians were at best ambivalent about being German, and most were French patriots. When they conscripted men from the region, they sent them as far from home as possible, to keep them from deserting. Eighty percent went to the Russian Front; thirty-eight thousand never returned. For the rest, it was the worst of both worlds. Young Alsatian men not only had to fight for the enemy, they had to do so on the world's most dangerous battlefields. They called themselves *Les Malgré-nous:* the Despite Ourselves.

"My grandfather was French and imprisoned by the Prussians in 1870," one conscript from Lorraine later wrote. "My German father was imprisoned by the French in 1918. Me, I'm French, and I was imprisoned by the Germans in 1940, drafted by force into the Wehrmacht in 1943, and imprisoned by the Russians in 1945. You see, sir, we have a very particular sense of history: We are always on the wrong side of it. When there's a war, we always end up in prison clothes. It's our only permanent uniform."

One day, Gabriel Arnold showed me a list of the men drafted from Bartenheim—152 in all. "Most of them were conscripted by force," the deputy mayor said. "If there were any volunteers, no one ever spoke of it." The Wehrmacht began with twenty-two- to twenty-six-year-olds in August of 1942, then turned to younger and older men as the war went on. By September of 1944, all men between ages sixteen and sixty had been declared eligible for conscription. Arnold's father fled to Mont-de-Marsan, in southwestern France. His uncle Martin went to Algeria and joined the Free French Forces under General Tassigny. His uncle Joseph stayed in Bartenheim, was drafted and sent to Russia, and ended up in Tambov, the infamous Russian prisoner-of-war camp. "The Russians were even worse than the Germans," Arnold said. "He survived, but for a long time nobody talked about what happened to him."

The more urgently the Germans needed men, the more likely those men were to die in the field, and the more desperate they were to avoid conscription. By one count, as many as forty thousand Alsatians fled to France and Switzerland. Others had to be more inventive. Robert Wagner, the Nazi leader of Alsace, had instituted a system of *Sippenhaft,* or collective punishment: Whole families could be deported if any of their members committed a crime. This gave would-be draft evaders no choice but to stay home and get conscripted, or try to get the Wehrmacht to reject them.

Arnold's uncle Jean went shirtless in the winter, hoping to get pneumonia. He covered himself in coats and sweaters so he would overheat and look like he had a fever. But he never got sick and the soldiers came for him one evening. Marcel Kielwasser, the mayor's son, considered half a dozen stratagems. He could flee to Switzerland, have a friend break his arm, or get some surgery done—a gynecologist he knew had put him in touch with a surgeon who offered to remove his appendix. But the first option would endanger his family, and the others would buy only a little time. Luckily, his father had ingratiated himself with a secretary in the local war office. Kielwasser would bring him an occasional gift of eggs, rabbits, chickens, or ham, and the secretary would let him know whenever draft notices were going out. If Marcel was on the list, he would change addresses so the notices never reached him.

Others weren't so clever nor so connected. Some Bartenheimers hid in basements or barns or threw themselves off rooftops to break their own limbs. Others claimed disabilities of various sorts: "If we are to believe the census figures for those unfit for military service," one commentator wrote after the war, "there were four times as many mental deficients in Alsace as in Baden, and twice as many men with tuberculosis." Marcel's second cousin, Charles Kielwasser, stuck his foot under the wheel of a harvest wagon loaded with beets. Then he did it again for good measure. When doctors in Strasbourg examined him later, they declared the break self-inflicted—how else could the wagon have gone over the same foot twice?—and Charles was imprisoned. Once healed, he was drafted by the SS and sent to Normandy, where he deserted and was recaptured. He was slated for execution when the Americans freed him. Another cousin shot himself in the thigh near Leningrad. He was on his way home on a German hospital ship when the Soviets torpedoed it as it crossed the Baltic Sea. But he managed to escape on a lifeboat and make his way to Denmark, where he stayed until the end of the war.

They were the lucky ones. Forty-one of Bartenheim's *Malgré-nous* never came home. Many of the rest were physically and psychologically ravaged, especially those captured by the Russians. Tambov lay three hundred miles southeast of Moscow, surrounded by swamps and birch forests. More than twenty-four thousand men died there of hunger, cold, disease, and exhaustion. "The days began with the burial of friends who had died in the night," Marcel later wrote, recalling what one of his friends told him after returning from the camp. "Heaped onto dozens of carts drawn by cadaverous men who were themselves exhausted and often had only a few days to live, then thrown into mass graves dug in frozen ground. . . . Then it was back to forced and demented labor, to cabbage water offered as soup and a hunk of bread if there was any. Yes, Tambov, the horror of those who passed the hardest hours of their lives there remains etched in the memory of a whole generation of Alsatians."

The Alsatian prisoners should have been sent home, since they had been drafted by the Germans illegally. For a time, after petitions from General de Gaulle and other Allied leaders, the Soviets did separate out some Alsatians and release them. (To tell them apart from Germans, Marcel was told, the Soviets sometimes showed them an umbrella and asked what it was; the Germans would say *Regenschirm*, the Alsatians *parapluie*.) But as the war dragged on, they stopped making distinctions and imprisoned them all.

.   .   .

Karl knew what awaited the *Malgré-nous*. To send a soldier to Russia was as good as a death sentence. And he knew these boys. By the time the Alsatian draft began in the summer of 1942, Karl had lived in Bartenheim for nearly two years. He had taught its students and discussed them with their parents. He had had cups of coffee with farmers, carpenters, merchants, officials, and construction workers. He had heard Frau Schöpfer's gossip as she served him dinner or his one egg in the morning. The villagers wanted no part of this war. To force their sons to fight for Germany was unjust, and many would never come home. This they all knew.

Karl could tell who was fit to serve and who was not; who was faking an injury and who was hiding in a barn. "He used to say, 'If I reported all the people who broke rules in Bartenheim, half the village would be deported,'" François Grienenberger, the village priest, told me. Still, it was one thing to ignore an illegal hog killing; another to interfere with the war effort. If word got out that a young man was hiding from the draft, the authorities would send a military detachment to find him and encircle his family's house with barking dogs.

Karl had come to a crossroads. He could give the draftees away or help them stay hidden. One way would risk their lives; the other way would risk his. Undermining the occupation was a grave offense. "*Feind hört mit!*" the black silhouettes on storefronts warned. The enemy is listening. But colluding with draft dodgers was a capital crime. Any German caught doing so could be unceremoniously shot. The Gestapo's investigations reached into "the very bosom of the family," a report from Mulhouse later noted. "The slightest gesture seemed to be under surveillance." And yet, by risking the Gestapo's wrath, Karl wound up saving his own life.

One afternoon in the fall of 1944, Karl was in the neighboring village of Blotzheim, when he ran into Georges Tschill. In my mother's video of Tschill years later, this was his most revealing story—the one that showed the men's trust in each other and their necessary caution. When Karl greeted him in his usual way—"Tschill, what's new?"—the Alsatian shook his head. He knew how close they were to the end of the war. He had contacts in the Resistance and a whisper network throughout the region. "I've told you before, the French are coming, and the English and Americans, too," Tschill said. Then he smirked and added, "If you want to give me up to the Germans, you can, but you don't have much time."

Karl laughed, but Tschill was only half joking. For two years, Karl had been the most powerful figure in Bartenheim. If he never seemed to abuse that authority—and sometimes even used it to protect people—he was still the ruling hand of the Nazi Party. The villagers had no choice but to submit to his orders. What would they do when the tables were turned?

"I need to ask you, because it's come to this," Tschill said, fixing Karl with a hard stare. "Do you have anything on your conscience?" If Tschill was going to stick his neck out for this German, he needed to make sure the man was worth it. "Have you killed anyone or done anyone harm?" Karl shook his head. "Okay then, I'll help you. If they put you in prison, call me. And if someone comes to you and says, 'Tschill sent me,' go with them. That's when you should leave."

·   ·   ·

On the evening of November 19, 1944, the villagers of Bartenheim were cooking their Sunday dinners when the road began to quake outside. A platoon of tanks and armored trucks was rolling down the main road, led by Lieutenant Jean Carrelet de Loisy. They bore the double cross of Lorraine, symbol of the Free French Forces. The day before, de Loisy's squadron had left the area of Blamont, forty miles to the west, with orders to fight their way through German forces until they reached the Rhine. After brief skirmishes in the villages of Seppois and Bisel, they found only clear road and abandoned countryside ahead. By the time they reached Bartenheim, it was dusk and they were hurtling full throttle toward the river, headlights flaring. They were the first French army to reach the Rhine.

They were a little ahead of themselves. Although the Germans had retreated north for the moment, they were far from ready to cede the territory. Four days later, Lieutenant de Loisy would lose his life to a tank shell in Mulhouse, and Nazi forces would hold on to the "Colmar Pocket" in central Alsace deep into the winter. Still, on that evening in November when de Loisy's squadron came barreling through, the people of Bartenheim considered themselves free. "What's that noise?" Alphonse Huttenschmitt, who was seventeen at the time, remembered his mother saying. Then he ran into the street and saw a row of tanks. "Someone said, 'They aren't French! They can't be French! *You* ask them, since you speak the language.' So I said, '*Êtes-vous de la première armée française, ou êtes-vous des allemands?*' And they said, '*Ah non!* We're French. We're the liberators!' And everyone started to cheer."

That same afternoon, Karl gathered his things in Weil and prepared to cross the Rhine, perhaps for the last time. He had known for a while that the French were coming. It was the reason he was away from home for weeks at a time that fall. The Nazis were losing their grip on Alsace. Half the time, Karl was fielding desperate work orders from Mulhouse; the rest of the time he was placating the villagers or writing appeals on their behalf. "*Alles ging bachab*," as my mother put it, when we were visiting Bartenheim. Everything was going to hell.

The Tschills had invited us for lunch that Sunday, at the chalet that Jean-Georges had built for their retirement, north of town. Afterward, we sat on the porch and watched their grandchildren play in the yard, and my mother began to talk about the fall of 1944. She remembered her father coming home from France one day with a package on the back of his bicycle. It was full of doll furnishings: a dresser, table, and four chairs, all beautifully carved from mahogany by a woodworker in Bartenheim. "Oh Karl, those are too expensive," her mother said. "At least wait and give them to her at Christmas." The toy furniture cost thirty marks—half a month's rent—but Karl insisted. Edeltraut should have them now, he said. "Who knows what Christmas will bring?"

When word finally came that the French were in Alsace, Emma pleaded with Karl to stay home. But he couldn't be swayed. It may be that he was driven by a last vestige of party loyalty, or by an urge to face judgment. Or perhaps, as Emma later explained to my mother, he hoped to shield the villagers from the Nazis' parting cruelties. "I can't leave those people in the lurch," he told her. Whatever the reason, it was an amalgam of conscience and misguided duty, like everything he had done in Alsace.

Karl put on his uniform, climbed onto his bicycle, and waved goodbye to my mother and her brothers at the window. "I think he thought that he would die before the war was over," my mother said. "Either the Germans would kill him or the French would." As he was pedaling across the Rhine, Karl later told her, he stopped on the bridge and took out the pistol he had been issued as party chief. Then he tossed it into the river.

•   •   •

Lieutenant de Loisy's men were waiting on the other side. When Karl reached Rosenau, they arrested him, stripped off his shoes and socks, and marched him the three miles to Bartenheim. By the time they arrived at the main square, Karl's feet were torn and bloody. "He should never have come back," Gérard Kielwasser, the mayor's son, told me. The place was in an uproar. Some villagers were shouting in the street, delirious with joy; others sat at home with their head in their hands, flooded with relief, fear, or grief. "Everyone knew that the war wasn't over," as Marcel Kielwasser put it. "Some thought of their sons who would never return, others of those still engaged in bloody battles on the Russian front." The villagers who had bet on the wrong regime were terrified. Those who hadn't were enraged at what they had been forced to endure, and they took their vengeance where they could.

They began by gathering every picture and portrait, banner and bust of Hitler and tossing them in a pile to burn. Then they rounded up the most prominent Nazi collaborators and locked them in a barn. This was where the soldiers took Karl that evening. Eugène Liebis, the mayor who had replaced Kielwasser, was already inside along with a few others. They could smell the smoke in the streets outside and hear windows shattering. At the height of the frenzy, a local farmer named Würtlin grabbed Karl's landlady, Josephine Schöpfer, and dragged her to a restaurant near the center of town. Then he and others shaved her head and paraded her up and down the main street. "She hadn't done anything wrong," François Grienenberger told me with a weary frown. "She had only given your grandfather a room to rent, nothing more."

What happened next was the story that Georges Tschill told my mother, when they first met in Bartenheim. The soldiers unlocked the barn and marched the prisoners outside, then bound them to a large tree. The French collaborators were haggard with sleeplessness and dread. All of them had been party members and administrators under the occupation and were likely to be imprisoned for it. But Karl had much more to fear. Louis Obrecht, the schoolteacher and army veteran, was urging the soldiers to shoot him on the spot. The Germans had executed countless prisoners without a trial. Why treat this Nazi any differently? Karl was standing against the tree trunk, watching the soldier in front of him prepare to raise his gun, when Tschill's voice reached him: "What's going on here?"

Tschill had been walking across the square when he spotted the prisoners bound to the tree and the squadron chief heading toward them. "I said, wait a minute, this isn't right," he told my mother. He knew this man, Gönner. And as far as he knew—"And I know everything that happens in this town"—it was because of Gönner that no family from Bartenheim had been deported. That no one had died in a camp.

Tschill was not a man for speeches, but he spoke with a gruff force that brooked no argument. The soldiers glanced around at the other villagers, nodding or looking away, and slowly lowered their guns. Tschill had all the prisoners untied and taken into custody, then turned to the soldier in front of Karl. "Give him back his stockings and his shoes," he said. "Send him to a prison camp or somewhere. If he's guilty of something—if we find out that he's done anything bad to anyone—I'll be the first to let you know."

A week later, Karl was on a prison transport heading west. Alive.

15

PRISONER

PRISONER NO. 816922 ARRIVED AT DEPOT NO. 86 AT ARC-ET-
Senans on December 1, 1944. Two weeks later, he was transferred to
Depot No. 142 near the town of Pont d'Ain. His path took him
southwest along the Swiss border, down sinuous river valleys and up
forested slopes, high into the Jura Mountains. As he clattered from
camp to camp that winter, his view from the train was like a time-
lapse film of French history: from la Belle France of Courbet and
Pointelin, with its waterfalls and romantic overlooks, to blasted cities
and prison cells. After four years at the border, riven by ambivalence,
Karl was plunging into the country's bitter heart.

All around him, the war thundered on. It would be another five
months before Hitler shot himself in a bunker and the Germans surrendered unconditionally. More than a hundred prisoner-of-war

camps would spring up across France in that time, their inmates brought in by railcar and truck, beaten and spat upon along the way. Over a million German prisoners of war were detained in France between 1944 and 1948, and put to work rebuilding the places they had destroyed. They planted crops and dug tunnels, chiseled quarries, cleared land mines, and reconstructed bridges. Some prisoners wouldn't be released until late 1948, and more than forty thousand died.

Arc-et-Senans was one of France's former glories. Situated on the plains west of the Jura, the prison camp was housed in a former salt factory. Commissioned by Louis XV when salt was still traded like gold, its cavernous halls were designed by Claude Nicolas Ledoux, the famed architect of the Enlightenment. A great stone arch, fronted by Doric columns, greeted the prisoners when they arrived. Beyond it lay a luminous green pavilion encircled by what looked like Greek temples. The prisoners were held in two brick edifices, five stories high and 260 feet long, where enormous kettles of brine had once bubbled over open furnaces. Ledoux envisioned his Royal Saltworks as the centerpiece of a utopian village, arrayed on a semicircle like the sun's arc across the sky: the most beautiful factory in the world.

Karl must have felt like he had gone to Valhalla, but it was just a holding pen for beaten men. It was the same place where the Vichy regime had imprisoned more than two hundred Roma between 1941 and 1943. There was no glory in it, only misery. Soon he was back on a truck headed south, to a place more befitting his station.

·   ·   ·

Trundling along the same road three generations later, retracing Karl's path in my rental car, I wound down through the vineyards of the Côtes du Jura onto the plains of Bresse. As morning passed, the sun broke through in patches, illuminating hardwoods cloaked in ochre and rust. Here and there, an onion-domed church stood vigil on a hill.

I knew the names of Karl's camps from a pair of identity cards that the French Red Cross had sent me. The prisons themselves were long gone, I assumed, replaced by a strip mall or Monoprix. I should have known, by then, how tightly people hold on to their history—even the worst of it. Arc-et-Senans was the first surprise. I hadn't realized that the prison camp was in the royal saltworks, a UNESCO World Heritage site and one of the great monuments of French history. But Karl's next stop was less promising. Pont d'Ain was just a small town in Auvergne, unremarkable except for its excellent fishing. I had driven well past the city limits before I realized that I had arrived.

I was doubling back to make inquiries when I caught a glimpse of something off to the left, well away from the road. I followed the next turn behind some houses and there it was: the prison camp. Its abandoned barracks were arrayed on a field, their barred windows open to the wind and rain. I later learned that French Muslims had been detained there in the late 1950s, during the Algerian war for independence. A decade earlier, this was where Karl lived and nearly died.

What my mother knew about his time there was mostly written on his body: rail thin and wrung pale by fever when he came home a year later, bones jutting beneath his cheeks and chest. He never talked about the location of the camps or his journey there, across an enraged and unshackled country. The few stories he did tell all seemed to revolve around food. How little he was given. How he forced himself to take small mouthfuls and chew until nothing was left—a habit he passed on to my mother. How his hunger, desperate as it was, was nothing compared to the other prisoners' craving for cigarettes. So he traded the few he had for crusts of bread. Waves of dysentery swept through the camp, squeezing any last substance from the already withered men, till they were thin as broom handles.

More than sixteen thousand German prisoners died in French prisoner-of-war camps in 1945 alone. Karl could tell that a man was about to pass on when he quit washing himself, so he made sure to do so even when he could barely stand.

There is nothing so unnatural as a prison, nothing so inhuman as the logic of shutting people in cells. I thought of the twenty thousand prisoners who had been murdered by the Nazis at Natzweiler-Struthof. There was rough justice in the turnabout here—the perpetrators had become the prisoners. But it was hard to see the point of so much pain. Camps like this were brutally indiscriminate: war criminals, foot soldiers, and functionaries like Karl, all thrown into the same cells and meted out the same punishment. They were about vengeance more than justice.

The old washrooms were in ruins now, the prison cells covered in graffiti. Outside, the town had built a skate park where Karl and the other prisoners once lined up in the winter cold, quivering with illness. Inside, the broken walls were like an anarchist art exhibit, covered in curses, tags, and twisted cartoons, superheroes and psychedelic angels. THE WORLD BELONGS TO ME! one wall announced, next to a sketch of a barking policeman. I imagined the boys in cargo shorts and baggy shirts that came there now, vaulting off ramps with their long hair flying, and had to laugh. The place had a lawless energy— a cracked sense of fellow feeling—that seemed the perfect antidote to its bleak, unyielding history.

As I left the cells and stepped out into the open field, I saw that someone had marked the entrance in black spray paint: JUSTICE, it read. THE TIME OF OPEN HEARTS.

·   ·   ·

Two hundred miles to the northeast, Emma and the children were doing their own best to survive. The day after Karl was arrested in

Alsace, the French began to rain shells on the German towns across the Rhine. The bombardment continued at steady intervals from six that night until the next morning, blanketing Weil from the river to the Tüllinger Berg. It was a confirmation of all Emma's fears. Her husband was probably dead, and the enemy was coming. For the third time in five years, she made the children throw their clothes into suitcases and flee for the train station with her. Sigmar was thirteen, my mother nine, and Winfried barely six years old. They were heading to the Black Forest again to stay with Karl's relatives in Herzogenweiler, but this time they had no idea when they would be coming home—or what would be left when they did.

Gernot, the oldest, was off to war by then. He had been listening to illegal Swiss broadcasts about it for years, hiding under his bedcovers at night. He had joined the Hitler Youth and trained as a glider pilot, then fought with the Wehrmacht that spring. He was sixteen. "It's one of those moments I remember perfectly," my mother told me. "We were in the courtyard of the Bläserhof when they drafted him. How my mother cried! It was such insanity to take these young boys and make them go to school by day and shoot down planes by night." Gernot's *Gymnasium* was in Lörrach, north of Weil; his flak unit was stationed in Steinen, a four-mile walk east of the school. They were supposed to protect the canal locks from bombers, but Gernot was myopic like his sister and had to rely on a friend to guide his shots: "To the left! Now up a little!" His unit still managed to down four planes, but the memories that stayed with him were less than heroic. They pulled one English pilot from the Rhine, eels twined through his corpse. They dragged another from burning wreckage. Afterward, the boys roasted a wild rabbit for dinner. When Gernot tried to eat it, he threw up: The pilot's blood was still under his fingernails.

Gernot was part of the *Volkssturm*—the final uprising of citizens meant to bring German victory at last. But by mid-January the storm was already breaking, and the head of the flak unit told the boys to go home. Herzogenweiler was eighteen hours away on foot. The French had already crossed the border, and Gernot had nothing but a grenade in a shoulder bag to protect himself. When he stopped at a farmhouse to ask for food, the woman who came to the door took one look at his uniform and yanked him inside. Didn't he know that the French would shoot him on sight? She left him in the hall and came back a few minutes later with a shirt, a pair of pants, and a piece of bread spread with artificial jam. The clothes were her husband's, she said, before he went missing in the war. Then she shooed Gernot outside and locked the door.

When a French patrol stopped him a little later, it was the bread that saved him. "What's in the bag?" they wanted to know. Gernot hesitated, then reached in and pulled out his hand covered in jam. They laughed and drove off, and he threw the grenade into a field.

Herzogenweiler had long been the family refuge—a place out of time, safe from hunger and bombs. But when Gernot arrived two days later, an eerie silence hung over it. The men had all left for war, leaving only women, children, and a few grandfathers and invalids. Yet the fields still needed harvesting, the fences mending, the livestock herding and milking. Farms that usually kept a whole family working from dawn to dusk had to survive on half the labor. Gernot and his family were just more people to feed. My mother was staying with her cousin Hedwig; Emma and Winfried were with a family nearby, and Gernot joined Sigmar at Gerhard and Manfred's house. Gernot was so hungry by the time he came, and his aunt had so little food to spare, that he snuck into the barn when she wasn't looking. He opened a milk jug, stuck a piece of straw inside, and sucked just enough cream from the top that no one would notice.

·   ·   ·

That winter was one of the coldest in memory. My mother would lie awake in the early morning and think of her father. Where was he and when would he come home? Why didn't he write? Then she would watch the snow pile up to the windowsill, counting the minutes till her aunt stomped in and rousted her from bed. She had to milk the cows every morning and evening, watch the little ones, and help cook dinner. Her brothers would gather wood in the forest in the afternoon and bring it in by sled at night, their path lit by kerosene lamp. The next day, Gernot and Sigmar would chop the logs while Winfried hunted for eggs under the thresher and other spots that only his little hands could reach. With their father gone, Gernot tried to keep everyone in line, but they were too busy to cause much trouble. At night, the dishes done and potatoes on the stove for breakfast, they sat around the flickering firelight and told stories from before the war. But even then they were working—weaving, sewing, patching, and mending torn clothes. Hedwig's pants were made of pieces of repurposed carpet.

The village was as tightly wound as a cuckoo clock, my mother sometimes thought, its people popping in and out of doors and windows, repeating the same tasks on the same revolving schedule. Almost everything had to be done by hand, each chore leading to the next and the next and the next, in cycles within cycles. Every four weeks they did laundry, boiling the clothes in a tub as big as a cattle trough. Every two weeks they baked bread, mixing the *Mischbrot* in big bowls of rye, wheat, and spelt flour. They kneaded the dough, shaped it into huge round loaves, and slid them into the ashes of the wood-fired oven. When the loaves rang hollow, they set them to cool on boards, then hung them from the ceiling by chains to keep the mice away.

The war, meanwhile, ran on its own schedule. Surveillance planes passed overhead, bombs detonated in the distance and rumbled over the hills, and rumors of French advances skittered from house to house. Beginning in 1942, a ragged procession of prisoners of war made its way to Herzogenweiler as part of the *Arbeitseinsatz*—the Nazi forced-labor program. There were eight or nine of them when my mother arrived, between sixteen and eighteen years old: a Belgian, two Frenchmen, and several *Ostarbeiter*—"eastern workers" deported from occupied Ukraine. One of them was a girl named Olga. They stayed in barracks at the edge of town or lived with families and shared meals with them. A few of the Ukrainians grew so close to their keepers that they promised to write to them after the war, but not Olga. Her overseer was a *Sauhund,* Gerhard told me. He kept her locked up at night, barefoot even in winter, and beat her mercilessly. As for the French and Belgian prisoners, they vanished into the forest as soon as the Allies crossed the border.

The Black Forest had always been a closed, secretive world, its families interwoven for generations. But outsiders had begun to shoulder in and wrench it open. To my mother, as a child, the most memorable of the foreigners was her aunt Regina, the soothsayer. Stylish and beautiful, with long black hair and extravagant manners, Regina was from Transylvania, a part of Romania where ethnic Germans had lived since the twelfth century. Her husband was a foreman at a watch factory in Villingen and her father had made a small fortune in America, so she lived in fine style. Her house had running water—a rare luxury in Herzogenweiler—and she always wore dresses in the latest fashion, which she changed every afternoon. Tante Gini, as my mother called her, was unusually kind to her. She gave my mother a white dress for first communion, and taper candles wrapped with asparagus flowers cut from the garden. My mother would never forget the imperial bearing with which Regina swept down the staircase in her gown. But among the other women she could be an object of fear as well as fascination.

Regina had learned to tell fortunes in Transylvania and honed her skills in the war, when they were much in demand. With so many sons and husbands away from home, their fate suspended by a thread in the forests of Russia or the plains of Belgium, the wives and mothers of Herzogenweiler longed for any news at all, even from a soothsayer. Regina would read their palms or serve them coffee in her parlor, then peer at the grounds in the bottom of the cup. When she finally spoke, it was in dream images and darkly suggestive fragments, strangely spiced by her Romanian accent, with its hooded vowels and burred syllables. Even Karl, once so haunted by the spirit world, hadn't been able to resist going to see her when he was on leave from Alsace a few summers earlier. My mother, who had been allowed to tag along, watched as Regina took her father's cup and studied the patterns inside, then glanced up at him with startled, unfocused eyes. "I see you and your children," she said. "You can see them and hear them, but you can't go to them. Something is keeping you apart."

Tante Gini was just telling stories, Karl told my mother afterward. But she would remember her aunt's words years later, and wonder if they had come true after all.

.   .   .

The war had reached them at last. In that spring of 1945, when Hedwig and my mother walked to school in Pfaffenweiler, two miles to the east, they kept an ear cocked for a drone of engines. When a plane appeared above the trees, they scrambled into the ditch beside the road. Then they lay flat on their bellies, hands clamped over their ears, and waited for the roaring to stop. There were no military targets in Herzogenweiler, no munitions factories or heavy guns. But in the first flush of excitement over Hitler, a local farmer had painted a swastika on his roof. He tried to remove it later, when the French were drawing near, but the shadow of the symbol was still visible from the sky.

One afternoon in late April, my mother was feeding the chickens in the farmyard of Gerhard's house, when a terrible noise erupted behind her. The French were lobbing incendiary shells into Herzogenweiler from Villingen, five miles to the east. One of them tore through the roof of the house and exploded in the attached barn. Another struck the road in front of the neighbor's house, toppling the chimney and igniting the rafters inside. A soldier named Paul Treichel was in the house, sitting on a bench by the fireplace, and a one-year-old boy, Josef, was asleep in his crib. Treichel was struck dead instantly by shrapnel. The baby seemed unscathed, but the shockwave had damaged his hearing and his brain. He never learned to speak properly.

My mother stood frozen in the farmyard. She had been taught to run into the house in case of attack and hide in her aunt's bedroom. But what now? She didn't know where to turn. First she ran to the house next door and hid under a mattress with the neighbors. Then someone shouted that they should go to the Hirsche inn, which had a deep cellar, and soon they were all stampeding across the street, tumbling down the stairs in a ragged herd. A series of blasts shook the ground above them, and someone threw a blanket over them as they huddled in the dark. My mother could hear Sigmar moaning beside her, but she was sure he was faking it—just another one of his jokes. Then a candle was lit and she saw the blood. Sigmar had been sitting in the outhouse when the shell exploded, and the blast had sent a shard through the wall and into his left hand. It was a mangled mass of blood and bone.

When the bombing stopped and they emerged from underground, there was a ten-foot-wide crater in the street. Cows were bolting from burning sheds and a line of villagers was tossing water onto Gerhard's house, leaving the soldier's house to the flames. They could save only one. They took Sigmar to the schoolhouse, where some German soldiers wrapped a bandage around his hand. Then Emma sat him in a small wagon, grabbed the handle, and began to pull him to the hospital in Vöhrenbach. Thankfully, some soldiers stopped along the road and offered to drive them the rest of the way. They reached the hospital before nightfall.

Anesthesia was for only the severely wounded, Emma was told. The boy would just have to bear the pain. A doctor pulled the splinters of metal and bone from Sigmar's hand and set the shattered fingers as best he could. They would be twisted into a hook for the rest of his life, as if he were forever crossing his fingers. When the doctor had stitched up Sigmar's wounds, he rebandaged his hand and gave him a small blanket as a reward for his courage.

.   .   .

By the time they came home, the village was in pandemonium. The main road was filled with German soldiers: the battered remnants of the Black Forest Army, abandoning their vehicles along the road for want of fuel. The French were coming to burn the village down, it was said. Everyone had to get out now. Some people frantically loaded their belongings onto trucks. Others led horse-drawn carts out of the village. One woman brought her dairy cow. Then everyone walked into the forest. It was an ancient impulse, deep in the blood—an ancestral memory of robber barons and mercenaries, mad kings and the Thirty Years' War, when a fifth of the German people died, often slaughtered by marauding armies. When the killers come, you hide in the trees.

The entire village slept in the woods that night, clustered in and around two foresters' huts. But sleep wasn't the word for it. The ground was soft with moss and a thick bed of pine needles, but the forest was anything but silent. All night, my mother lay wide-eyed in the dark between Winfried and Emma, as bursts of gunfire and screeching shells flew overhead, from one side of the forest to the other. The place they had chosen to hide, as it turned out, was squarely between two armies—the advancing French and the retreating Germans. At any moment, it seemed, soldiers would come charging through the trees with their bayonets, or a bomb would drop among them, obliterating them all.

No one said a word at first. They were stoics, these farmers' wives, so they lay side by side in total silence, and their children knew to keep quiet, too. Then, slowly, a whimpering rose from the ground, and a long, low sob. It was Tante Gini. After years of divining the other villagers' fates, she had come face-to-face with her own. She was alone without children, far from her homeland, with her husband in Villingen, where the French were attacking. Soon she was wailing and crying and praying so loudly that she almost drowned out the shells. "You can't imagine it," my mother said. "They kept coming and coming. You would hear the whistling and imagine the arc across the sky and think, 'Will it hit us this time?' And then the terrible explosion. I think we all thought we were going to die."

By morning the shelling had stopped. The villagers, numb with shock, picked themselves off the ground and gathered their children, then trudged back home. Anything seemed safer than the forest now. Not long after they returned, the enemy arrived. They were French Moroccans, soft-spoken and courteous, and to my mother's nine-year-old eyes, strikingly beautiful. It was a new world.

·   ·   ·

The Germans surrendered two weeks later. In June, my mother and her family packed their things and spent two days hitchhiking back to Weil, trading potatoes and vegetables for rides in lorries and vans.

The country lay in a silent stupor around them, its cities demolished, its supply lines broken, its highways pocked with craters. Gasoline was in such short supply that the few vehicles on the road, aside from military convoys, often had balky, wood-fired engines, belching smoke as the cars rattled from town to town on wooden wheels. The roads were so deserted that year, my father once told me, that they became his playground. On idle summer days, he would lash a broomstick to his toy wagon, tie a bedsheet to it, and sail up and down the Autobahn.

By the time my mother's family arrived at the Bläserhof, another family was living in their apartment. The owners' daughter had been bombed out of her house in Mannheim. Finding the apartment un-occupied, she had moved in with her husband and three children. They had no intention of leaving. Emma and her children were put in the old servant's quarters on the ground floor—a single bedroom and toilet for five people. There was no kitchen or living room, so they had to use those in the main house at off hours. To my mother this was all entrancingly romantic—like living in a painted caravan. But to Emma, the world was falling apart. She had no money, no work, and no real home. She had four children, little food, and her husband was missing or dead. The war had taken everything, just as she knew it would.

Her first decision was the hardest: She had to send Winfried back to the Black Forest. There was still plenty of food on the farms in Herzogenweiler, and she could keep his ration card to get an extra thousand calories a day for the family. Besides, she told herself, it was for only a few months. Winfried would end up staying for two years. Decades later, when he had a family of his own, he was still haunted by the vague fear that he was a burden to someone. At family re-unions, his son Christian told me, Winfried would insist on staying at a hotel, even if there was plenty of room at one of his brothers' houses. *Aber wieso denn?* Christian would think. But why?

Sending Winfried to Herzogenweiler gave the family a little more food, but still no income. Emma had always loved teaching, and positions weren't hard to get with so many instructors lost to the war. But between the school day and caring for three children at night, she was soon more exhausted than she had been on the farm. That fall, Emma petitioned the city for a new apartment and was assigned a second-story flat on the east side of town. It was a heartbreaking move for my mother—her childhood paradise, gone—but even harder for Emma. The downstairs neighbor had lost her only son to the war, and the sound of two boys and a girl, tromping across the floorboards above her, drove home her bitterness and heartache. When she heard that Emma's husband was a party member, she took to shouting up the stairwell: "Nazi pig!"

Was Karl even alive? Emma still didn't know. For months after he was arrested, the French sent no word of his whereabouts—the postal system was in pieces like everything else. There were rumors that Karl had died months earlier. That he had been tied to the back of a tank and dragged through a village. That he had been held down and shot in a prison camp. Then one day, nearly a year after his family last saw him, Karl sent a postcard. He had been released from a French prisoner-of-war camp, he wrote in a spidery, uncertain script. He would be home soon.

"How happy we were to get the news that you are in Freiburg," Gernot wrote to tell him that November. "Mama told us about everything you've been through; it seems a miracle that you endured it. I was most afraid for you when I was still with the flak unit. You must have heard the cannons thundering; those were the hardest days of the war for us young soldiers, too." He hoped that his father would come home very soon, he added, "and stay with us forever."

∙   ∙   ∙

The man who shuffled off the train on November 23, 1945, wasn't the father they had known. They could see that even through their tears. He had always been a little undernourished—gristle and bone held together by spirit. But now he looked like a living ghost. His skin hung thin and sallow from his frame; his eyes were sunk low in their sockets, so dull that they both seemed made of glass. He was half in and half out of the world.

When he left for Alsace, Karl had weighed 140 pounds. Now he weighed less than a hundred. He was too weak to work, too trauma-tized to think straight, yet there was no food to build back his strength. At the Bläserhof, they had never gone hungry even at the height of the war. There was an orchard and a vegetable garden and a court-yard where Karl kept his bees for honey—pale gold in the late spring, when the linden trees were in bloom; amber in the summertime, when Karl would truck his hives to the Black Forest and let the bees forage among the pines. There was schnapps in the fall, when the wasps would get drunk on the fermented fruit and fly wobbly circles around the yard, and *lebkuchen* in the winter. But the new apartment had no room for a garden much less for bees, and there was never enough food for anyone.

The worst times for the family were yet to come, in the *Hunger-winter* of 1946. But already, in late fall of 1945, the cupboard was half empty. When my mother went to get groceries, she was too small to reach the shelves where the best things were kept. Her fam-ily couldn't afford them anyway. "You can have all the vinegar you want," the storekeeper would tell her with a crooked grin, then dole out the family's rations of flour, butter, and milk. At home, Emma would bake a small *Mischbrot*, a fraction of the size of the loaves in the Black Forest. Then Karl would weigh out everyone's portion on a scale. Gernot and Sigmar would eat theirs right away—or spit on it to make sure no one else would. "As if that would have stopped us," my mother told me. Like the prisoners at Pont d'Ain, she sometimes traded her bread to her brothers for more nourishing fare—books, in her case, rather than cigarettes. She hid them under her blouse at the dinner table and asked to be excused, then read them in the bathroom as the others ate. After a while, she was so thin that one of her teachers looked at her one day and said, "There's nothing left but the soul."

She had spent so long yearning for her father to come home, and terrified that he never would. Now all everyone did was fight. Emma was worn-out, Karl's nerves so frayed that he could erupt at the smallest sound. But it was Gernot who took things the hardest. He had done his best to play the man of the house while Karl was gone, the substitute parent. Yet here he was being treated like a child again, fighting over scraps with his little brother. Sigmar had a shrewd mind and rollicking wit, and he knew just how to get under your skin. If my mother was Karl's favorite, Sigmar was Emma's—one more reason that they all didn't get along. At one point, Sigmar made Gernot so blindingly furious that the two of them went at each other with chairs. My mother ran out into the street, screaming for help, convinced that her brothers would kill each other. But no one came.

After a few weeks of this, Gernot stormed out of the apartment one day, vowing to never come back. But where could he go? The country was under military occupation, its cities overrun with refugees. Every spare bedroom and basement was filled. Should he leave or stay? On the morning of February 19, 1946, the decision was made for him. There came a rapping at the door, and when my mother went to answer it an armed French officer stood in the hall. "Does Karl Gönner live here?" he asked. Then he took her father away—first to a prison in neighboring Lörrach, then to the Citadel in Strasbourg. A man in Alsace had accused him of murder.

16

ACCUSED

THE CITADEL IN STRASBOURG LAY HALF BURIED BESIDE THE
Rhine, like the carcass of some ancient sea beast. Its ramparts of
brick and pink sandstone slanted up from the ground as if thrust by
the bedrock, overtopped with berms of green grass. When Louis XIV
had them built in the 1680s, these walls formed a great five-pointed
star, strong enough to repel a cannonball. But only one side was left
by the time Karl arrived under guard; the rest had been reduced to
rubble. The Germans themselves had destroyed the Citadel seventy-
five years earlier, in the siege of Strasbourg. Now it was their turn to
be imprisoned in its remains.

The Citadel held the most notorious war criminals in Alsace.
Among them was Erich Isselhorst, the former head of the Gestapo
in the region. Born in Alsace-Lorraine when it was still part of the

German Empire, Isselhorst went on to join the SS and lead a squad of *Einsatzkommandos* in the Baltic states, in charge of hunting down and murdering Jews. He passed his days in prison writing a history of the Third Reich in Alsace in an easy, flowing hand. When I came across it at the Archives du Bas-Rhin in Strasbourg, it had an un-marked blue cover bound tight with a cloth band. Unlike the dog-eared documents in most of the archive, these pages were pristine and seemingly unread, as if the fountain pen had just left the page. The date on the manuscript read July 1947. Seven months later, Is-selhorst was sentenced to death for war crimes and shot by a firing squad.

Like Isselhorst, Karl was imprisoned below the ramparts, under thick courses of brick, mortar, and mounded soil. The cells were technically above ground but felt far beneath it. The cold and damp made Karl's joints ache, and the air was rank with sweat and stewing excrement. Lying on a straw mattress on the ground, Karl could feel the silence press in on his eardrums like deep water. His only human contact was with the jailer who brought him food and a nun who sat and talked with him every few days.

"He was so grateful to that nun," my mother told me, when we went to the Citadel together. "That a human being would talk to him like another human being. He never forgot her." We walked under the ramparts, down a dim tunnel that smelled of earth and iron, and up a spiral staircase that led onto the grassy berm. My mother looked out over the rambling gardens that covered the Citadel grounds, and the joggers skimming past in bright outfits. She had been here once before, when she was in high school and the Citadel was still in ruins. She wanted to understand what her father had been through, but almost everything she knew about the Third Reich had come by word of mouth. Her school was in the French zone of occupation, and her instructors had been forbidden from teaching any German history after 1871. "They said that Germans didn't know how to teach it," she said. The history they did read was full of dashing French heroes and stodgy, pugnacious Germans. "One day after class, I went to my teacher and said, 'Do we really have to read this stuff?' And he gave me a long look, and we never used that book again. He had lost a son in the war."

When Karl was first arrested, before he was brought to the Citadel, he was held in a prison not far from my mother's school. Every morning before class, she would swing by to see him with her brother Gernot. Sometimes, their father would open a window onto the prison yard and wave at them. Other days, he would talk to them through the fence, or through the bathroom window of a French family's house where he did some gardening. On weekends, when she and Gernot were out gathering wood for home, they would drop off a basket of apples and potatoes and some toasted flour that he could make into a soup. The prison was next to an elementary school, so Karl could hear the sounds of laughter and playing as he talked to his son and daughter across the fence. It was just as Regina had foretold in the Black Forest: He could see and hear children, but his own were out of reach.

Then one January afternoon in 1947, nearly a year after Karl was arrested, he was gone. Transferred to the Citadel in Strasbourg, the guard said. My mother stared at him, in shock. As long as her father was standing across the fence, she could imagine him being set free one day. But Strasbourg seemed a continent away. All through that spring, summer, and fall, Emma wrote letters to the French military government, to no avail. The prisoner was under investigation until further notice, she was told. The *épuration* had him in its grip.

·   ·   ·

Alsace was in an agony of mutual recrimination. The great majority of its people had stayed true to France during the war: Fewer than three thousand had volunteered for the Wehrmacht or the Waffen-SS, as against the hundred thousand who were conscripted. Still, four years of occupation had left few people uncompromised. Some seventy-four thousand Alsatians worked as Nazi block and cell wardens, keeping watch over their communities for any signs of disloyalty to the Reich. And while most Alsatians were ecstatic to rejoin France, the whiplashing demands of yet another regime change took their toll. Once again, the official language was changed, books replaced, signs repainted—only German was banished this time instead of French. "*C'est chic de parler français*," one paper declared, adding: "Yes . . . but . . . you have to know how. And there's the rub."

It was a liberation laced with fear. No sooner had the Germans been driven off than the French turned on one another. Who were the patriots and who were the collaborators? Who was to blame for the disaster of this war? The *épuration*, or purification, could claim anyone. Nearly a third of a million people were charged with treason or collaboration over the next five years, and more than half were tried. Others never had the privilege of a trial. They had their heads shaved or their homes ransacked, were beaten by mobs, branded with swastikas, or shot by firing squads. In one village, a man had to walk the streets with a bell around his neck; in others, women were paraded about with their "Nazi babies" in their arms. "The *épuration* is neither a bout of fever nor communicable madness," a local liberation group declared. "Its aim is to facilitate the convalescence, healing, and even survival of the nation as a whole by pitilessly eliminating morbid germs." It was a national spasm of self-disgust, and the people of Alsace, as usual, were among the first suspected.

One of the worst crimes of the occupation, it soon became clear, had involved a group of Alsatians. On the afternoon of June 10, 1944, in west-central France, an SS tank division descended on the small farming community of Oradour-sur-Glane. The soldiers herded the citizens into the market square and surrounded them with machine guns. They announced that a cache of weapons and munitions had been hidden in the town by terrorists, and demanded to know where it was. When no one came forward, the men from the village were locked into six nearby barns, while the women and children were barricaded in the church. Then the men were shot and the church burned down.

All told, 642 villagers were killed that day. Among the perpetrators were thirteen Alsatian conscripts and one Alsatian volunteer. The massacre became a byword for complicity, yet the courts and the French public were bitterly divided over it. Were the Alsatians forced to join in the killing or were they willing participants? Did it matter? When a military tribunal in Bordeaux found all fourteen men guilty of war crimes, six thousand Alsatians gathered in Strasbourg to protest the verdict. Meanwhile, in Limousin, the region where the massacre occurred, public opinion demanded the death penalty.

Ten days after the verdict, the French Parliament granted amnesty to all Alsatian conscripts. The fourteen men condemned in Bordeaux were eventually released—including the Alsatian who had volunteered for the SS. It was an act of national reconciliation, some politicians said. But if a crime so horrific could be pardoned, what of the war's other complicities, great and small?

.   .   .

"De Gaulle's great mistake was saying, '*Le peuple jugera!*'" Gérard Kielwasser, the son of Bartenheim's former mayor, told me. "How were the people to judge? After a liberation, these jealousies and resentments explode into the open. There were false accusations. There were people who had fought the Germans who were put in prison, and others who were killed for nothing. People just wanted revenge and executed them. *C'était des conneries.*" It was foolishness. He sighed and shook his head. "When there is no justice, people make justice themselves."

No sooner had Bartenheim been liberated than a struggle for power began. Gérard's father, hoping to be reinstated as mayor, went home and dug up three boxes that he had buried in the cellar before the war. The first was full of French banknotes; the second held Swiss gold coins; the third had an old French flag and the mayor's ceremonial sash. With these items secured, Kielwasser marched to the town hall to reclaim his office. Louis Obrecht, the schoolteacher and former soldier, was there to greet him. He was standing in the doorway in his military uniform with a tricolored armband, Kielwasser later recalled. By order of Commander Communal of the Third Battalion of the Sixth Regiment of the Colonial Infantry, Obrecht declared, he was now in charge of the village. If Kielwasser signed a statement renouncing his claim to the mayorship, nothing would happen to him. If not, "One fine morning, you and your son will find yourselves with a bullet in your guts."

Obrecht had vowed to clear out the rot of occupation—to summon "the moral and spiritual forces necessary for the rebuilding of France," as he put it in one newspaper story. But to many villagers this just seemed an excuse to prosecute old grudges. "An arriviste," they called him later, "a poor wretch," or simply "a bad sort." As Gabriel Arnold, the deputy mayor, put it in his mild way: "I've heard that he was not a very congenial person."

Obrecht had always been something of an outsider in Bartenheim. He was born fifty miles to the north, in Herbsheim, and the war had been hard on him. As a soldier, he was forced to surrender to the Germans. As the school principal, he had to cede his position to Karl. As a teacher, he had to sign an oath to Hitler before he could enter a classroom. A welter of conflicting emotions seemed to drive him, the villagers said: jealousy and hunger for authority, contempt for collaborators and envy of their access to power. In Colmar, I found a letter from Charles Reymann, Bartenheim's first party chief, to the Nazi leadership in Mulhouse. It was written in December 1940, when the party must have already had some misgivings about René Kielwasser's loyalties. "It's hard to find a successor with experience in local politics," Reymann wrote. "But in case you still need a replacement, I can only suggest Herr Obrecht."

Even after the French freed Alsace, Obrecht didn't believe it at first. When a small German troop crossed the Rhine five miles north of Bartenheim, Obrecht fled the village with his wife. "He was frightened," Georges Tschill later recalled. "He spread the word that people should flee, that the Germans were coming back." Still, Obrecht lost no time in returning when all was clear. Brandishing his captain's rank, he declared himself interim mayor and took charge of Bartenheim's Purification Commission. On December 22, 1944, the commission sent a list of supposed Nazi sympathizers to French authorities in Mulhouse. Kielwasser was at the top. "Bartenheim is sick of this mayor," Obrecht wrote. "He is neither French nor German, but a perfect egotist who, as *Ortsgruppenleiter* Gönner has said, knows only his own pocket. . . . His return to power would trigger a real riot in Bartenheim." By March, Kielwasser was in prison.

.   .   .

A vacuum had opened up in Bartenheim's politics, and all the old disputes rushed to fill it. One faction, led by Obrecht and a local café owner named Charles Charpillet, aligned itself with the former Blacks and fancied itself the party of the Resistance—if for no other reason than Kielwasser and the Reds were in charge during the occupation. Obrecht's group hoped to stack the town council with their candidates, reclaiming the power they had lost to the Reds in the 1936 election. In the voting that followed, a number of their candidates were elected, but Charpillet was not, and the new council chose a rival villager for mayor.

Afterward, Charpillet confronted the councilmen at his café in a drunken rage. They had swindled the people of Bartenheim! It would be best if they were blown up at their first meeting along with the city hall. Charpillet claimed to have a stockpile of arms and munitions, and threatened to throw a grenade into the new mayor's bedroom while he slept. But when police searched his property—they had received a tip that the weapons were hidden under some lumber and straw in Charpillet's barn—they found nothing.

Obrecht was a more resourceful adversary. In the months leading up to Kielwasser's trial for collaboration, he did his best to dig up evidence against the former mayor. He sent copies of Kielwasser's wartime speeches and Nazi correspondence to the military court. He joined with other locals to testify against the former mayor and sent letters to the mayors of villages that had hosted the Bartenheimers during the evacuation. Did Kielwasser show signs of Germanophilia? Obrecht wondered. Did he sell goods intended for the refugees and keep the proceeds? The mayors responded with a wariness typical of those paranoid times. They weren't surprised by Obrecht's questions—*pas du tout!*—but they had nothing substantial to share. Perhaps Kielwasser hid his Nazi leanings from them, they suggested. He must have known what staunch French patriots they were.

Purification left no room for ambiguity. History had to be rewritten in black and white, patriots and collaborators. It was no longer enough for Kielwasser to be an opportunist, playing both sides. He was an "enraged Nazi," as Obrecht put it in his letters and testimony to the military court in Mulhouse. He had lied and betrayed the Alsatian population, and made the world believe that everyone in Bartenheim was "enchanted by the Nazi regime." Now that the French were in power again, Obrecht argued, Kielwasser wanted to pretend that he'd been a good Frenchman all along. "And as his brother-in-law is a secretary at the town hall, all the compromising documents have disappeared."

Obrecht described himself as a freedom fighter. He had "sabotaged German teaching" in Bartenheim, he wrote, and stayed behind "to organize the Resistance." And yet, in Kielwasser's own account to the military court, it was Obrecht who openly consorted with German officers. It was Obrecht who engineered "a veritable coup d'état" after the war.

The trial that followed, on January 31, 1946, could only confirm both sides. Ten witnesses testified against Kielwasser. They accused him of denouncing citizens to the Nazis for their anti-German sentiment, of having villagers sent to Schirmeck, and of depriving them of refugee allotments during the evacuation. Kielwasser countered with a statement signed by ninety-two citizens of Bartenheim. Far from denouncing and imprisoning villagers, they claimed, the mayor had worked to have them released. He had helped numerous men avoid conscription and had kept the Gestapo from punishing veterans who had deserted the German army in the First World War. He had helped bring back a woman who was deported to Germany and prevented another from being sent to Finland to work for the Wehrmacht. He was an unwavering patriot, Kielwasser's allies maintained, whose sole purpose had been to protect them from Nazi terror.

It was a familiar spectacle: a French village divided against itself, each side marshaling its private loyalties and grievances. Was Kielwasser a turncoat or a double agent? A collaborator or a secret patriot? Both, perhaps, but the judge could choose only one: Kielwasser was acquitted, but he would never again hold office.

Two months later, Karl was taken to the Citadel. This time, Obrecht couldn't fail to get his man.

17

DEFENDANT

THE FRENCH INSPECTOR REPEATED THE CHARGES, GLANCING
at a typed sheet as he spat out the words. Wasn't it true that Karl's
sole purpose in coming to France was to turn the people of Bartenheim into Nazis? That he sent dozens of letters to the Gestapo and
Nazi leadership, denouncing the villagers under his rule? That he
could have saved young Alsatians from conscription, yet refused to
sign their appeals? "You are indirectly responsible for their deaths!"
the inspector shouted. "You brought to your duties a zeal and a tyrannical fervor without equal!"

Karl sat ramrod straight in his chair, his good eye bloodshot with
fatigue. He knew who was behind these charges—the inspector was
reading from Obrecht's signed statement. Karl tried to answer as
calmly and carefully as he could. But what was the point? The in-

spector took him for a monster—albeit an oddly ineffective one. According to Obrecht, Karl was both an evil mastermind and a bumbling figurehead. He led a reign of terror yet imprisoned only one man for a few months. He denounced Obrecht to the Gestapo, yet failed to get him arrested. He threatened to take Obrecht's apartment above the school, then meekly moved in with Frau Schöpfer. He came to Alsace with the sole purpose of indoctrinating its citizens into National Socialism, yet spent his time fruitlessly writing letters to Nazi bureaucrats. "The district leadership even complained because he wrote them too often," Obrecht noted in his testimony.

It made no sense. Yes, Karl had organized political meetings and Hitler Youth activities, he told the inspector. That was his duty as party chief. No, he didn't denounce villagers to the Gestapo or send their sons to the Eastern Front. "It's impossible for me to believe that Herr Obrecht, in signing this document, took all of these lies and defamations seriously," Karl said. "The whole thing is an outpouring of hatred with no basis in reality." It was all the more astonishing, Karl added in a subsequent interrogation, because it was he who had had Obrecht released from a German camp in 1940, when Obrecht was a prisoner of war. "After his liberation, Obrecht frankly rallied to the German cause and worked for the party as an organization leader," Karl said. "I could tell that he was an opportunist when he ceased all party activity after the German army's first reversal of fortune."

Obrecht dismissed these allegations out of hand. Like the Kielwasser case, this one contained two incompatible narratives. But this time, Obrecht wasn't an outsider accusing one of Bartenheim's own. He was a captain in the French army, and the defendant was a Nazi.

·　　·　　·

Obrecht's most serious charge—the one that led to Karl's rearrest—was accessory to murder. Karl was responsible for the death of a great patriot, Obrecht claimed. The incident occurred on the morning of October 4, 1944. American and British forces had liberated Normandy the previous summer and fought their way east to Champagne, joined by the Free French Forces along the way. In a month, they would reach Strasbourg. In six weeks, Bartenheim would be liberated. The Germans believed that Alsatians were duty bound to fend off the attack, but the villagers had begun to push back. The fiercest resister was a man named Georges Baumann.

Baumann was a farmer and war veteran. Born in Alsace when it was under German rule, he had served in the Wehrmacht during the First World War, but he had no love for the German occupation. On the morning in question, he was standing in front of his house, preparing to head to the fields to feed his cows, when a police chief named Anton Acker arrived. Baumann was late for his mandatory work detail, Acker said. The army was digging trenches along the Rhine and needed some wooden pallets built. Baumann waved him off. He had no intention of working for "those German swine," he said, according to Acker's later report. When Acker threatened to arrest him, Baumann shoved him away, shouting, "But you won't be the one to do it!"

By then, the pair had been joined by Baumann's wife, son, and daughter, and their neighbor Jeanne Kielwasser. Another neighbor, Anna König, was standing nearby. A number of them later testified that Acker slapped Baumann in the face—so hard, according to König, that Baumann's hat flew off. In the ensuing scuffle, Acker reached for a rifle strapped on his bicycle but was disarmed by Baumann's family. He tried to pull his revolver next, but the others jumped on him again, joined by König, who had come running to help. When the group had taken away the revolver, they dragged Acker into König's kitchen, where they were joined shortly by three military police who had come to check on the commotion. The police promptly sided with the family. One of them asked Acker if he was drunk on schnapps. When Acker was finally released, he stalked off in a fury to the police station in Sierentz, two miles north of Bartenheim.

An hour later, he returned with five officers.

"This is where they came for him," Gérard Kielwasser, the president of Bartenheim's historical society, told me one night. We were standing in front of Baumann's house, a handsome, half-timbered building on a quiet side street on the north end of town. Kielwasser—no relation to Gérard Kielwasser, the son of the former mayor—lived just four houses up the block from the Baumanns as a boy. His mother, Jeanne, was the neighbor who was standing with the Baumanns that morning when Acker first arrived. It was she who sent for the millitary police after the fighting broke out. When Acker returned later with reinforcements, they arrested Baumann in the fields and took him to Sierentz. That afternoon, his wife and daughter were arrested as well. His teenage son, Georges Jr., had fled the scene.

Almost as soon as they entered the police station, the two women were savagely beaten and interrogated, then locked in a secure room. When it was over, the police had extracted a statement from Baumann's wife saying that her husband was a brutal, vindictive man, always on edge and prone to violence. "The whole village knows that I've had to endure terrible things with him," she said. That night, the police shot Baumann in the pelvis and knocked him unconscious with repeated blows from the butt of a rifle. He was dead by morning. His wife was released a few hours later, so battered that she could barely walk. She later retracted her statement about her husband, saying that it had been "torn out of her."

Baumann's son was the only one to escape unharmed. He ran to the church to get help from the priest, René Luttenbacher, who told him to hide in a vineyard nearby. That's where Georges Tschill found him that night: The priest had told the boy to whistle when he saw Tschill coming. Tschill stashed him in the hollow space under his front stoop, where he usually stored preserves. When the Germans had given up searching for him, Georges Jr. moved to a room upstairs, where he hid until the liberation came six weeks later. Fräulein Ruff, the German teacher who was boarding with the Tschills, never saw him, though she always swore that the house was full of strange shadows.

The killing of Georges Baumann was one of the most brutal incidents of the German occupation of Bartenheim. To the villagers, it became a tale of heroic resistance: the moment when one of their own stood up to the Nazis. The street where Baumann lived was renamed Rue de la Résistance after the war. But Obrecht wanted more than an empty tribute. He wanted retribution. Anton Acker was charged with Baumann's murder in 1946, but he fled the area and was never tried. (His case file ends in the fall of 1947, when he was still a fugitive.) But Acker was just the henchman, Obrecht insisted. It was Karl who had set the whole crime in motion. As party chief, he had issued the work orders that were "the direct cause of the death of a brave farmer, a veritable patriot . . . traitorously shot by German police," Obrecht told the investigators. In the name not just of Georges Baumann but of all the victims of the occupation, Karl Gönner should be imprisoned and sentenced to forced labor.

·   ·   ·

There was no truth in it, Emma told herself. There couldn't be. Karl had told her for years about Obrecht and his machinations. It was no surprise that the man would turn on him now, when the French were in power. By December of 1946, when Emma first got word that Karl had been transferred to the Citadel, it had been nearly a year since he was taken into custody. Her appeals to the French government had fallen into a void, and now Karl was in solitary confinement. How could she help prove his innocence when she couldn't even see him?

Then, the following February, Emma got a letter from a lawyer named René Weinum. Karl had written to him—the court or one of the villagers from Bartenheim must have given him the address—and asked if the lawyer would represent him. Weinum agreed. "I will try my best to complete this matter as soon as possible," he wrote to Emma. "I am in touch with my client and intend to visit him in the next few days to discuss various details."

Weinum was forty-five years old. The son of a tailor, born and raised in the village of Bischheim just north of Strasbourg, he had worked as an interpreter for the French army and had been a well-respected lawyer for twenty years. Emma was surprised that he took the case. Weinum shared a last name with the most famous Alsatian resistance fighter—Marcel Weinum, leader of a network of young saboteurs called *Le Main Noir*—and he was said to be Jewish. Weinum's hometown was one of the oldest and largest Jewish communities in Alsace. In 1349, when an angry mob massacred more than a thousand Jews in Strasbourg, accusing them of poisoning the city's wells, it was to Bischheim that many survivors fled. Why would a man with such a background want to defend a Nazi?

Her assumptions were only half right. When I stopped by Bischheim on one of my trips to Bartenheim, I found Weinum's birth and residency certificates in the basement of the town hall. On one of the forms, he had listed his nationality, defiantly, as Alsatian rather than French. But under religion he had written Catholic.

Weinum's correspondence with Karl and Emma, in any case, was brisk but encouraging. Two weeks after his first letter to Emma, Weinum wrote Karl to say that she had sent him some notes about the case and Karl's accuser: "I am personally of the opinion that the indictment, particularly as framed by Mr. Obrecht, is certainly exaggerated on many points." Weinum planned to interview witnesses soon. He might have a hard time recouping his expenses and fees, he added, but they could discuss that later.

Weinum's challenge was this: His client wasn't accused of murdering Baumann with his own hands. That would have been easy to
disprove. Baumann was killed in Sierentz, not Bartenheim, and Karl
wasn't there when it happened. But Karl did order people in Bartenheim to join work details, and that led indirectly to Baumann's death.
To Obrecht, and perhaps to a like-minded tribunal, Karl's real crime
was being a brutal Nazi administrator. And that was more than
enough to make him an accessory to murder. To win Karl's freedom,
Weinum would have to prove that his client wasn't the terror of
Bartenheim. He was that strange and contradictory figure that villagers like Alphonse Huttenschmitt later described to me: a reasonable
Nazi. Was there even such a thing? And who would risk defending
him in the middle of a purification campaign?

Emma had nearly given up hope when another letter arrived, this
time from Switzerland. It was from the daughter of Eugène Liebis,
the former mayor of Bartenheim who was arrested with Karl in
1944 and later released. She had heard that Karl was imprisoned at
the Citadel and wanted to help with his defense. If Emma would
write letters to the villagers in Bartenheim, Liebis's daughter and
Josephine Schöpfer, Karl's former landlady, could pass them along.
"He's been terribly slandered," Schöpfer wrote to Emma on December 2, 1946. "But I think here, too, justice will get the upper hand.
The pastor has promised to do what he can, and I'll also try to gather
testimonials and send them to Herr Gönner." If Emma would just
ask for people's help, perhaps they would give it—no matter what the
risk.

All that winter of 1946 and 1947, Emma sent letters across the
Rhine. She wrote to Schöpfer, Weinum, and the priests in Bartenheim and Sierentz. She made lists in German and her impeccable
French of all the villagers whom he had helped in Bartenheim and
how he had helped them. Then she tried to reach them by mail or
through Schöpfer or a local police captain named Leber. Emma

knew that the court would render its verdict soon. Anyone willing to testify on his behalf had to do so now. They couldn't wait for the purification campaign to die down.

Late in February, Schöpfer sent Emma a note to reassure her, though it might have done the opposite. "I have not been idle," she wrote. "I've passed along the various addresses of people who have told me that Herr Gönner stood up for them when they were in need, wrote appeals for them, and so forth. But you have to understand that they're all afraid of putting something in writing."

Schöpfer knew firsthand what rancor and mistrust the war had left behind. Hadn't those boys shaved her head and paraded her through Bartenheim? "I just wonder when this eternal torture of human beings will end," she wrote. "Any shitbird can take revenge right now. I could sing a tune as well! You know how we used to say, 'swallow your anger'? Well, you can always talk, but it's of little use. Hopefully you'll get some good news soon."

·   ·   ·

There was nothing left to do but wait, and now the *Hungerwinter* had come. It had settled over Germany like a rain cloud that wouldn't lift. Even the worst days of the war hadn't felt so hopeless. The countryside was ravaged, its livestock massacred, its farmers driven away or killed in flight. What harvests the fields provided were meager, with fertilizer and farming equipment in such short supply. Winter temperatures were at back-aching lows, freezing the waterways so supply ships couldn't reach their ports. The ports were often destroyed in any case. Coal was so scarce that whole families froze to death. Other countries offered to send vegetables, lard, fish, and nuts in trade, but the Germans had no machinery or steel left to barter.

At first, rations in the occupied zones could contain up to twenty-six hundred calories per day—no worse than in the hardest-hit Allied countries. But in cities overwhelmed with refugees, the calorie count soon dropped to fourteen hundred or less. After seven years of wartime rationing, many people were undernourished before the *Hungerwinter* began. Now they were too weak to fight off infections and their children couldn't develop properly. In Stuttgart, where the population more than doubled between 1945 and 1948 as evacuees returned, meat rations fell to a tablespoon a day, to go with five ounces of bread. That was barely enough to keep a small child alive; for an adult it meant slow starvation. By 1948, the infant mortality rate in East Germany was nearly double that of some of its neighbors. At one point, so many Germans above the age of seventy were starving to death in the American zone that their mortality rate increased by 40 percent in three months. One man resorted to drinking his wife's breast milk to stay alive.

My mother was eleven years old that winter. She had never liked going into town to get rations, but now she could hardly bear it. The people were so desperate and mean. Roughly half of Germany was buying goods on the black market—though a loaf of bread could cost half a week's wages—and many of the rest wanted the death penalty for those who did. Everyone thought everyone else was getting more than their share. Some simply stole what they needed, especially ration cards and food. "*Zuerst kommt das Fressen, dann die Moral,*" they said, quoting Bertolt Brecht. First comes food, then morality.

One morning, my mother went to the bakery to get bread for the family. She was standing in line with a friend, reminiscing about a family that had served fourteen cakes at a birthday party once, when the woman in front of them wheeled around. "*Wer war das?*" she wanted to know, fixing them with hard, glimmering eyes. Who was that? My mother shrank back, shaking her head. She couldn't remember, she said. It was too long ago. If she gave the lady a name, she knew, someone would get hurt.

The birthday party was just a fond memory anyway. No one had that much food anymore, and gas and coal were so scarce that the house was always freezing. When Germans after the war were asked what worried them most, lack of food or clothing, they almost always said food. That winter, they said clothing. Emma had only enough fuel to cook one meal a day—not that there was food for more. In the fall, my mother and her brothers had gathered beechnuts in the woods. They had spiky shells and a bitter taste—if you ate too many, they would twist your stomach in a knot—but they were full of fat and protein. In the winter, there wasn't even that.

Sometimes, the family walked to the Swiss border to meet two of Karl's cousins who lived in Basel. They talked to them across the barbed-wire fence, then caught the packages that the nuns threw over the top—chocolate, a rubber ball, and once, best of all, five pounds of pork fat. When even that ran out, Emma had no choice but to go begging. She would bundle up one of her little ones and head into the countryside, stopping at farmhouses to ask for a few potatoes, a rutabaga, an egg or two. Some farmers gave them what they could; others shook their heads or wouldn't come to the door. It might not be long before they were hungry, too.

After school, if they still had the energy, Sigmar and Gernot would go scavenge for food—"hamstering," they called it. Emma would give them a tablecloth or another household item that she could spare, and the boys would use it for barter. Sigmar was especially gifted at this. He learned to collect the soles from discarded shoes, melt them with a solvent to make a rubber cement, and use it to patch bicycle tires. People would pay him in money or butter, but there was never close to enough. The country was full of women like Emma, with children to feed and their husbands lost to war. Some resorted to prostitution just to keep their families fed.

•   •   •

For weeks, Emma had nothing to show for all her letters to Alsace. The only testimonials she had received were written months earlier, soon after Karl was arrested. They were dated April 4, 1946. Most of France was hunting down Nazis and their collaborators then, but two villagers had wanted Emma to know that her husband had done them no wrong. "I declare that the *Ortsgruppenleiter,* Herr Gönner, never held anything against me, although I was a Frenchman first and an enemy of the Nazis," a man named Georg Hassler wrote. "Herr Gönner helped me out of an unpleasant situation when I was politically denounced by an Alsatian. For his work and petitions on my behalf, he never accepted anything." Another villager, named Eugen Ott, wrote that Karl had helped him apply for money for child support and housing, although Ott, too, hated the Nazis.

That was it for nearly a year. Then, finally, the following spring, more letters began to arrive, in a trickle then a stream. They almost all took the same form. First a declaration of French patriotism, then a denunciation of Nazism, and finally an acknowledgment, no less emphatic, that this Nazi was not like the others. "Of the eighteen hundred souls in our town, not one was deported," a villager named Josef Merzisen wrote. "Although he knew that several young men had hidden themselves." A widow's son had been imprisoned for in-juring himself to escape the draft, but Karl had had him released. Another woman was nearly deported when the German authorities opened an anti-Nazi letter she had written, but Karl intervened. One letter began, simply, "Husband, wife, daughter, and niece all freed from prison by his requests."

They were brief statements, written in a cramped and laborious script. Their grammar was often poor, their wording stilted. But each told a story of how life was lived during the war—what choices were made, what wrongs committed and occasionally set right. "*Très important!*" a villager named Albert Doppler began. "My son, A. Doppler, who was arrested while fleeing to France and taken to

Schirmeck, was able, through Herr Gönner's appeals on our be-half, to obtain his freedom. When he was drafted by the Wehrmacht and went into hiding, Herr Gönner never gave him away." Even the former mayor, René Kielwasser, spoke up for his old adversary. Yes, it was indisputable that the man was "a perfect Nazi," he said, when summoned as a witness for the prosecution. But Karl used "persuasion rather than force to impose his ideas," and no one was hurt under his command.

Emma copied out the letters in her clear schoolteacher's hand and forwarded them to Weinum. As the number of testimonials grew, the lawyer's replies became more encouraging. "My personal impression is as follows," he wrote in mid-March, six weeks after he took the case. "Herr Obrecht has cast the facts in a false light, and I am firmly con-vinced that I can provide evidence that will invalidate the charge."

If any of Karl's witnesses convinced Weinum, it was probably René Luttenbacher, Bartenheim's priest. The Nazis had set politi-cians and priests at odds like never before, yet Luttenbacher proved to be Emma's best ally. Karl's arrest had put him in an awkward position, he admitted in one letter: Captain Obrecht was one of his parishioners, and Hitler and his representatives were so despised in Bartenheim "that their every word and every action, even if meant well, is harshly judged." Still, Luttenbacher wrote, "when a human life is at stake, and when a wife and children fear for a father and wait for his return, a priest must not hesitate to give voice to the truth." Karl had been a dutiful Nazi Party member, no doubt. "Yet his dos-sier shows that he had a good heart and was always ready to do good for the population."

·   ·   ·

The court's verdict was brief and to the point. It was issued on July 21, 1947, by the Military Tribunal of the Sixth District in Metz, and published in both French and German: "The so-named Karl Gönner, detained in Strasbourg and accused of imposing forced labor on French civilians in regard to military operations, has been granted a notice of dismissal." Karl couldn't be held responsible for the work order or the murder that resulted from it, the tribunal ruled. He had merely passed along the order—"like any other man in his position, French or German"—and even participated in the work himself. "We therefore declare that there is no reason to prosecute the accused and order that the so-named Gönner be freed immediately."

In all, seventeen villagers had testified on Karl's behalf. Some had even gone to Strasbourg to defend him. "They were certainly well disposed toward you," Luttenbacher assured him in a letter. "That is, they spoke the truth and blamed you for none of the charges pressed by the prosecution." Those testimonials alone might have sufficed to convince the court. But at the last moment another piece of evidence found its way to the judges. Gérard Kielwasser, the village historian, told me about it on the night we visited Georges Baumann's house. We were on our way out the door, when he ducked into his office and returned with a thick sheaf of documents. They were given to him by Georges Boulay, a former deputy mayor of Bartenheim, not long before he died. On the cover, Boulay had scrawled "Secret" and underlined it twice. Most of the documents concerned René Kielwasser and Louis Obrecht, but Boulay had added a postscript to his note:

I also have at my disposal a dossier on Karl Gönner, the former party chief and school principal in Bartenheim during the occupation, whom this same Captain Obrecht wanted to have shot during the Liberation. When the Germans left, I found a voluminous personal file at the town hall, which clearly detailed how Gönner, though in the grip of the Nazi ideal, was of enor-

mous service to the entire population of Bartenheim. The entire
file, with a panegyric written by Reverend Luttenbacher, I immediately handed over to the judge in charge of Gönner's case.

Karl was released from prison eight days after the verdict. His
discharge papers were issued by the Ministry of Foreign Affairs,
signed by the commissioner of police, and sent to the Citadel by
courier. A soldier was ordered to unlock his cell, and Karl walked
down the dark tunnel a final time, beneath the ramparts and out
through the iron gate. Into the dazzling sun of a July afternoon.

"Loyalty is no empty delusion," he later wrote, recalling that day.
"Emma was so desperately worried about me and had almost wasted
away with sorrow. How elated she was when so many Alsatians sent
her their testimonies, and she learned that I could come home fully
acquitted. That night at eleven, when I called up to the lighted
kitchen window, our children tumbled out of their beds and there
was nothing but happiness in that kitchen."

.   .   .

He was a free man. He was in limbo. To his family, he still seemed a
ghost, an uneasy revenant. They couldn't quite believe that he was
home to stay. To the German government, he was more suspect still.
They had yet to decide if he was fit to teach children. The French
purification commissions were mirrored, across the Rhine, by an
elaborate system of *Entnazifizierung*, or denazification. More than
four hundred thousand Germans were detained in internment camps
by the Allies, who hoped to purge the government and military of
party leaders and their ideology. It was a monumental task: Germany had eight and a half million party members, and more than
half its population had been involved in party organizations. Nazi

industrialists and bankers often had long-standing ties to American and British businesses and were seen as essential to the country's reconstruction. Nazi researchers, like the rocket scientist Wernher von Braun, were useful in the Cold War. Those who weren't as well connected could use their influence to solicit false witness in their favor. Even Gestapo officers claimed to have had no choice in their actions, though joining the secret service was voluntary.

By the late 1940s, denazification had been handed over to the Germans—the Allies had lost patience for it. The results were predictable. In the entire state of North Rhine Westphalia, the historian Eric Johnson wrote in his book *Nazi Terror*, only ninety former Nazis were convicted of serious crimes. Karl would surely have benefited from the same leniency. But his situation was different from most. He had no business ties or political connections, and though his case was adjudicated by German courts, the French military government had the final say. In the year and a half after his release, his denazification file grew to more than a hundred pages, including teacher records, prison records, testimonials, and statements from purification commissions.

In the meantime, he took any jobs he could find. The years in prison had left him with "a sorrow that still darkens my mind and disturbs the balance of my soul," he wrote to the denazification board a year after he was released. All he could do was lose himself in hard work. He removed barbed-wire fences between France and Germany. He mixed mortar on a construction site and taught math to railroad employees. For the little money that he and Emma earned, they found a flat in a workers' settlement by the railyards in Weil, in a cheerless grid of new-built apartments. Their place had electricity but no toilet, just a hole down to a sump. Still, it was a relief to escape their catcalling neighbor. The *Hungerwinter* was over, but food was still scarce. No sooner had Winfried come home from the Black Forest than my mother was sent to Switzerland, to distant relatives who owned an electrician's shop and could afford to feed her.

Finally, on October 15, 1948, eight years after Karl was sent to France, a decision was reached on his status as a citizen. At first, an investigative committee in Lörrach classified him as one of the *Minderbelasteten*—"Less Responsible"—and recommended a two-year probation. Then the purification commission in Freiburg overruled them, reclassifying him as one of the *Entlasteten*—"Exonerated." "The accused strikes this chamber as an unconditionally honest character," they declared. "It is only just that he be absolved of all guilt." A month later, the French military government overruled them both. "Okay to be reintegrated," its ruling tersely noted. "But the commission's conclusion is incorrect."

Among the documents used to decide Karl's case was the letter he wrote in 1934, complaining about his church choir in Aulfingen. The words "my open commitment to National Socialism" were underlined in pencil. Karl belonged neither to the less responsible nor to the exonerated, the judges concluded. He was a *Mitläufer*—a "Fellow Traveler." Or as the French translation put it, with an ink stamp on the cover of the verdict, a *Sympathisant*. A Nazi sympathizer. "The burden of the accused lies primarily in his role as a Nazi Party chief in Alsace from 1942 to 1944," the German court conceded, when the case was sent back to them. "But this activity was largely offset by a series of good testimonials." Karl seemed to be innocent of any injustice, though he had ample opportunity for it in Alsace. "But the above facts do not suffice to classify him as exonerated."

Karl would always be in limbo, it seemed. But he was free to teach in a school again. Earlier that winter, he had received a letter from his lawyer, René Weinum. Reverend Luttenbacher had paid Weinum a visit recently and shared some interesting news. Karl's old enemy, Captain Obrecht, was under investigation and might soon face sanctions. "His superiors are outraged by his political posturing, by which he tried to gain the greatest benefit at other people's expense," Weinum wrote. He sent his best wishes to Emma, who had worked so hard on her husband's case, and to Karl himself. "I've come to know you as an honorable man," Weinum concluded.

Karl put the letter away in his desk, along with those from the villagers in Bartenheim. He rarely talked about Alsace again.

18

GRANDFATHER

ONE SUMMER AFTERNOON IN 2005, A PACKAGE ARRIVED AT my parents' house in Wisconsin, where they had moved a few years earlier. The postmark said Weil am Rhein. When my mother peeled away the brown paper wrapping, she found a shoebox underneath filled with yellowed envelopes and ink-smudged transcriptions. There was a note inside from my aunt Gerda, Gernot's wife. Karl had kept these letters in his desk all his life, she wrote. She found them after his death and put them away in the attic, then rediscovered them when the house was sold. She thought my mother would like to see them.

My mother picked up the letters one by one and peered at the words. They were all about her father's time in Alsace, she realized. Some were handwritten by the villagers in Bartenheim; others had been typed out by a clerk and stamped by a notary. But a few had been transcribed from the originals by her mother. Those were the ones that stopped her breath. She remembered the scratching of her mother's fountain pen at night, and the dim glow of the kitchen lamp when the children were supposed to be asleep. She kept a picture of Emma on her bedstand, standing outside in a rumpled dress, her weary face just managing a smile. But she rarely talked about her, as if doing so might dim the memory. In a childhood full of fear and unease, Emma was her secret resting place.

Reading the villagers' testimonials that day, my mother felt something unspool inside her. For the villagers to defend an accused collaborator like Kielwasser took some courage after the war. But only a profound sense of debt or decency could have prompted them to defend a member of the Nazi Party. "You have to realize that everything was *Spitz auf Kopf*," my mother told me. "You could get shot for the smallest thing. So these scraps of paper—there was *sehr viel Tapferkeit* behind them." A good deal of bravery. If Georges Tschill rekindled her belief in her father, these testimonials, and Emma's faith in gathering them, washed away her deepest doubts.

Among the letters that Gerda sent my mother was one that Karl wrote on April 15, 1947, from his prison cell in the Citadel. It was the only letter of his that survives from that time. "Dear Gernot!" it begins. "Just a few weeks from today you will celebrate your birthday. Nineteen years. How great was our joy when we took you into our arms, a healthy child in body and soul. Now the years of your youth are behind you. Before you lies the world, and you stand brave and carefree, ready to venture into its great machinery and test your youthful strength and daring against it. That is only right. We old folks are more contemplative and have learned through bitter experience to deliberate before we dare."

Karl goes on to explain just how grim the family's situation is. They have no savings and no insurance. Emma's income is barely enough for food and the simplest clothing. "I have no idea if my fate will take a turn," he writes. "But even if it does, worries upon worries will remain." Karl knows that his son has his heart set on going to university, but that's out of the question. Gernot needs to start earning a salary. "Even in the best case, if I'm released and rehired, we'll be short two thousand marks a year," Karl goes on to write. In the meantime, Winfried is in the Black Forest, living with relatives for want of food at home, and he's only nine years old. "If such a tender little plant is kept from his parents even an hour longer than is necessary, that is a crime. I'm sure that you, as the eldest, wouldn't want to be the cuckoo who pushes his siblings from the nest."

My mother never liked this letter. She took it personally, I think—to be dismissed as nothing but a burden to her brother, a helpless chick—and she felt terrible for Gernot. For five years, he had helped hold the family together while their father was away in France. Now the war was finally over, and Gernot still had to give up his dreams. My mother could imagine nothing crueler.

And yet, given what Karl had been through and what he still faced, there is a bracing optimism to his words, a stubborn hope. His bleak bookkeeping complete, Karl goes on to suggest some possible career paths that Gernot can take, as if Germany's shattered economy still has plenty to offer. He could work in customs or finance, find a job in the chemical industry or become a vocational instructor. Or he could become a teacher like both his parents. "In no other field are you so free to follow your own peculiar interests," Karl writes. "Moreover, you'll have a chance to shape the finest material known to the world, the human soul."

I've thought of that letter again and again these past few years, as the world has seemed to spin to pieces around me: war, terrorism, mass shootings, and climate disasters, racism, pandemic, and a deepening gulf between rich and poor. My grandfather had seen even more terrible things outside his prison cell. He had been handcuffed and beaten, wasted by disease and driven half mad with solitude. He had seen cities razed and sixty million people killed and his own ideology exposed as a murderous sham—a lie that engulfed the world. Yet he still believed that the future was full of promise. That his son could land a job, find a vocation, and help piece his country back together. That the world the Nazis had nearly destroyed was worth inheriting.

·   ·   ·

The last time my mother was in Germany, in 2015, she and I took a walk along the Rhine. It was a gusty Saturday afternoon in Weil, and the riverbank was spangled with spring flowers. People were gathered for picnics under the acacias and wild cherries, or strolled across the footbridge that spanned the water—the longest of its kind in the world. Some spoke French, some German or Swiss German, but it was hard to tell from which side of the river they came. My mother was unsteady on her feet that day, her eyes weaker than ever. She had to squint to read the sign at the entrance to the bridge: WER SCHWANNEN FÜTTERT, FÜTTERT AUCH RATTEN. Those who feed swans also feed rats. Then I took her hand, and we walked across the river to France.

Alsace is a different place now. There is little need for passports or identity cards, and most people are bilingual. In Bartenheim, schoolchildren are taught in both French and German, to prepare them for well-paying jobs across the river and in Switzerland, and the villagers shuttle seamlessly between countries. When my mother and I were visiting the Tschills, they proudly told us that their sons live in France but work in Switzerland. Michel is a truck mechanic, Marc a cabinetmaker, and both are volunteer firemen in Bartenheim like their father. Every summer, their brigade throws a party with the firemen across the Rhine in Efringen-Kirchen, where my father's father once raised rabbits admired by a Nazi administrator. Water under the bridge.

When we reached the opposite shore, my mother turned back to look at her hometown. Her father was right about one thing: His country had rebuilt itself. Where bunkers and broken roofs once lay, there were now parks and modern apartment blocks. Karl's children, too, had thrived. Gernot took his father's advice and earned an education degree; he became a beloved middle-school principal in Weil. Sigmar and Winfried were both engineers, with numerous patents under their names, and my mother had earned a PhD, raised five children, and taught history at university. Only Emma never lived to see the *Wirtschaftswunder*—the economic miracle of postwar Germany—in full flower. She died of ovarian cancer in the fall of 1956.

Karl didn't see it coming. The disease must have lain inside Emma a long time, but she kept it tamped down somehow. In April, she was still doing well—in bed but free of pain. Two days later, she was taking her first tentative steps, but her stomach had begun to ache. By late September she was dead. Karl had snuck some holy water from Lourdes into her food, but it was no use. "Mama's grave is decorated with pine needles and a wreath of evergreen and moss," he wrote to Sigmar that November. "It would be lovelier if she were here with us."

He threw himself into his work after that, thinking he could shake off his solitude and bitterness. He would be over it by spring. Instead, he had a heart attack in May, at the age of fifty-eight. "My stupid heart rebelled," he later wrote. "I could no longer see much sense in all the efforts to save my life. I wouldn't have minded if I never woke from anesthesia."

Yet even he was granted a second act. A year before Emma died, Karl was named principal of Karl-Tschamber Elementary School in Weil. He reentered politics, first joining the Free Democratic Party, then the Social Democrats—the one party in the Reichstag that had voted against giving Hitler unlimited legislative power in 1933. He was elected to two terms as a city councilman and learned, little by little, to live without Emma. The older one gets, he wrote to his half brother Xaver, the more one can feel "a worm gnawing in the heartwood that no one can reach. Might as well let it drill and gnaw. I know some old trees that are completely hollowed out and yet they bloom and bear leaves and fruit."

Two years after Emma died, Karl sent a letter to a cousin of hers, Emmy Boll, at my mother's urging. Emmy was fifty-seven and had never married. For more than thirty years, she had kept house for a professor in Munich and raised his four children. Now, like Karl, she faced a solitary retirement. Perhaps they could keep each other company.

Karl's first letter was more business proposal than billet-doux. "This transaction isn't primarily about mutual profit," he assured her. "Though I believe it could be beneficial to both of us." He had no time for empty promises; nothing to offer other than his own un-varnished need. "If no part of me pleases you, don't hesitate to run away," he told her. Yet his candor slowly won her over. Soon, he was composing poems and coining nicknames—Heartbug, Rascal, Little Bee. "Well, my Sunday Child, bring only pure joy into our house," he wrote, not long before they married. "I've muddled along, sick in soul and body. . . . Enough of that. We'll head toward the sun."

· · ·

When he died, on April 20, 1979, his passing was warmly noted by the local papers. "A Schoolmaster in the Truest Sense of the Word," the headline in the *Weiler Zeitung* read. "Very Popular with Students, Parents, and Teachers." To his relatives, he would always be a Black Forest farmer, earthy and profane; to the German govern-ment, both an honored veteran and a discredited Nazi Party mem-ber; to his grandchildren, a kindly but discomfiting figure, with his rigid bearing and baleful eye. His school records are full of intimate personal details: electrocardiograms, notes on his appendix and hernia operations, a graphic map of his teeth. But his deeper history goes unmentioned—the string of identities he left behind, like foreign passports in a secret agent's drawer.

My mother had just begun to study Vichy France when he died, and to slowly circle back to him. It's no surprise, I think, that she chose that moment to revisit her family history. She was in her early forties, about the same age as her father at the end of the war. She had five children—one more than he had—and knew in her bones how it would feel to leave them behind. How could he have done it?

She came to think of him as a soul undone by history and then spared by it—a man whose reckless, blinkered idealism led him to the Nazis, then gave him the nerve to resist them. "*Angst het er nit g'ha*," she told me. Fear wasn't in him. But she could never truly forgive him. After she moved to America in 1962, she asked her father again and again to visit, but he never came. "He said to me, 'You were the ones who left me. You are the ones who have to come back,'" she recalled that day, on the footbridge over the Rhine. "And I thought, 'You were the one who left *us* during the war.'"

I was too young to register his absence then, much less to judge him. Even now, with all I know about my grandfather, I'm left with an impossible accounting. Does his courage in Alsace balance his moral blindness earlier? Or was he only able to help the villagers because of his own complicity in their oppression? Was his willingness to stand up to his party, first by defending his colleague in Aulfingen, then by ignoring his orders in Bartenheim, proof of a moral awakening? Or does it make his failure to see Hitler's other inhumanities even worse? There is no perfect sum to be made of his contradictions, no equation that can solve for his soul.

The last time my mother and I saw him, the year before he died, there was little left to love or resent. My family was living in southern France then, and we had driven to Germany to visit him. He had just turned seventy-nine and had been moved to a nursing home outside of Weil. The police had twice caught him driving the wrong way on the road. They issued no ticket and levied no fine—as if everyone ended up on the wrong side sometimes. But he was becoming a danger to himself even at home.

Lying in bed, in the pale light from his window, he looked nearly as gaunt as he once was as a prisoner of war. My mother sat beside him and held his hand, but he just glared at her, bewildered and un-recognizing. A few nights earlier, one of the orderlies told her, he had tried to run away from the facility after dinner. They found him in the woods across the road hours later, wandering around in his paja-mas in the dark. He was retracing the same path again and again, as if looking for something he had lost.

What do we owe the past? Why does it have such a hold on us? The more I know about my grandfather—the longer I stumble along in his footsteps—the more those questions echo beyond my own family history. What seemed like a German problem when I began has become an American one, too—though of course that was true all along. Friends who used to nod sympathetically, or with carefully blanked expressions, when I talked about my grandfather now tell me about their own ancestors who owned slaves, or their great-uncle who was a McCarthyite or a member of the Klan. They talk about their cousin or sister-in-law who believes in QAnon or white suprem-acy. They feel both betrayed by their history and implicated in it. What to do with our poisoned heritage? How to make peace with it without perpetuating its wrongs? We live in an unforgiving time, im-patient to pass judgment and rectify the past. But the guilt that drives us can reach beyond penance or restitution to a conviction that something in us, or in our culture, is broken beyond repair. That our history is irredeemable.

I have never believed that. Not when I first went searching for my grandfather's past and even less so now. It's not just that his story belies the idea of irredeemable sin, or that Germany has been so utterly transformed since the war. It's that the better I know him, the more I see how deeply personal his choices were—how bound up in the events of his life and the peculiarities of his mind. Like millions of Germans, Karl came to the Nazis in his own way and through his own weaknesses. Only he could bear the weight of that decision, and only he, and other Germans like him, could summon the strength to change. He was my mother's father. I have his hollow cheeks and downturned eyes, his stiff shoulders and earnest stare. But his conscience was his own.

"Yes, I had a plan, but this is how things are," he wrote, in his letter to Gernot from the Citadel in 1947. "Let us leave the past behind us. Try to wrest some beauty and goodness from life. A fine little tune can give more joy than the latest scientific discovery, the results of which are often just used to ruin people. And so, onward into your twentieth year, full of energy and light, and all will be well. Your Papa."

———— • ————

ACKNOWLEDGMENTS

For a long time, I wasn't sure that I could finish this book. The story was too close to home and hard to tell, and full of holes I didn't know that I could fill. I knew the rough outline of my grandfather's years in occupied France—the beginning and end and major turning points—but not the crucial details in between. As often as not, starting a new chapter felt like standing at the edge of an abyss, with only a thin rope of dates and anecdotes suspended across it.

If I've managed to reach the other side, it's thanks to dozens of friends and colleagues in Brooklyn, Berlin, Alsace, and the Black Forest, at the offices of Penguin Random House and *The New Yorker*. Elyse Cheney, my wonder of an agent, kept faith for years while I wavered between projects, then found the perfect home for this book. My editor, Robin Desser, understood the project's risk and promise and never lost her passion for it. I can't imagine a better collaborator: brilliant, clear-eyed, and deeply insightful, with a pitch-perfect ear and a near telepathic sense of what I'm trying to say. I'm grateful to David Remnick, Andy Ward, and the late Sonny Mehta for their patience and belief in this book when it seemed like it might never get done, and to Hilary Redmon and the Random House staff for shepherding it so ably to its publication.

Along the way, a succession of historians and archivists have illuminated my grandfather's time for me and helped find needles in haystacks across Europe: Gerhard Blessing, Sabine Bode, Dominique Dreyer, Heinz Fehlauer, Brigitte Guyot, Marie-Josèphe Guyot, Stephen Harp, Manfred Hennhöfer, Konrad Jarausch, Eric Johnson, Julian Klein, Edward Lengel, Jochen Rees, Philippe Renaud, Mélanie Alves Rolo, Hans-Joachim Schuster, Konrad Stuhlmacher, Pierre Taborelli, Jean-Pierre Thirion, and Friedbert Trendle, among others. An extraordinary group of early readers—Kathryn Bowers, Atul Gawande, David Grann, Joel Harrington, Eric Johnson, and Raffi Khatchadourian—helped fine-tune the tone and key passages of the book, as did Cressida Leyshon, my beloved and preternaturally gifted editor at *The New Yorker*. Molly Montgomery, Pauline Peek, Sameen Gauhar, Emily Ulbricht, and Ena Alvarado saved me from countless errors and infelicities while bringing other details into sharper focus. This book is immeasurably better for all their help.

Like my parents, I've spent most of my life far from my roots. So it was strange to find, when I sat down to write about them, that I'd been preparing to do so the whole time. All my oddities were suddenly essential to the task. My school years in France and Germany helped me to sift archives on both sides of the Rhine. My family connections opened doors in secretive villages. My obscure German dialect put my elderly sources at ease: It was just like the Alsatian they spoke as children. Some of this was inevitable—the virtuous circle of writing what you know—but I also relied on a great deal of luck and goodwill. My uncles Sigmar and Winfried sat for long, thoughtful interviews, as did my aunts Heidi, Christel, and Gerda, and my cousins Karin, Silvia, Sabine, Thomas, Christian, and Susan. My brother, Martin, and my sisters Eva, Monika, and Andrea filled essential gaps in my memory, and my daughter Ruby nearly froze her toes off in northern France following her great-grandfather's trail through the trenches of Champagne. She and my son, Hans, and my daughter Evangeline have vetted hundreds of sentences, paragraphs, covers, and photographs, and pulled me from the brink of any number of clumsy phrases and misguided metaphors. Most of all, I'm thankful to my wife, Jennifer Nelson—my first and best reader—for her boundless patience and love, and to my mother, who had the courage and faith to set the whole story in motion.

Again and again, while writing this book, the events I was describing were reenacted in the day's news, whether by racist attacks and the rise of the far right, or the invasion of Ukraine. In the darkest moments, when the world seemed doomed to endlessly repeat its mistakes, it was always a comfort to return to Alsace. The villagers in Bartenheim have lived through the worst of history's cycles and somehow emerged with their wisdom and sharp wit intact. I'm grateful to Gabriel Arnold, Alfonse Huttenschmitt, René Kannengieser, Georges and Marie-Rose Baumann, the Grienenberger family, and both Gérard Kielwassers for inviting me into their homes and speaking honestly about their history. Above all, I'm indebted to Georges Tschill for befriending my mother forty years ago, and to Jean-Georges and Monique Tschill for extending that friendship to me. Without their generosity and grace, this book would not exist.

Alsace is a far more peaceable, prosperous place than it was in my grandfather's time, but it, too, has had its losses. With the borders open and customs checks gone, France and Germany have grown less distinct—they have the same Ikeas, Starbucks, and Uniqlos— even as their deeper connections have faded. Kindred dialects once bound the people across the Rhine even when war intervened. Now most children speak High German or the French of the Academy and leave Alsatian and Alemannisch to their parents. Before the war,

Bartenheim was full of storks in the spring, nesting on rooftops and clattering their beaks to greet one another. Now they're gone. They miss the rough, companionable sound of Alsatian, the old-timers say.

My family has never stopped coming back: first my parents, for visits short and long, then my wife and I as exchange students, and finally a stream of my grandfather's great-grandchildren, in a kind of reverse migration. Ruby and Hans moved to Germany after college, as did three of my nieces, and Evangeline may not be far behind. It's hard to say how long they'll stay—America has more to lure them back than Germany did for my parents after the war. But for now it's an equal exchange: Five of us emigrated in 1962, and five have returned. I like to imagine them all aloft on the same night: my children's jet drifting past my parents' propeller plane, high above the Atlantic. They peer through their windows at one another, and for just a flash, a crease in time, they recognize themselves. They have the same apprehension in their eyes—the same fear of bad blood and unbridgeable distances—and the same hope.

NOTES

CHAPTER 1: SUSPECT

3. **The man in the interrogation room:** The descriptions of Karl's interrogation, including quotations, come from the following interrogation files: "Déclaration concernant l'attitude de l'allemand Karl Gönner, instituteur pendant les années d'occupation," interrogation report, Gouvernement Militaire de Württemberg, Tuttlingen, 1946; "Interrogatoire de Karl Gönner par Otto Baumgartner, Justiz-Inspektor," interrogation report, Gouvernement Militaire de Lörrach, March 13, 1946, Dépôt Central d'Archives de la Justice Militaire, Le Blanc, France.

4. **Georges Baumann:** The details of Georges Baumann's murder come from the following police and military reports: "Concernant Goenner Karl alias Genner Karl, Témoins et renseignements," military report, Tribunal Militaire Permanent de Metz, 1947; "Meurtre du Français Baumann, Georges," military report, Ministère de la Justice, Strasbourg, 1946; "Procès-verbal de renseignements, Affaire Baumann, de Bartenheim. Victime par crime de guerre," police report, Gendarmerie Nationale, Mulhouse, 1945; "Renseignements complémentaires sur l'affaire Baumann, de Bartenheim (H-R), victime par crime de guerre," police report, Gendarmerie Nationale, Mulhouse, 1946; "Renseignements judiciaires: Affaire Baumann, Georges, de Bartenheim (Haut-Rhin), victime par crime de guerre," police report, Gendarmerie Nationale, Mulhouse, 1945, Dépôt Central d'Archives de la Justice Militaire.

CHAPTER 2: SUBJECT

10. **"We in Germany":** Karl Jaspers, *Die Schuldfrage: Zur politischen Haftung Deutschlands* (Munich: R. Piper, 1965), 7 (author's translation).

10. **"We don't want":** Jaspers, *Die Schuldfrage*, 15.

17. **the Black citizens:** Chelcey Adami, "Stillwater Men Helped Integrate City's Neighborhoods," *Stillwater News Press*, January 16, 2010, stwnewspress.com /news/stillwater-men-helped-integrate-citys-neighborhoods/article_a87967b3 -641d-51ca-bf7e-5c29c0e5a9b3.html. Michelle Charles, telephone interview, May 20, 2022.

19. **Some forty million:** "German-American Day: October 6, 2021," news release, United States Census Bureau, last revised October 8, 2021, census .gov/newsroom/stories/german-american-day.html.

20. **nearly twice as:** U.S. Census Bureau, American Community Survey, 2019: ACS 1-Year Estimates Detailed Tables, Table C04006, data.census.gov/cedsci /table?q=ACSDT1Y2019.C04006&tid=ACSDT1Y2019.C04006&hide Preview=true.

20. **"The notion that":** Daniel Jonah Goldhagen, *Hitler's Willing Executioners: Ordinary Germans and the Holocaust* (New York: Doubleday, 2007), 408.

21. **"in alphabetical order":** " 'Be Nice to the Germans,' " *New York Times*, July 20, 1990, nytimes.com/1990/07/20/opinion/be-nice-to-the-germans .html.

21. **"capacity for excess":** " 'Be Nice to the Germans.' "

21. **"Germany is never":** Roger Cohen, "An Unreliable Germany and the Volkswagen Debacle," *New York Times*, September 28, 2015, nytimes.com/2015 /09/29/opinion/roger-cohen-volkswagen-unreliable-troubling-germany .html.

23. **"Life can't be":** Karl Gönner to Sigmar Gönner, November 24, 1956.

CHAPTER 3: FATHER

28. ***Adieu, Emile:*** Rod McKuen, "Seasons in the Sun," recorded 1965, Track B8 on *Seasons in the Sun*, Stanyan Records (vinyl).

31. **"These all differ":** Julius Caesar, *The Commentaries of Caesar*, trans. William Duncan (London: Dodsley, 1779), B2; Julius Caesar, *The War for Gaul: A New Translation*, trans. James J. O'Donnell (Princeton, NJ: Princeton University Press, 2021), 1–3. The original text can be viewed here: Gaius Julius Caesar, *Caesar's Commentaries* (London: Whittaker, 1857), 1–3, google.com/books /edition/Caesar_s_commentaries_De_bello_Gallico_b/wYcCAAAAQAAJ ?hl=en&gbpv=1&dq=Germanis,+qui+trans+Rhenum+incolunt&pg=PA3 &printsec=frontcover.

31. ***Germanis, qui trans:*** Gaius Julius Caesar, *Caesar's Commentaries* (London: Whittaker, 1857), 3, google.com/books/edition/Caesar_s_commentaries_De _bello_Gallico_b/wYcCAAAAQAAJ?hl=en&gbpv=1&dq=Germanis,+qui +trans+Rhenum+incolunt&pg=PA3&printsec=frontcover.

31. **"tall of body":** Diodorus Siculus, *The Library of History*, Vol. 3, Loeb Classical Library (Cambridge, MA: Harvard University, 1939), penelope.uchicago .edu/Thayer/E/Roman/Texts/Diodorus_Siculus/5B*.html.

31. **The Germans were:** Tacitus, *The Germany and the Agricola of Tacitus*, Project Gutenberg, May 17, 2013, section 4, gutenberg.org/files/7524/7524-h/7524 -h.htm#linknoteref-144.

31. **"fierce blue eyes":** Tacitus, *The Agricola and Germania*, trans. A. J. Church and W. J. Brodribb (London: Macmillan, 1877), 87–110, reprinted by Paul Halsall in "Medieval Sourcebook: Tacitus, the Germania, excerpts," Fordham University, July 1998, sourcebooks.fordham.edu/source/tacitus-germania -excerp.asp#:~:text=All%20have%20fierce%20blue%20eyes,Government.

31. **Best to keep:** Caesar, *War for Gaul*, 155.

31. **Caesar invented Germany:** See, for example, Susan P. Mattern, *Rome and the Enemy: Imperial Strategy in the Principate* (Berkeley: University of California Press, 2002), 76; Michel Reddé, "Roman *Germania*? What *Germania*?" in *The Oxford Handbook of the Archaeology of Roman Germany*, ed. Simon James and Stefan Krmnicek (Oxford: Oxford University Press, 2020), 559.

34. **When the war:** Edeltraut Bilger, "The German-Americans in Oklahoma During World War I, as Seen Through Three German-Language Newspapers" (master's thesis, Oklahoma State University, 1976), 1, 73–74, 85–86.

34. **"There was no":** Bilger, "German-Americans in Oklahoma," 91–92.

34. **"The new generation":** Bilger, "German-Americans in Oklahoma," 91–92.

34. **When the United States:** Bilger, "German-Americans in Oklahoma," 91–92.

35. **"It is with a heavy":** Julian Jackson, *France: The Dark Years, 1940–1944* (Oxford: Oxford University Press, 2003), 126.

36. **"lose her soul":** Edeltraut Bilger, "The Reconstruction of France: Marshal Pétain's Policies, 1940–1942, as Evaluated by American Journalists and Scholars" (dissertation, Oklahoma State University, 1984), 28, 165–66.

36. **"beat the Fascists":** Bilger, "Reconstruction of France," 6.

36. **"shining symbol of":** "France: Pétain Joins Up," *Time*, May 27, 1940, content.time.com/time/subscriber/article/0,33009,884102,00.html.

CHAPTER 4: ANCESTOR

40. **"Your Blood":** Author's translation of *Ahnenpaß* (Dortmund: Westfalia), 45.

40. *Nazi Ancestral Proof:* For more information about the Nazis' genealogical programs, see Eric Ehrenreich, *The Nazi Ancestral Proof: Genealogy, Racial Science, and the Final Solution* (Bloomington: Indiana University Press, 2007).

41. **"The blood that":** Isolde Kurz, from "Allgemeines vom Menschendasein," as printed in *Ahnenpaß* (Dortmund: Westfalia), 48 (author's translation).

44. **"Death to Germans":** "Historic Graffiti at Germany's Reichstag Stirs Controversy," CNN, July 18, 1999, edition.cnn.com/WORLD/europe/9907/18 /reichstag.graffiti/index.html.

45. **"People murdered in":** Jas Chana, "Plan for Holocaust Memorial 'Stumbling Stones' Takes a Tumble," *Tablet*, August 5, 2015, tabletmag.com/sections /news/articles/plan-for-holocaust-memorial-stumbling-stones-takes-a -tumble.

45. **In Villingen-Schwenningen:** The city has since reversed that decision: In 2020, the district council voted in favor of the plaques. In October 2021, the first Stolpersteine were installed, and twenty-two more were installed as recently as March 6, 2022. Roland Sprich, "Sie stellten sich den Nazis entgegen und wurden ermordet—Jetzt erinnern an sie Stolpersteine," *Südkurier,* March 6, 2022, suedkurier.de/region/schwarzwald/villingen-schwenningen /sie-stellten-sich-den-nazis-entgegen-und-wurden-ermordet-jetzt-erinnern -an-sie-stolpersteine;art372541,11067426.

45. **a poll of more:** Noah Rayman, "The U.S. Is No Longer the Most Popular Country in the World," *Time,* November 13, 2014, time.com/3583915 /germany-us-popular-country/.

45. **"The world voted":** Lauren Davidson, "The World Voted, and the Best Country Is . . . Germany?" *Telegraph,* November 12, 2014.

52. ***"Etwas ist nur wahr":*** Paraphrased from Friedrich Hölderlin, *Übersetzungen, philosophische Schriften* (Weimar: Erich Lichtenstein, 1922), 332.

CHAPTER 5: SON

54. **The village must have:** The descriptions of Herzogenweiler come from the author's conversations with Gerhard Blessing and from the following text: *Herzogenweiler 1208–2008: Auf der Suche nach Geschichte und Geschichten, Gerhard Bessing, Oskar Diringer, Sigfried Gütert, et al.* Heinrich Maulhardt, ed. (Villingen-Schwenningen: Verlag der Stadt Villingen-Schwenningen, 2008).

57. **"For more than a hundred":** *Herzogenweiler 1208–2008,* 89.

61. **They claimed:** Johann Scheible, ed., *Das sechste und siebente Buch Mosis, das ist: Mosis magische Geisterkunst, das Geheimniß aller Geheimnisse: wort- und bildgetreu nach einer alten Handschrift* (Stuttgart: Scheible, 1849), 8.

62. **"Siberian cold":** Heinrich Maulhardt, "Kirchengeschichte," in *Herzogenweiler 1208–2008: Auf der Suche nach Geschichte und Geschichten,* ed. Stadtarchiv Villingen-Schwenningen (Villingen-Schwenningen: Verlag der Stadt Villingen -Schwenningen, 2008), 29.

62. **"I have a duty":** Maulhardt, "Kirchengeschichte," 30.

63. ***Beim frühen Morgenlicht:*** Sebastian Pörtner, ed., *Katholisches Gesangbuch für den öffentlichen Gottesdienst in Würzburg* (Würzburg: Dorbath, 1828), 183.

63. **When morning gilds:** Henry Formby, ed., *Catholic Hymns* (London: Burns and Lambert, 1853), 44.

CHAPTER 6: SOLDIER

64. **They were camped:** The descriptions of Karl's company are drawn from a memoir written by veterans from his regiment: Gustav Seiz, ed. *Geschichte des 6. Badischen Infanterie-Regiments Kaiser Friedrich III. Nr. 114 im Weltkrieg 1914–1918.* (Zeulenroda: Sporn, 1932). The descriptions of his particular movements, locations, and timeline come from the following World War I unit roster records for the 114th Infantry Regiment, Generallandes-

archiv Karlsruhe: 456 C Nr. 1376, Bild 191, landesarchiv-bw.de/plink/?f=4
-777233-191; 456 C Nr. 1472, Bild 232, landesarchiv-bw.de/plink/?f=4
-782243-232.

64. ***"Es gilt die"***: Gerd Paul, *Es gilt die letzten Schläge, den Sieg zu vollenden! Zeichnet
Kriegsanleihe!*, lithograph, war poster (1918), photo, U.S. Library of Congress,
loc.gov/item/2004666141/.

66. **"Especially the never-ending"**: Seiz, *Geschichte*, 464.

67. ***Elle est détruite:*** Seiz, 467.

67. **his military records show:** Unit rosters (1915–1919), 114th Infantry Regiment, 456 C Nr. 1472, Bild 232, Generallandesarchiv Karlsruhe, landesarchiv
-bw.de/plink/?f=4-782243-232.

67. **memoir of the war:** Seiz, *Geschichte*.

67. **"At Tahure, death":** Seiz, *Geschichte*, 567.

68. **I stand at:** Seiz, *Geschichte*, 563.

69. **Lengel calls the Meuse-Argonne:** Edward Lengel, telephone interview,
October 19, 2017.

70. **The first two:** Unit rosters, 456 C Nr. 1412, Bild 17, landesarchiv-bw.de
/plink/?f=4-779182-17; 456 C Nr. 1376, Bild 191, landesarchiv-bw.de/plink
/?f=4-777233-191.

70. **The third page:** Unit rosters, 456 C Nr. 1472, Bild 232, landesarchiv-bw.de
/plink/?f=4-782243-232.

71. **"ill-suited to this age":** Adolf Hitler, "Kulturrede 1934," in *Reichstagung in
Nürnberg 1934*, ed. Julius Streicher (Berlin: Weller, 1934), 140–74.

71. **The secret note:** For more information, see Louis MacKay, "Negative
Typecasting," *London Review of Books,* May 27, 2015, lrb.co.uk/blog/2015/may
/negative-typecasting.

73. **"It has been determined":** "Gas Mask Command," letter from the German ministry of war to Infantry Regiment 114, June 4, 1918, Generallandesarchiv Karlsruhe.

74. **"friendly, clean little town":** Seiz, *Geschichte*, 474.

CHAPTER 7: CASUALTY

80. **The military camp:** The descriptions of the region come from the author's
conversations with Jean-Pierre Thirion.

82. **By late September:** As in Chapter 6, most of the descriptions of Karl's
company in this chapter are drawn from a memoir written by veterans from
his regiment: Gustav Seiz, ed. *Geschichte des 6. Badischen Infanterie-Regiments Kaiser Friedrich III. Nr. 114 im Weltkrieg 1914–1918.* (Zeulenroda: Sporn, 1932). A
few descriptions of the path of Karl's division come from archived logbooks
found in *War Diaries of German Units Opposed to the Second Division (Regular) 1918,*
Vol. 7, Blanc Mont (Part 1), trans. Gustav J. Braun and Trevor W. Swett
(Washington, DC: Second Division Historical Section, Army War College,
1931).

82. **"For what are you":** Propaganda leaflets, World War I Document Archive,

Brigham Young University Library, wwi.lib.byu.edu/index.php/Propaganda_Leaflets.

83. **"waving a red flag":** Reid Badger, "The Conquests of Europe: The Remarkable Career of James Reese Europe," *Alabama Heritage* 1 (Summer 1986), 45, worldwar1centennial.org/images/alabama/Readings_Resources/Alabama Heritage001_Badger.pdf.

83. **"It is important":** Rebecca Onion, "A WWI-Era Memo Asking French Officers to Practice Jim Crow with Black American Troops," *Slate*, April 27, 2016, slate.com/human-interest/2016/04/secret-information-concerning-black-troops-a-warning-memo-sent-to-the-french-military-during-world-war-i.html.

85. **"They looked like":** Edward G. Lengel, *A Companion to the Meuse-Argonne Campaign* (Chichester: Wiley Blackwell, 2014), 14.

85. **"There is no necessity":** Lengel, 269–70.

86. **"The combat method":** Braun and Swett, *War Diaries*.

86. **"A runner was":** Braun and Swett, *War Diaries*.

87. **"The plane moves":** Fliegerbeschießung (collection of instructional leaflets from the German army in the First World War), Generallandesarchiv Karlsruhe.

87. **the captured German logs:** Braun and Swett, *War Diaries*.

88. **"The armed forces":** Lengel, *Companion to the Meuse-Argonne Campaign*, 1.

88. **Just after dawn:** Seiz, *Geschichte*, 494.

88. **To recover any semblance:** Braun and Swett, *War Diaries*.

88. **The trucks took them:** Seiz, *Geschichte*, 494.

89. **"So great was":** Seiz, *Geschichte*, 496.

90. **"For a long time":** Karl Gönner to Emmy Boll, October 25, 1957, copy in author's possession.

90. **One winter morning:** The anecdote comes from the author's conversations with Jean-Luc Evrard.

91. **It was here:** Unit rosters (1915–1919), 114th Infantry Regiment, 456 C Nr. 1376, Bild 191, landesarchiv-bw.de/plink/?f=4-777233-191; Unit rosters (1915–1919), 114th Infantry Regiment, 456 C Nr. 1472, Bild 232, Generallandesarchiv Karlsruhe, landesarchiv-bw.de/plink/?f=4-782243-232.

91. **Karl's regimental history:** Seiz, *Geschichte*, 495.

CHAPTER 8: GHOST

93. **villagers in Herzogenweiler:** Gerhard Blessing (local historian), in conversation with the author, September 22, 2016.

100. **"Three times a week":** Michael Mittermeier, interview by Soraya Sarhaddi Nelson, "Germany: A Comedy Renaissance," *All Things Considered*, National Public Radio, July 25, 2017.

102. *Der Struwwelpeter:* Heinrich Hoffman, *Der Struwwelpeter* (1845) (Erlangen: Pestalozzi Verlag, 1985).

103. *The Forgotten Generation:* Sabine Bode, *The Forgotten Generation*, trans. Robert Brambeer (Stuttgart: Verlag Klett-Cotta, 2004).

CHAPTER 9: TEACHER

108. **He arrived:** Unit rosters (1915–1919), 114th Infantry Regiment, 456 C Nr. 1472, Bild 232, Generallandesarchiv Karlsruhe, landesarchiv-bw.de/plink /?f=4-782243-232.

109. **Before he went to war:** Melde- und Personalbogen I Karl Gönner, personnel file, Staatsarchiv Freiburg. Karl's file contains records on his time in Sasbach, his two war injury compensation requests, his qualifications to become head teacher, and the jobs he held up until 1948.

109. **But this was a bit:** "Reichsversorgungsgesetz, 22. Dez. 1927," *Zeitschrift für ausländisches öffentliches Recht und Völkerrecht* 1 (1929): 561–97, zaoerv.de/01_1929 /1_1929_2_b_561_2_597.pdf.

109. **Fear of the Lord:** The motto is taken from Psalm 110:10, biblegateway.com /passage/?search=Psalm%20110%3A10&version=ESV.

110. **The year Karl graduated:** Adam Smith, *Paper Money* (New York: Summit Books, 1981), 57–62.

110. **Der Geißt ist:** The English translation of this Bible verse appears in John 6:63, biblegateway.com/passage/?search=john+6%3A63&version=NKJV.

110. **Gerechtigkeit erhöht ein Volk:** Proverbs 14:34, biblegateway.com/passage /?search=Proverbs%2014%3A34&version=NKJV.

112. **"If you were my wife":** Karl Gönner to Xaver and Regina Blessing, December 23, 1955, copy in author's possession.

112. **"I'm a person":** Karl Gönner to Emmy Boll, October 19, 1957, copy in author's possession.

113. **But when Susan:** The anecdote comes from the author's conversation with Susan Gönner, March 2019.

113. **"Dearest one":** Emma Egle to Karl Gönner, January 25, 1926, in author's possession.

114. **She had been:** "Jubiläum: Vor 200 Jahren konnten Mädchen in Basel erstmals zur Schule gehen," *bz Basel*, January 4, 2013, bzbasel.ch/basel/basel-stadt /jubilaum-vor-200-jahren-konnten-madchen-in-basel-erstmals-zur-schule -gehen-ld.1957540.

114. **But German law didn't allow:** Claudia Huerkamp, *Bildungsbürgerinnen: Frauen im Studien und in akademischen Berufen, 1900–1945* (Göttingen: Vandenhoeck & Ruprecht, 1996), 221–222.

115. **Aulfingen:** Jakob Josef Hoffmann, *Handbuch für Stellenbewerbung (Schulstatistik). Nachtrag* (Bonndorf: Spachholz & Ehrath, ca. 1905).

115. **"From my personal experience":** "Auf Einkunft der Bewerberliste von der O.B. Aulfingen," memo, district school board, Konstanz, 1930, Staatsarchiv Freiburg.

120. **That a village:** Joseph Goebbels, *Das Tagebuch von Joseph Goebbels 1925–1926*, ed. Helmut Heiber (Berlin: de Gruyter, 1961), 27.

123. **"The undersigned urges":** Karl Gönner, "Antrag des Hauptl. K. Gönner um Erstellung eines Kachelofens mit Backgelegenheit," letter to mayor, July 21, 1931, Ortsarchiv Aulfingen.

124. **Many teachers had:** Hans-Joachim Schuster (archivist), in conversation with the author and fact checker Emily Ulbricht, February 2022.

125. **"Their masses grow":** Cited in Konrad Hugo Jarausch, *The Unfree Professions: German Lawyers, Teachers, and Engineers, 1900–1950* (New York: Oxford University Press, 1990), 92.

126. **"In my great educational work":** Cited in Martyn Housden, *Resistance and Conformity in the Third Reich* (London: Taylor & Francis, 2013), 68.

126. **The source of that groundswell:** Jarausch, *Unfree Professions*, 164–65. For more on the role of teachers in Hitler's ideology, see Dieter Hoffmann-Axthelm, *Wie kommt die Geschichte ins Entwerfen?: Aufsätze zu Architektur und Stadt* (Braunschweig: Vieweg, 1987), 133; and Gottfried Feder, *Das Programm der N.S.D.A.P. und seine weltanschaulichen Grundgedanken* (Munich: Eher, 1933), 51.

127. **By 1938:** Jarausch, *Unfree Professions*, Table 6.2, 165.

127. **"What is speed?":** Cited in Milton Mayer, *They Thought They Were Free: The Germans, 1933–45* (Chicago: University of Chicago Press, 1955), 196.

CHAPTER 10: BELIEVER

129. **"There were jobs":** Milton Mayer, *They Thought They Were Free: The Germans, 1933–45* (Chicago: University of Chicago Press, 1955), 48.

129. **"A man saw":** Mayer, 61.

129. **"Oh, Mother, Mother":** Mayer, *They Thought They Were Free*, 50.

129. **"speak truth to":** H. Larry Ingle, "Milton Mayer, Quaker Hedgehog," *Quaker Theology*, February 18, 2020, quakertheology.org/milton-mayer-quaker -hedgehog-2/.

130. **"there were two truths":** Mayer, *They Thought They Were Free*, 52.

130. **"Now I see":** Mayer, *They Thought They Were Free*, viii–ix.

132. **threw a pine cone:** Karl Gönner, "Unfall des Schülers Oswald Gut," letter to school board, Konstanz, December 12, 1938, Ortsarchiv Aulfingen.

132. **"Their shining little eyes":** Karl Gönner to Emmy Boll, October 22, 1957, copy in author's possession.

134. **Winter Relief Agency:** "Interrogatoire de Karl Gönner."

134. **"welfare idiocy":** Cited in Peter Hammerschmidt, *Die Wohlfahrtsverbände im NS-Staat. Die NSV und die konfessionellen Verbände Caritas und Innere Mission im Gefüge der Wohlfahrtspflege des Nationalsozialismus* (Wiesbaden: Springer VS, 2013), 135.

134. **"No one shall":** "Keiner soll hungern! Keiner soll frieren! Winterhilfswerk des deutschen Volkes 1934/35," propaganda material, 1934/35, Staatsarchiv Freiburg, deutsche-digitale-bibliothek.de/item/TGTO5OOC GUWESLBRRNWXQK7WTLBQUANW.

135. **party was officially closed:** This claim appears in a letter Karl wrote to the military government in 1945, describing his life up until that point and requesting to receive his teaching license again. Karl Gönner, "Bitte des Hauptlehrers Karl Gönner, Weil am Rh., um Wiederverwendung als Volks-

schullehrer," letter to the military government, December 1945, Staatsarchiv Freiburg.

135. **"open commitment to National Socialism":** Karl Gönner, "Zur Kenntnisnahme an das Bad. Kreisschulamt Konstanz," letter to the mayor and the head of the Catholic parish, November 11, 1934, Ortsarchiv Aulfingen.

135. **"Get to work":** Karl Gönner to Sigmar Gönner, March 12, 1957, copy in author's possession.

136. **"Radio is the mouthpiece":** F. Frik to the mayors of the district of Engen, March 1936, Ortsarchiv Aulfingen.

137. **a speech that he gave:** "Schöne Ortsgruppenversammlung der NSDAP in Bartenheim," *Mülhauser Tagblatt*, December 15, 1940.

137. **"Nothing's eaten":** sprichwort-plattform.org/sp/Nichts%20wird%20so %20hei%C3%9F%20gegessen%20wie%20es%20gekocht%20wird.

137. **"a tolerable relation":** "Text of Hitler's Speech to Reichstag at Nuremberg," *New York Times*, September 16, 1935.

139. **"It is shocking":** Lisa Pine, *Education in Nazi Germany* (Oxford: Berg, 2010), 29.

139. **"Song of the Faithful":** Reich and Prussian ministers for ecclesiastical affairs to all church authorities, August 28, 1936, Ortsarchiv Aulfingen.

139. **"It was cold":** Karl Gönner to the Badisches Kreisschulamt Konstanz, December 11, 1933, Ortsarchiv Aulfingen.

140. **"For some time now":** Heinrich Ganninger to the Badisches Kreisschulamt Villingen, June 25, 1938, Ortsarchiv Aulfingen.

140. **wrote a testimonial:** Karl Bihler, "Bescheinigung," December 14, 1945, copy in author's possession.

142. **"Dissidents, nondenominationalists":** Minister des Innern, "An die Berzirksämter," letter to district offices and police headquarters in Baden-Baden, July 31, 1933, Ortsarchiv Aulfingen.

143. **"I have recently received":** "Racial Research Bulletin," July 31, 1933, Ortsarchiv Aulfingen.

143. **denied citizenship:** to district offices and police headquarters in Baden-Baden, July 31, 1933, Ortsarchiv Aulfingen.

143. **"the male Jews":** Bezirksamt Engen, "Judenkartei," letter to the mayors of the district, Ortsarchiv Aulfingen.

143. **"Possible grounds for":** Bezirksamt Donaueschingen to the mayors of the district, Ortsarchiv Aulfingen.

144. **properly cared for:** Dr. Best (SS) to Gestapo and state police departments, Ortsarchiv Aulfingen.

144. **"In the winter":** Karl Gönner, "Fußballverein," letter to mayor of Aulfingen, March 16, 1938, Ortsarchiv Aulfingen.

146. **"spied upon":** Konrad H. Jarausch, *Broken Lives: How Ordinary Germans Experienced the 20th Century* (Princeton, NJ: Princeton University Press, 2018), 73.

146. **"Today Head Teacher Müller":** Karl Gönner to the district leadership of the National Socialist Teachers League, October 23, 1934, Staatsarchiv Freiburg.

147. **"It has come to":** Minister des Innern, "Verwahrung und Unfruchtbar-machung," bulletin to district office, June 8, 1934, Ortsarchiv Aulfingen.

149. **February 24, 1940:** Minister des Innern, "Verlegung von Anstaltsinsassen im Rahmen besonderer planwirtschaftlicher Maßnahmen," secret bulletin to Wiesloch nursing home and care facility, February 24, 1940, Fold3.

150. **Parents were either assured:** Franz Peschke, "Schreck's Abteilung—Die Wieslocher 'Kinderfachabteilung' im Zweiten Weltkrieg," publication series of the working group "Die Heil- und Pflegeanstalt Wiesloch in der Zeit des Nationalsozialismus" 2 (1993): 19–41.

150. **children had died:** Lawrence A. Zeidman, *Brain Science Under the Swastika: Ethical Violations, Resistance, and Victimization of Neuroscientists in Nazi Europe* (Oxford: Oxford University Press, 2020), 387.

152. **"Anti-Nazis":** Mayer, *They Thought They Were Free,* 74–75.

152. **in the same era:** Mayer, *They Thought They Were Free,* 181.

152. **during World War II:** Mayer, *They Thought They Were Free,* 75.

152. **"What happened here":** Mayer, *They Thought They Were Free,* 166.

153. **top marks:** Karl Gönner, report to the Badisches Schulamt in Konstanz, October 20, 1936, Ortsarchiv Aulfingen.

153. **"They tried to":** Hans Müller to Karl Gönner's lawyer, May 25, 1947, copy in author's possession.

154. **requested a transfer:** Karl Gönner to school board in Villingen, April 12, 1938, copy in author's possession.

154. **"Nazi friends":** Mayer, *They Thought They Were Free,* 186.

154. **"Let my thanks":** Karl Gönner to the school board in Villingen, April 12, 1938, Staatsarchiv Freiburg.

CHAPTER 11: INVADER

159. **"the very picture":** Karl Tschamber and Ludwig Keller, *Geschichte der Stadt Weil am Rhein* (Weil am Rhein, 1961), 201.

163. **man's stupidity:** Robert E. Terk, letter to the editor, *Worcester Telegram & Gazette,* September 28, 2016, telegram.com/story/opinion/letters/2016/09/29/letter-monuments-to-stupidity-of-man/25297907007/.

163. **riding a bicycle:** "Enquête sur l'histoire de l'occupation et de la libération de la France dans le Département du Haut-Rhin, Ville de Mulhouse," Ministère de l'Éducation Nationale, Commission d'Histoire de l'Occupation et de la Libération de la France, 1950, I, Archives Départementales du Haut-Rhin, Colmar, France.

164. **top of their lungs:** "Enquête sur l'histoire" (Mulhouse), 4.

165. **"By four o'clock":** Eugène Dessoud, *Pfastatt: Dans la tourmente 1940–1944* (unpublished manuscript), 5, Archives Départementales du Haut-Rhin.

165. **"Nearly everyone wept":** "Enquête sur l'histoire de l'occupation et de la libération de la France dans le Département du Haut-Rhin, Commune de Lutterbach," Ministère de l'Éducation Nationale, Commission d'Histoire de

l'Occupation et de la Libération de la France, 1950, I, Archives Départementales du Haut-Rhin.

166. **"We're not bad":** Dessoud, *Pfastatt*, 1.

166. **"You never learned":** "Enquête sur l'histoire" (Mulhouse), I.

166. **governor of Alsace:** Jean-Laurent Vonau, *Le Gauleiter Wagner: Le bourreau de l'Alsace* (Strasbourg: La Nuée bleue, 2011), 21.

167. **"If an Alsatian comes":** Cited in Lothar Kettenacker, *Nationalsozialistische Volkstumspolitik im Elsass* (Stuttgart: Deutsche Verlags-Anstalt, 1973), 73.

167. **signed a certificate:** "Enquête sur l'histoire" (Mulhouse), I, V.

168. **houses were ransacked:** "Enquête sur l'histoire de l'occupation et de la libération de la France dans le Département du Haut-Rhin, Commune de Magstatt-le-Bas," Ministère de l'Éducation Nationale, Commission d'Histoire de l'Occupation et de la Libération de la France, 1950, Archives Départementales du Haut-Rhin.

168. **The misery:** "Enquête sur l'histoire" (Magstatt-le-Bas).

169. **"This war has put us":** Philippe Husser, *Journal d'un Instituteur Alsacien, 1914–1951* (Paris: Hachette, 1989), 63.

170. **some two thousand Alsatians:** Husser, *Journal d'un Instituteur Alsacien, 1914–1951*, 172.

170. **The rest were issued:** Husser, *Journal d'un Instituteur Alsacien, 1914–1951*, 174.

170. **"The French yoke":** Husser, *Journal d'un Instituteur Alsacien, 1914–1951*, 297.

170. **"So here I am":** Husser, *Journal d'un Instituteur Alsacien, 1914–1951*, 461.

171. **"his beret ripped":** "Enquête sur l'histoire" (Lutterbach), I.

171. **"For me":** Tomi Ungerer, *Tomi: A Childhood Under the Nazis* (Boulder, CO: TomiCo, 1998), 28.

172. **"If you were to chat":** Hansi, (Jean-Jacques Waltz), *L'Histoire d'Alsace Racontée aux Petis Enfants par l'Oncle Hansi* (Paris: H. Floury, 1916) 3.

173. **"A Frenchman":** Johann Wolfgang von Goethe, *Goethe's Faust: The Original German and a New Translation and Introduction by Walter Kaufmann* (New York: Anchor Books, 1961), 227.

173. **"They were not":** Ungerer, *Tomi*, 30–31.

173. ***"Hinaus mit dem":*** Ungerer, *Tomi*, 50–51.

173. **longer phrases:** "Besprechung beim Gauleiter," memo to all chief officers, April 26, 1941, Archives Départementales du Haut-Rhin.

174. **worthy of a scolding:** This anecdote comes from a memoir written by Kielwasser's son, Marcel Kielwasser: "Mémoire" (unpublished manuscript), p. 26.

174. **Kantstrasse:** French street names and German cited in "Enquête sur l'histoire de l'occupation et de la libération de la France dans le Département du Haut-Rhin, Ancienne Commune de Bourtzwiller," Ministère de l'Éducation Nationale, Commission d'Histoire de l'Occupation et de la Libération de la France, 1950, VII, article 3. Archives Départementales du Haut-Rhin.

174. **Müller-Möhner:** French last names and German revisions cited in "Enquête sur l'histoire" (Mulhouse), II, VII.

174. **"The whole Nazi mechanism":** Ungerer, *Tomi,* 60.

175. **acts of anti-Semitic vandalism:** Ruth Beryl Schachter, "Our Little Country: National Identities of Alsatian Jewry Between the Two World Wars," Master of Arts thesis for the University of Maryland, College Park, 2006, 39.

176. **"So, jetzt seid Ihr":** Dessoud, *Pfastatt,* 3.

177. **"He clicked his heels":** Ungerer, *Tomi,* 38.

CHAPTER 12: OCCUPIER

178. **live among people:** The description of Emma's thinking comes from the author's conversations with his mother.

178. **Josephine Schöpfer:** Details about Karl's stay with Josephine Schöpfer are from the author's conversations with Alphonse Huttenschmitt.

179. **against his will:** Karl Gönner, "Der Unterzeichnete bittet um Wiederverwendung" (letter to the military government in Lörrach, Weil am Rhein, December 1945), Staatsarchiv Freiburg.

179. **no political duties:** "Interrogatoire de Karl Gönner."

179. **volunteered for the posting:** Karl Rahäuser, "Bescheinigung," testimonial letter to the Denazification Commission, May 22, 1947, Staatsarchiv Freiburg.

179. **a twenty-two-page report:** Karl Gönner, Chef der Zivilverwaltung im Elsass, Abteilung Erziehung, Unterricht und Volksbildung, "Die Schulhäuser im Elsass, Schule 1, Bartenheim, Mülhausen," Archives Départementales du Haut-Rhin.

185. **students would pass around:** Interviews by author with former students in Bartenheim.

186. **bazookas into haystacks:** Lisa Pine, *Education in Nazi Germany* (Oxford: Berg, 2010), 105.

186. **"The purpose of education":** Erika Mann, *School for Barbarians: Education Under the Nazis* (New York: Modern Age Books, 1938), 46.

187. **well under way:** Richard Grunberger, *The 12-Year Reich: A Social History of Nazi Germany, 1933–1945* (New York: Holt, Rinehart and Winston, 1971). The sources for most of the author's descriptions of Nazi teaching practices in Alsace are from Grunberger's work, Erika Mann's *School for Barbarians,* Lisa Pine's *Education in Nazi Germany,* and Tomi Ungerer's *Tomi.*

187. **"a pagan fire":** "Enquête sur l'histoire de l'occupation et de la libération de la France dans le Département du Haut-Rhin, Ville de Pfastatt," Ministère de l'Éducation Nationale, Commission d'Histoire de l'Occupation et de la Libération de la France, 1950, I, 4, Archives Départementales du Haut-Rhin.

188. **"How much":** Pine, *Education in Nazi Germany,* 52.

188. **"what is a Jew?":** Tomi Ungerer, *Tomi: A Childhood Under the Nazis* (Boulder, CO: TomiCo, 1998), 42.

189. **"The adolescent brain":** Adolf Hitler, *Mein Kampf* (Munich: Zentralverlag der NSDAP, 1938), 464.

189. **"Your real father":** Ungerer, *Tomi,* 78.

192. **a summer vacation:** Ungerer, *Tomi*, vii.
193. ***Songbook for Alsatian Educators:*** *Liederbuch für die Erzieherschaft im Elsaß,* *1940* [Nazi songbook], 1940, Archives Départementales du Bas-Rhin, Strasbourg, France.

CHAPTER 13: PARTY CHIEF

195. **had to help:** "Interrogatoire de Karl Gönner."
196. **The previous party chief:** René Kielwasser, "Zur Aufnahme in der Presse unter Lokalnachrichten Bartenheim," letter announcing the appointment of an interim party chief, June 7, 1941, Archives Départementales du Haut-Rhin.
196. **"In war":** Gönner, letter to the military government in Lörrach.
196. ***"Mit der Bevölkerung":*** Gönner.
196. **The local papers:** Unless otherwise noted, the newspaper stories cited are from the *Mülhauser Tagblatt,* published by the Nationalsozialistische deutsche Arbeitspartei, 1941–1945.
201. **"Little One Ear":** Marcel Kielwasser, "Mémoire" (unpublished manuscript). Unless otherwise noted, the following descriptions and anecdotes relating to René Kielwasser are mainly drawn from this memoir.
202. **"A real dandy!":** Kielwasser, "Mémoire" 12.
202. **"Faced with a ferocious":** Kielwasser, "Mémoire" 19.
202. **shield the village:** René Kielwasser, "Une période historique, au service de la commune," speech, 1975, copy in author's possession.
203. **horse-drawn cart:** Gérard Kielwasser, interview by author, November, 24, 2019.
203. **Nazi bonfires:** René Kielwasser, "Une periode historique."
203. **"Out with this French filth":** Albert Keiflin, testimony submitted to Albert Gutzwiller and Justin Guillemin, Gendarmerie Nationale, March 14, 1945, Dépôt Central d'Archives de la Justice Militaire.
203. **keep them for himself:** "An den Gauleiter Herrn Robert Wagner" (unsigned letter to the *Gauleiter,* January 1941), Archives Départementales du Haut-Rhin.
204. **reception was always:** Marcel Kielwasser, "Mémoire," 28–30.
204. **a pin map:** René Kielwasser, "Une période historique."
204. **he confiscated:** "Interrogatoire de Karl Gönner."
204. **"emergency slaughter":** René Kannengieser, interview by author, November 25, 2019; Marcel Kielwasser, "Mémoire," 22.
205. **implacable foes**: Kielwasser, "Mémoire," 19.
205. **"he never did":** Kielwasser, "Mémoire" 3.
205. **Kielwasser told Karl:** René Kielwasser, "Une période historique."
206. **"To manage a community":** Kielwasser, "Une période."
207. **a series of letters:** Unless otherwise noted, the following descriptions of Kielwasser's mayoral rule come from "René Kielwasser Mayoral Correspondence," 1940–45, Archives Départementales du Haut-Rhin.

208. **"risky game":** Marcel Kielwasser, "Mémoire," 17.

208. **At one Hitler Youth meeting:** Witness depositions by Ernest Runser and René Groellin to the Gendarmerie Nationale, Compagnie du Haut Rhin, February 7, 1945, 1–2, Dépôt Central d'Archives de la Justice Militaire.

208. **"I was called in":** René Kielwasser, "An den Herrn Landkommisar, Mülhausen," letter to Nazi authorities, December 20, 1942.

209. **refused to sign:** Marcel Kielwasser, "Mémoire," 34.

209. **"the German victory":** Gauschatzmeister Sievers, "Aufnahmeablehnung des Vg. Renatus Kielwasser," letter to the Reich leadership of the NSDAP, July 12, 1944, Archives Départementales du Haut-Rhin.

210. **"It's high time":** Karl Gönner, quoted by Kreisgeschäftsführer Wilhelmi, letter to Landkommissar Schäfer, Mülhausen, January 30, 1943, Archives Départementales du Haut-Rhin.

210. **relieved of his duties:** René Kielwasser, "Une période historique."

CHAPTER 14: TRAITOR

213. **The last time:** Karl Tschamber and Ludwig Keller, *Geschichte der Stadt Weil am Rhein* (Freiburg, Germany: Rombach & Co GmbH, 1961), 201.

214. **"the hay harvest":** Kamill Keiflin, "An die Dienststelle der Einheit Feldpostnummer 34489 C" (letter to the council of Bartenheim, May 10, 1943), Archives Départementales du Haut-Rhin.

215. **"had a milk bottle":** Georges Tschill, interview by Edeltraut Bilger, Bartenheim, 1992, in author's possession. Quotes and descriptions of events involving Tschill are drawn from this interview, as well as her previous conversations with Tschill.

216. **when they burned down:** Marcel Kielwasser, "Mémoire" (unpublished manuscript), 70.

221. **He sent letters:** Descriptions of these letters come from a collection of villagers' testimonials that Karl's wife, Emma, put together and had certified: Emma Gönner, "Collected Testimonials," March 21, 1947, copies in author's possession.

221. **"For two and a half years":** Karl Gönner to Emmy Boll, October 7, 1957, copy in author's possession.

223. **"all French sentiment":** "Enquête sur l'histoire de l'occupation et de la libération de la commune de Rosenau," Ministère de l'Éducation Nationale, Commission d'Histoire de l'Occupation et de la Libération de la France, 1950, Archives Départementales du Haut-Rhin.

223. **from the sidelines:** René Kielwasser to the district leadership of the NSDAP, March 12, 1941, Archives Départementales du Haut-Rhin.

223. **five came home:** Mélanie Alves Rolo, Memoriale Alsace-Moselle, Schirmeck, correspondence with author, November 26, 2019; Gérard Kielwasser, interview by author, November 21, 2019; René Kielwasser to the Préfet du Haut-Rhin, Service de l'Épuration, Colmar, August 29, 1945, Archives Départementales du Haut-Rhin.

224. **"Prussians in 1870":** Fabrice Virgili, Rouquet François, and Martine Allaire, *Les Françaises, Les Français et L'épuration: De 1940 à nos jours* (Paris: Gallimard, 2018), 269.

225. **By one count:** Kevin Heller and Gerry Simpson, *The Hidden Histories of War Crimes Trials* (Oxford: Oxford University Press, 2013), 153.

225. **half a dozen stratagems:** Kielwasser, "Mémoire," 105.

225. **"are to believe":** Virgili, François, and Allaire, *Les Françaises*, 283.

226. **managed to escape:** Kielwasser, "Mémoire," 123.

226. **"demented labor":** Kielwasser, "Mémoire," 115.

231. **was already inside:** Georges Tschill, interview by Edeltraut Bilger (author's mother); Georges Baumann, interview by author, July 30, 2019.

231. **At the height:** René Kannengieser, interview by author, November 25, 2019.

232. **was urging the soldiers:** Georges Boulay, "Correspondence échangé par le Capitaine Obrecht" (cover letter addressed to Gérard Kielwasser, president of the Bartenheim Historical Society), copy in author's possession.

CHAPTER 15: PRISONER

233. **Prisoner No. 816922:** Karl Gönner, arrest and prisoner-of-war certificates, International Committee of the Red Cross, Geneva, January 21, 2015.

237. **had been listening:** Details about Gernot in this chapter come from conversations with Edeltraut Bilger and Gerda Gönner.

240. **French advances:** Gerhard Blessing, *Herzogenweiler 1208–2008: Auf der Suche nach Geschichte und Geschichten* (Villingen-Schwenningen: Verlag der Stadt Villingen-Schwenningen, 2008), 135–36. Many of the stories about the war in Herzogenweiler are drawn from this book, in addition to conversations with Gerhard Blessing and Edeltraut Bilger.

242. **Paul Treichel:** Blessing, *Herzogenweiler* 133.

243. **French were coming:** Blessing, *Herzogenweiler* 134.

243. **slept in the woods:** Blessing, *Herzogenweiler* 134.

248. **decision was made:** Tribunal Militaire, "Ordre d'écrou" (Karl Gönner's arrest report, Lörrach, February 19, 1946), Dépôt Central d'Archives de la Justice Militaire.

CHAPTER 16: ACCUSED

252. **Alsatians worked:** Descriptions of the *épuration* are mainly drawn from Fabrice Virgili, Rouquet François, and Martine Allaire, *Les Françaises, Les Français et l'épuration: De 1940 à nos jours* (Paris: Gallimard, 2018), 269.

252. **In one village:** Anatoly M. Khazanov and Stanley Payne, eds., *Perpetrators, Accomplices and Victims in Twentieth Century Politics* (London: Routledge, 2009), 80.

252. **"bout of fever":** Virgili, François, and Allaire, *Les Françaises, Les Français*, 285.

254. **dug up:** Marcel Kielwasser, "Mémoire" (unpublished manuscript), 36–38.

254. **"One fine morning":** René Kielwasser to the Préfet du Haut-Rhin.

254. **"the moral and spiritual":** Louis Obrecht, quoted in "Helfrantskirch in Festimmung," *Mülhauser Tagblatt,* August 28, 1945.

254. **outsider in Bartenheim:** Gérard Kielwasser (son of René Kielwasser) in conversation with the author, November 21, 2019.

255. **"It's hard to find":** Charles Reymann to the district of the NSDAP, December 15, 1940, Archives Départementales du Haut-Rhin.

255. **"He was frightened":** Tschill, interview with Edeltraut Bilger.

255. **"Bartenheim is sick":** Louis Obrecht to the Sous-Préfet de Mulhouse, November 20, 1944, Dépôt Central d'Archives de la Justice Militaire.

255. **One faction:** René Kielwasser, "Une période historique, au service de la commune," speech, 1975, copy in author's possession; René Kielwasser to Monsieur Laporterie, November 3, 1945, copy in author's possession.

255. **the town council:** Kielwasser, "Une période historique."

256. **dig up evidence:** Descriptions of Obrecht's activities during the *épuration* come from interviews and a series of letters written by and about Obrecht, to the following persons: Sous-Préfet de Mulhouse, November 20, 1944; Préfet des Landes, November 24, 1944; mayor of Bascons, July 9, 1945; president of the Commission d'Épuration des Landes, September 5, 1945; mayor of Tartas, August 24, 1945; Sous-Préfet de Mulhouse, October 8, 1945, copies in author's possession.

256. **"enraged Nazi":** Louis Obrecht, testimony submitted to Albert Gutzwiller and Justin Guillemin, March 14, 1945, Dépôt Central d'Archives de la Justice Militaire.

256. **lied and betrayed:** Louis Obrecht to the Capitaine de la Gendarmerie à Mulhouse, Bartenheim, February 27, 1945, Dépôt Central d'Archives de la Justice Militaire.

256. **"And as his":** Obrecht, letter to the Gendarmerie Nationale.

257. **"a veritable coup d'état":** René Kielwasser to the Préfet du Haut-Rhin.

257. **sole purpose:** Kielwasser to the Préfet du Haut-Rhin.

CHAPTER 17: DEFENDANT

258. **"You are indirectly":** "Interrogatoire de Karl Gönner." All statements by Louis Obrecht come from "Déclaration concernant l'attitude de l'allemand Karl Gönner, instituteur pendant les années d'occupation," interrogation report by Gouvernement Militaire de Württemberg, Tuttlingen, 1946, Dépôt Central d'Archives de la Justice Militaire.

260. **The incident occurred:** The description that follows draws on archival material from 1944, 1945, and 1947. During those years, a number of witnesses involved in the incident gave multiple testimonies to investigators, as did the police chief, Anton Acker. Unless otherwise noted, the witness testimonies come from Marie Baumann, Anna Pfaff, and Anna König and appear in the following documents: "Procés Verbal sur actes de resistance," report to the Procureur du Tribunal de Mulhouse, October 5, 1944; "Meurtre du Français Baumann, Georges," report to the Ministère de la Justice, February 22, 1946;

"Inventaire des pièces de la procédure suivie contre les nommés: GOENNER Karl alias GENNER Karl, ACKER Anton," report to the Tribunal Militaire Permanent de Metz, October 14, 1947, Dépôt Central d'Archives de la Justice Militaire.

261. **of a rifle:** The description of Baumann's injuries comes from the testimonies of Dr. Robert Fournier, "Procés-verbal de renseignements Affaires Baumann," December 24, 1945, and of Ernest Charles Kientz, "Procés-verbal d'Information, Tribunal Militaire Permanent de la 6e Région," May 7, 1947, Dépôt Central d'Archives de la Justice Militaire.

261. **"torn out of her":** Statement by Marie Baumann, "Inventaire," Tribunal Militaire Permanent de Metz, Dépôt Central d'Archives de la Justice Militaire.

261. **found him:** Georges Tschill, interview by Edeltraut Bilger; Jean-Georges Tschill, interview by author, November 21, 2019.

262. **"cause of the death":** "Déclaration concernant l'attitude."

263. **got a letter:** René Weinum to Emma Gönner, February 11, 1947, in author's possession.

263. **"I am personally":** René Weinum to Karl Gönner, February 25, 1947, in author's possession.

264. **real crime:** "Déclaration concernant l'attitude."

264. **"terribly slandered":** Josephine Schöpfer to Emma Gönner, December 2, 1946, in author's possession.

265. **"not been idle":** Josephine Schöpfer to Emma Gönner, February 25, 1947, in author's possession.

266. **breast milk:** Manfred J. Enssle, "The Harsh Discipline of Food Scarcity in Postwar Stuttgart, 1945–1948," *German Studies Review* 10, no. 3 (1987): pp. 481–502. Descriptions of the *Hungerwinter,* including this anecdote (p. 493), are largely drawn from this article.

268. **"I declare":** The following quotes are all from original letters and their transcriptions. Emma Gönner, "Collected Testimonials," in author's possession.

269. **"a perfect Nazi":** Tribunal Militaire Permanent de la 6e Région Militaire, "Procès-verbal d'Information" (trial minutes), 1947, Dépôt Central d'Archives de la Justice Militaire; Kielwasser, "Une période historique."

269. **"My personal impression":** René Weinum to Emma Gönner, March 18, 1947, in author's possession.

269. **"their every word":** René Luttenbacher to Emma Gönner, March 6, 1947, in author's possession.

270. **"The so-named Karl":** Tribunal Militaire permanent de Metz, issuance of a verdict in the case against Karl Gönner, July 21, 1947, Staatsarchiv Freiburg.

270. **on Karl's behalf:** Emma Gönner, "Collected Testimonials," in author's possession.

270. **Some had even gone:** René Luttenbacher to Karl Gönner, June 14, 1947, in author's possession.

270. **"They were certainly":** Luttenbacher to Karl Gönner, June 14, 1947.

270. **"I also have":** Georges Boulay, "Correspondence échangé par le Capitaine Obrecht."

272. **Even Gestapo officers:** Eric A. Johnson, *Nazi Terror: The Gestapo, Jews and Ordinary Germans* (New York: Basic Books, 1999), 64.

272. **serious crimes:** Johnson, *Nazi Terror,* 479.

272. **"a sorrow":** Karl Gönner, "Spruchkammer, I. Abteilung," letter to the denazification board in Freiburg, August 24, 1948, Staatsarchiv Freiburg.

272. **to railroad employees:** Conversations with Edeltraut Bilger; "Beschäftigungsdaten Karl Gönner" (list of positions held by Karl Gönner), ca. 1949, Staatsarchiv Freiburg.

273. **"Less Responsible":** Untersuchungsausschuss Lörrach, "Einlage zum Revisionsantrag Gönner" (explanation of the reasons for the verdict), March 1, 1948, Staatsarchiv Freiburg.

273. **"Exonerated":** Badisches Staatskommissariat für politische Säuberung, "Entscheidung" (decision in the Karl Gönner case), August 19, 1948, Staatsarchiv Freiburg.

273. **"Okay to be":** Gouvernement Militaire de la Zone Française d'Occupation en Allemagne, "Dénazification de M. Gönner, Karl" (ruling in the Karl Gönner case), September 14, 1948, Staatsarchiv Freiburg.

273. **"The burden of":** Badisches Staatskommissariat für politische Säuberung, "Begründung/Exposé des Motifs" (explanation of the reasons for the verdict), October 15, 1948, Staatsarchiv Freiburg.

273. **teach in a school:** Badisches Staatskommissariat für politische Säuberung, "Wiedereinstellung des Gönner, Karl" (letter to the Baden Ministry of Culture and Education about reappointment of Karl Gönner), March 12, 1949, Staatsarchiv Freiburg.

274. **"His superiors are":** René Weinum to Karl Gönner, November 24, 1948, in author's possession.

CHAPTER 18: GRANDFATHER

276. **"Dear Gernot!":** Karl Gönner to Gernot Gönner, April 15, 1947, copy in author's possession.

279. **fall of 1956:** Emma died on September 21, 1956. Her death certificate was issued a day later. See Standesamt Weil am Rhein, "Sterbeurkunde," death certificate of Emma Gönner, September 22, 1956, Staatsarchiv Freiburg.

279. **doing well:** Karl Gönner to Sigmar Gönner, April 14, 1956, copy in author's possession.

279. **first tentative steps:** Karl Gönner to Sigmar Gönner.

279. **holy water from Lourdes:** Karl Gönner to Sigmar Gönner, November 24, 1956, copy in author's possession.

279. **"Mama's grave":** Karl Gönner to Sigmar Gönner.

279. **over it by spring:** Karl Gönner to Emmy Boll, September 7, 1957, copy in author's possession.

279. **"My stupid heart":** Karl Gönner to Sigmar Gönner, May 14, 1964, copy in author's possession.

280. **"a worm gnawing":** Karl Gönner to Xaver Blessing, December 30, 1952, copy in author's possession.

280. **"This transaction":** Karl Gönner to Emmy Boll, August 31, 1957, copy in author's possession.

280. **"Well, my Sunday":** Karl Gönner to Emmy Boll.

280. **"A Schoolmaster":** "Bewegender Abschied von Karl Gönner," *Weiler Zeitung,* April 27, 1979.

281. **hernia operations:** Kreisschulamt Lörrach, "Meldung," letter to the Ministry of Culture and Education, October 28, 1952, Staatsarchiv Freiburg.

281. **of his teeth:** Kreisschulamt Lörrach, "Kostenvorschlag für Zahnersatz des Hauptlehrers Karl Gönner," letter to the Ministry of Culture and Education, September 14, 1950, Staatsarchiv Freiburg.

BIBLIOGRAPHY

Amit, Aviv. *Regional Language Policies in France During World War II*. London: Palgrave Macmillan, 2014.

Arendt, Hannah. "The Aftermath of Nazi Rule: Report from Germany." *Commentary*, October 1950.

Atkinson, Rick. *An Army at Dawn*. The Liberation Trilogy, vol. 1. New York: Henry Holt, 2013.

———. *The Day of Battle*. The Liberation Trilogy, vol. 2. New York: Henry Holt, 2013.

———. *The Guns at Last Light*. The Liberation Trilogy, vol. 3. New York: Henry Holt, 2013.

Baker, Chris. *The Battle of the Lys, 1918: North: Objective Ypres*. Barnsley, UK: Pen & Sword Books, 2018.

Bammer, Angelika. *Born After: Reckoning with the German Past*. New York: Bloomsbury, 2019.

Barry, John M. *The Great Influenza: The Story of the Deadliest Pandemic in History*. New York: Penguin, 2005.

Bashford, Alison, and Philippa Levine, eds. *The Oxford Handbook of the History of Eugenics*. New York: Oxford University Press, 2010.

Bauer, Frieder, and Jörg Vögele. "Die 'Spanische Grippe' in Der Deutschen Armee 1918: Perspektive Der Ärzte Und Generäle." *Medizinhistorisches Journal* 48, no. 2 (2013): 117–52.

Baussan, Charles. "General Gouraud." *Studies: An Irish Quarterly Review* 7, no. 27 (1918): 400–415.

Benbassa, Esther. *The Jews of France: A History from Antiquity to the Present*. Translated by M. B. DeBevoise. Oxford, UK: Princeton University Press, 2001.

"'Be Nice to the Germans.'" *New York Times*, July 20, 1990.

Bergère, Marc. *L'Épuration en France*. Paris: Presses Universitaires de France, 2018.

Bilger, Edeltraut. "The German-Americans in Oklahoma During World War I, as Seen Through Three German-Language Newspapers." Master's thesis, Oklahoma State University, 1976.

———. "Reconstruction of France: Marshal Petain's Policies, 1940–1942, as Evaluated by American Journalists and Scholars." Dissertation, Oklahoma State University, 1984.

Binder, Peter. "8.7.1915: Preußische Schulen führen die Sütterlin-Schrift ein." *SWR*, July 1, 2020.

Bode, Sabine. *The Forgotten Generation*. Translated by Robert Brambeer. Stuttgart: Verlag Klett-Cotta, 2004.

"Bombs Dropped on Amiens." *New York Times*, September 26, 1914.

Bradbury, Jim. *The Capetians: Kings of France 987–1328*. London: Bloomsbury, 2007.

Branting, Susan M., and Ida Piller-Greenspan. *When the World Closed Its Doors: Struggling to Escape Nazi-Occupied Europe*. Abingdon, UK: Taylor & Francis, 2015.

Bruce, Robert Bowman. *Pétain: Verdun to Vichy*. Washington, DC: Potomac Books, 2008.

Byerly, Carol R. *Fever of War: The Influenza Epidemic in the U.S. Army During World War I*. New York: New York University Press, 2005.

Caesar, Julius. *Caesar's Commentaries*. London: Whittaker, 1857.

———. *The Commentaries of Caesar*. Translated by William Duncan. London: Dodsley, 1779.

———. *The War for Gaul: A New Translation*. Translated by James J. O'Donnell. Princeton, NJ: Princeton University Press, 2021.

Canaday, Margot, Nancy Cott, and Robert O. Self, eds. *Intimate States: Gender, Sexuality, and Governance in Modern US History*. Chicago: University of Chicago Press, 2021.

Canoy, Jose Raymond. *The Discreet Charm of the Police State: The Landpolizei and the Transformation of Bavaria, 1945–1965*. Boston: Brill, 2007.

Carrol, Alison. *The Return of Alsace to France*. Oxford: Oxford University Press, 2018.

Catholic Hymns. Edited by Henry Formby. London: Burns and Lambert, 1853.

Ceesay, Alpha. "Reclaiming Remembrance: 'I thought it was a white event'." BBC News. November 12, 2017, bbc.com/news/uk-england-41917784.

Chana, Jan. "Plan for Holocaust Memorial 'Stumbling Stones' Takes a Tumble." *Tablet*, August 5, 2015.

Churchill, Winston. *The Second World War, Vol. 4, The Hinge of Fate*. London: Orion, 2015.

———. *The Second World War, Vol. 2, Their Finest Hour*. London: Cassell, 1949.

Clark, Lloyd. *Blitzkrieg: Myth, Reality, and Hitler's Lightning War: France 1940*. New York: Grove Atlantic, 2016.

Cohen, Roger. "An Unreliable Germany and the Volkswagen Debacle." *New York Times,* September 28, 2015.

de Gaulle, Charles. *The Complete War Memoirs of Charles de Gaulle.* New York: Simon & Schuster, 1968.

de Jong, Mayke, and Justin Lake. *Confronting Crisis in the Carolingian Empire: Paschasius Radbertus' Funeral Oration for Wala of Corbie.* Manchester, UK: Manchester University Press, 2020.

Dessoud, Eugène. *Pfastatt: Dans la tourmente 1940–1944* (unpublished manuscript).

D'Este, Carlo. *Patton.* New York: HarperCollins, 1995.

Deutsches Lesebuch für Volksschulen. Zweiter Band (Lahr: Schauenburg, 1942).

Diamond, Hanna. *Fleeing Hitler: France 1940.* Oxford: Oxford University Press, 2007.

Douglas, R. M. *Orderly and Humane: The Expulsion of Germans After the Second World War.* New Haven, CT: Yale University Press, 2012.

Ehrenreich, Eric. *The Nazi Ancestral Proof: Genealogy, Racial Science, and the Final Solution.* Bloomington: Indiana University Press, 2007.

Enssle, Manfred J. "The Harsh Discipline of Food Scarcity in Postwar Stuttgart, 1945–1948." *German Studies Review* 10, no. 3 (1987): 481–502.

"Erster Weltkrieg: Die Front fraß Offiziere und schrie nach mehr." *Süddeutsche Zeitung,* July 4, 2017.

Ewald, Paul W. *Evolution of Infectious Disease.* Oxford: Oxford University Press, 1994.

"France: Pétain Joins Up." *Time,* May 27, 1940.

Friedlander, Henry. *The Origins of Nazi Genocide: From Euthanasia to the Final Solution.* Chapel Hill: University of North Carolina Press, 2000.

Fröhlig, Florence. "Painful Legacy of World War II: Nazi Forced Enlistment: Alsatian/Mosellan Prisoners of War and the Soviet Prison Camp of Tambov." Master's thesis, Stockholm University, 2013.

"German-American Day: October 6, 2021." News release. United States Census Bureau. Last revised October 8, 2021.

Gilbert, Martin. *Churchill: A Life.* New York: Rosetta Books, 2014.

———. *The First World War: A Complete History.* New York: Henry Holt, 2004.

———. *Winston S. Churchill: Finest Hour, 1939–1941.* New York: Rosetta Books, 2015.

Glass, James. *Life Unworthy of Life: Racial Phobia and Mass Murder in Hitler's Germany.* London: Basic Books, 1999.

Goethe, Johann Wolfgang von. *Goethe's Faust: The Original German and a New Translation and Introduction by Walter Kaufmann.* New York: Anchor Books, 1961.

Goldhagen, Daniel Jonah. *Hitler's Willing Executioners: Ordinary Germans and the Holocaust.* New York: Doubleday, 2007.

Götze, Heinz, and Heinz Sarkowski. *History of a Scientific Publishing House: Part 1: 1842–1945 Foundation Maturation Adversity.* Berlin: Springer-Verlag, 1996.

Grann, David. *Killers of the Flower Moon*. New York: Doubleday, 2017.

"Greatest Battle in American History: Argonne-Meuse Struggle Described in Thrilling Detail from Official Records." *Current History* (1916–1940) 10, no. 3 (1919): 526–39.

Greenhalgh, Elizabeth. "1918: German Offensives." In *The French Army and the First World War*. Cambridge, UK: Cambridge University Press, 2014.

Grunberger, Richard. *The 12-Year Reich: A Social History of Nazi Germany, 1933–1945*. New York: Holt, Rinehart and Winston, 1971.

Halsall, Paul. "Medieval Sourcebook: Julius Caesar: The Germans, c. 51 BCE." Fordham University, August 1998.

———. "Medieval Sourcebook: Tacitus, the Germania, excerpts." Fordham University, July 1998.

Hansi (Jean-Jacques Waltz). *L'Histoire d'Alsace Racontée aux Petits Enfants par l'Oncle Hansi*. Paris: H. Floury, 1916.

Hatt, Christine. *The First World War, 1914–18*. London: Evans Bros., 2007.

Hecker, Mel, Geoffrey P. Megargee, and Joseph R. White, eds. *The United States Holocaust Memorial Museum Encyclopedia of Camps and Ghettos, 1933–1945*. Vol. 3, *Camps and Ghettos Under European Regimes Aligned with Nazi Germany*. Bloomington: Indiana University Press, 2018.

Heimannsberg, Barbara, and Christoph J. Schmidt, eds. *The Collective Silence: German Identity and the Legacy of Shame*. San Francisco: Jossey-Bass, 1993.

Heller, Kevin, and Gerry Simpson. *The Hidden Histories of War Crimes Trials*. Oxford: Oxford University Press, 2013.

Hengerer, Mark. *Adel im Wandel: Oberschwaben von der Frühen Neuzeit bis zur Gegenwart*. Edited by Elmar L. Kuhn. Ostfildern: Thorbecke, 2006.

Herzogenweiler 1208–2008 auf der Suche nach Geschichte und Geschichten. Gerhard Blessing, Oskar Diringer, Sigfried Gütert et al. Edited by Heinrich Maulhardt. Villingen-Schwenningen: Verlag der Stadt Villingen-Schwenningen, 2008.

Hitler, Adolf. "Kulturrede 1934." In *Reichstagung in Nürnberg 1934*. Edited by Julius Streicher. Berlin: Weller, 1934.

———. *Mein Kampf*. Munich: Zentralverlag der NSDAP, 1938.

Hitler's Table Talk, 1941–1944: His Private Conversations. Edited by Hugh Trevor-Roper. New York: Enigma Books, 2008.

Hoffmann, Jakob Josef. *Handbuch für Stellenbewerbung (Schulstatistik). Nachtrag*. Bonndorf: Spachholz & Ehrath (ca. 1905).

Hohendorf, Gerrit. "The Extermination of Mentally Ill and Handicapped People under National Socialist Rule, Mass Violence & Résistance." Mass Violence and Resistance, Research Network, November 17, 2016, sciencespo .fr/mass-violence-war-massacre-resistance/en/document/extermination -mentally-ill-and-handicapped-people-under-national-socialist-rule.html.

Hölderlin, Friedrich. *Übersetzungen: Philosophische Schriften*. Weimar: Liechtenstein, 1922.

Hornblower, Simon, and Anthony Spawforth, eds. *The Oxford Classical Dictionary*. Oxford: Oxford University Press, 1999.

Housden, Martyn. *Resistance and Conformity in the Third Reich*. London: Taylor & Francis, 2013.

Husser, Philippe. *Journal d'un Instituteur Alsacien, 1914–1951*. Paris: Hachette, 1989.

Jackson, Julian. *France: The Dark Years, 1940–1944*. Oxford: Oxford University Press, 2003.

Jahner, Harald. *Aftermath: Life in the Fallout of the Third Reich*. Translated by Shaun Whiteside. New York: Knopf, 2022.

James, Simon, and Stefan Krmnicek, eds. *The Oxford Handbook of the Archaeology of Roman Germany*. Oxford: Oxford University Press, 2020.

Jarausch, Konrad H. *Broken Lives: How Ordinary Germans Experienced the 20th Century*. Princeton, NJ: Princeton University Press, 2018.

———. *The Unfree Professions: German Lawyers, Teachers, and Engineers, 1900–1950*. New York: Oxford University Press, 1990.

Jaspers, Karl. *Die Schuldfrage: Zur politischen Haftung Deutschlands*. Munich: R. Piper, 1965.

Johnson, Eric A. *Nazi Terror: The Gestapo, Jews and Ordinary Germans*. New York: Basic Books, 1999.

Judt, Tony. *Postwar: A History of Europe Since 1945*. New York: Penguin, 2005.

Kamphoefner, Walter D. *Germans in America: A Concise History*. London: Rowman and Littlefield, 2021.

Kaufmann, J .E., et al. *The Maginot Line: History and Guide*. Barnsley, UK: Pen and Sword Military, 2011.

Kettenacker, Lothar. *Nationalsozialistische Volkstumspolitik im Elsass*. Stuttgart: Deutsche Verlags-Anstalt, 1973.

Khazanov, Anatoly M., and Stanley Payne, eds. *Perpetrators, Accomplices and Victims in Twentieth Century Politics: Reckoning with the Past*. New York: Routledge, 2009.

Kielwasser, Marcel. "Mémoire" (unpublished manuscript).

Lane Herder, Brian. *The Meuse-Argonne Offensive 1918: The American Expeditionary Forces' Crowning Victory*. Oxford, UK: Bloomsbury, 2020.

Lengel, Edward. *A Companion to the Meuse-Argonne Campaign*. Chichester, UK: Wiley Blackwell, 2014.

———. *To Conquer Hell: The Meuse-Argonne, 1918*. New York: Henry Holt, 2008.

Lloyd, Nick. *Hundred Days: The Campaign That Ended World War I*. London: Viking, 2013.

———. *The Western Front: A History of the Great War, 1914–1918*. New York: Norton, 2021.

Mann, Erika. *School for Barbarians: Education Under the Nazis*. New York: Modern Age Books, 1938.

Marix Evans, Martin. *1918: The Year of Victories*. London: Arcturus, 2017.

Mastriano, Douglas V. *Thunder in the Argonne: A New History of America's Greatest Battle*. Lexington: University Press of Kentucky, 2018.

Mattern, Susan P. *Rome and the Enemy: Imperial Strategy in the Principate*. Berkeley: University of California Press, 2002.

May, Karl. *Winnetou.* Translated by David Koblick. Pullman: Washington State University Press, 1999.

Mayer, Milton. *They Thought They Were Free: The Germans, 1933–45.* Chicago: University of Chicago Press, 1955.

McCormack, John. *Over One Million Mercenaries: Swiss Soldiers in the Armies of the World.* London: Leo Cooper, 1993.

McDougall, Walter. *The Heavens and the Earth: A Political History of the Space Age.* New York: Basic Books, 1985.

Morgen, Daniel. *Mémoires retrouvées: Des enseignants Alsaciens en Bade, des enseignants Badois en Alsace: Umschulung 1940–1945.* Strasbourg, France: Do Bentzinger, 2014.

Office of United States Chief of Counsel for Prosecution of Axis Criminality. *Nazi Conspiracy and Aggression: Opinion and Judgment.* Washington, DC: U.S. Government Printing Office, 1947.

Onion, Rebecca. "A WWI–Era Memo Asking French Officers to Practice Jim Crow with Black American Troops." *Slate,* April 27, 2016, slate.com/human-interest/2016/04/secret-information-concerning-black-troops-a-warning-memo-sent-to-the-french-military-during-world-war-i.html.

Paul, Gerd. *Es gilt die letzten Schläge, den Sieg zu vollenden! Zeichnet Kriegsanleihe!* 1918. Photograph of lithograph, 86 cm X 58 cm. U.S. Library of Congress.

Pine, Lisa. *Education in Nazi Germany.* Oxford: Berg Publishers, 2010.

Pitte, Jean-Robert. *La France.* Malakoff, France: Armand Colin, 2009.

Rozett, Robert, and Shmuel Spector, eds. *Encyclopedia of the Holocaust.* London: Routledge, 2000.

Rundel, Otto. *Kurt Georg Kiesinger: Sein Leben und sein politisches Wirken.* Stuttgart: W. Kohlhammer Verlag, 2006.

Sachar, Howard M. *The Assassination of Europe, 1918–1942: A Political History.* Toronto: University of Toronto Press, 2014.

Scheck, Raffael, Julia Torrie, Fabien Théofilakis, and Julia Torrie, eds. *German-Occupied Europe in the Second World War.* New York: Taylor & Francis, 2019.

Scheible, Johann. *Das sechste und siebente Buch Mosis, das ist: Mosis magische Geisterkunst, das Geheimnis aller Geheimnisse: Wort- und bildgetreu nach einer alten Handschrift.* Stuttgart: Scheible, 1849.

Schiffman, Harold. *Linguistic Culture and Language Policy.* London: Taylor & Francis, 2012.

Schlant, Ernestine. *The Language of Silence: West German Literature and the Holocaust.* New York: Routledge, 1999.

Schröder, Martin Z. "Eine zackige Kehrtwendung." *Süddeutsche Zeitung,* April 20, 2005.

Schutz, Herbert. *The Carolingians in Central Europe, Their History, Arts and Architecture: A Cultural History of Central Europe, 750–900.* Boston: Brill, 2004.

Scofield, Devlin M. "Veterans, War Widows, and National Belonging in Alsace, 1871–1953." Dissertation, Michigan State University, 2015.

Seiz, Gustav, ed. *Geschichte des 6. Badischen Infanterie-Regiments Kaiser Friedrich III. Nr. 114 im Weltkrieg 1914–1918.* Zeulenroda: Sporn, 1932.

Siculus, Diodorus. *The Library of History*, Vol. 3, Loeb Classical Library. Cambridge, MA: Harvard University, 1939, accessed March 9, 2022, penelope .uchicago.edu/Thayer/E/Roman/Texts/Diodorus_Siculus/5B*.html.

Smith, Adam. *Paper Money*. New York: Summit Books, 1981.

Stachura, Peter, ed. *Unemployment and the Great Depression in Weimar Germany*. Basingstoke, UK: Palgrave Macmillan UK, 1986.

Strohn, Matthias, ed. *1918: Winning the War, Losing the War*. Oxford, UK: Bloomsbury, 2018.

Styron, William. *Sophie's Choice*. New York: Random House, 1979.

Tacitus. *The Germany and the Agricola of Tacitus*. Comments by Edward Brooks. Project Gutenberg, 2013.

Taylor, Frederick. *Exorcising Hitler*. London: Bloomsbury, 2014.

Teuteberg, Hans Jürgen, and Günter Wiegelmann. *Unsere tägliche Kost*. Münster: Coppenrath, 1988.

"Text of Petain's Address." *New York Times*, August 20, 1941.

Torrie, Julia S. *"For Their Own Good": Civilian Evacuations in Germany and France, 1939–1945*. Oxford, UK: Berghahn Books, 2010.

Tschamber, Karl, and Ludwig Keller. *Geschichte der Stadt Weil am Rhein*. Freiburg, Germany: Rombach & Co GmbH, 1961.

Ungerer, Tomi. *Tomi: A Childhood Under the Nazis*. Boulder, CO: TomiCo, 1998.

United Nations War Crimes Commission. *Law Reports of Trials of War Criminals*. London: H.M. Stationery Office, 1949.

Vidal-Naquet, Pierre, and Limor Yagil. *Holocaust Denial in France: Analysis of a Unique Phenomenon*. Tel Aviv: Tel Aviv University, 1995.

Vintras, Achille. *Medical Guide to the Mineral Waters of France and Its Wintering Stations*. London: J. & A. Churchill, 1883.

Virgili, Fabrice, François Rouquet, and Martine Allaire. *Les Françaises, les Français et l'Épuration: De 1940 à nos jours*. Paris: Gallimard, 2018.

Vlossak, Elizabeth. "Regimenting Unfree Labour: Alsace and Moselle." Working Papers of the Independent Commission of Historians Investigating the History of the Reich Ministry of Labour (Reichsarbeitsministerium) in the National Socialist Period. Working Paper Series A (9), 2017.

Vonau, Jean-Laurent. *Le Gauleiter Wagner: Le bourreau de L'Alsace*. Strasbourg: La Nuée Bleue, 2011.

Wagner, Esther-Miriam, Ben Outhwaite, and Bettina Beinhoff, eds. *Scribes as Agents of Language Change*. Boston: De Gruyter, 2013.

Walter, Hans-Henning. "Historische Produktionsverfahren für anorganische Salze." *Geschichte der Chemie: Mitteilungen*, no. 10 (1996): 72.

War Diaries of German Units Opposed to the Second Division [Regular] 1918, Vol. 7, Blanc Mont [Part I]. Washington, D.C.: Second Division Historical Section, Army War College, 1931.

Weindling, Paul. *Health, Race and German Politics Between National Unification and Nazism, 1870–1945*. Cambridge: Cambridge University Press, 1993.

Weißbrich, Thomas. "Giftgas." Deutsches Historisches Museum Berlin, September 1, 2014.

Wieviorka, Olivier. "Between Propaganda and Telling the Truth." In *France at War in the Twentieth Century: Propaganda, Myth and Metaphor.* Edited by Valerie Holman and Debra Kelly. New York: Berghahn, 2000.

———. *The French Resistance.* Translated by Jane Marie Todd. Cambridge, MA: Harvard University Press, 2016.

Wightman, Edith Mary. *Gallia Belgica.* Berkeley: University of California Press, 1985.

Wilkerson, Isabel. "The Nazis and the Acceleration of Caste." In *Caste: The Origins of Our Discontent.* New York: Random House, 2020.

Williams, Maude, and Bernard Wilkin. *French Soldiers' Morale in the Phoney War, 1939–1940.* London: Routledge, 2019.

Winkler, Willi. *Das braune Netz: Wie die Bundesrepublik von früheren Nazis zum Erfolg geführt wurde.* Rowohlt E-Book, 2019.

Yockelson, Mitchell. *Forty-Seven Days: How Pershing's Warriors Came of Age to Defeat the German Army in World War I.* New York: New American Library, 2016.

Zeidman, Lawrence A. *Brain Science Under the Swastika: Ethical Violations, Resistance, and Victimization of Neuroscientists in Nazi Europe.* Oxford: Oxford University press, 2020.

Zieger, Philipp. "Deutsche und Schweizer kämpften im grünen Regiment Seite an Seite—und prägten die Geschichte der Stadt Konstanz." *Südkurier,* June 2018.

PHOTO CREDITS

Chapter 1: Karl Gönner prisoner photos
(Dépôt Central d'Archives de la Justice Militaire)

Chapter 2: Hans and Edeltraut Bilger wedding photo
(from the collection of Edeltraut Bilger)

Chapter 3: Town hall, Bartenheim, France
(Archives de Bartenheim)

Chapter 4: Greiner farmstead, Herzogenweiler, Germany
(Ortsarchiv Herzogenweiler)

Chapter 5: Village chapel, Herzogenweiler, Germany
(Ortsarchiv Herzogenweiler)

Chapter 6: Military record, Karl Gönner
(Landesarchiv Baden-Württemberg, Generallandesarchiv Karlsruhe)

Chapter 7: Underground infirmary, Orfeuil, France
(courtesy of the author)

Chapter 8: Children playing by the ruined City Palace, Potsdam, Germany
(United Archives/Erich Andres)

Chapter 9: Archives, Aulfingen, Germany
(courtesy of the author)

Chapter 10: Karl and Gernot Gönner
(courtesy of the author)

Chapter 11: Town square blown up, Bartenheim, France
(Archives de Bartenheim)

Chapter 12: School room, Bartenheim, France
(Archives de Bartenheim)

Chapter 13: Nazi Teacher's League identification card
(Landesarchiv Baden-Württemberg, Staatsarchiv Freiburg)

Chapter 14: Crematorium, Natzweiler-Struthof, France
(1993 © MPP Michael Kenna)

Chapter 15: Prisoner barracks near Pont d'Ain, France
(courtesy of the author)

Chapter 16: French woman accused of sleeping with Germans near Marseilles, France
(Carl Mydans/The LIFE Picture Collection/Shutterstock)

Chapter 17: Testimonial letters from Bartenheim, France
(courtesy of the author)

Chapter 18: Three Countries Bridge between Weil am Rhein, Germany, and Huningue, France
(picture-alliance/ dpa | Rolf Haid)

ABOUT THE AUTHOR

Burkhard Bilger has been a staff writer at *The New Yorker* since 2001. His work has also appeared in *The Atlantic, Harper's,* and *The New York Times,* among other publications, and has been anthologized ten times in the Best American series. Bilger has received fellowships from Yale University, MacDowell, and the New York Public Library's Cullman Center. His first book, *Noodling for Flatheads,* was a finalist for the PEN/Martha Albrand Award. He lives in Brooklyn with his wife, Jennifer Nelson.

ABOUT THE TYPE

This book was set in Baskerville, a typeface designed by John Baskerville (1706–75), an amateur printer and typefounder, and cut for him by John Handy in 1750. The type became popular again when the Lanston Monotype Corporation of London revived the classic roman face in 1923. The Mergenthaler Linotype Company in England and the United States cut a version of Baskerville in 1931, making it one of the most widely used typefaces today.

The title was set in Sachsenwald, and the chapter headings, author name, running headings, and page numbers were set in Albertus. Both typefaces were designed by the German calligrapher and typographer Berthold Wolpe. Born to a Jewish family in Offenbach in 1905, Wolpe emigrated to Great Britain in 1935 to escape Nazi persecution. In 1941, he was arrested and deported to an internment camp in Australia for "enemy aliens." He was released the following year and became a naturalized British citizen in 1947.